PASTOR

Pastor

A Reader for
Ordained Ministry

William H. Willimon

Abingdon Press
Nashville

PASTOR
A READER FOR ORDAINED MINISTRY

Copyright © 2002 by Abingdon Press

This book is printed on recycled, acid-free, elemental-chlorine–free paper.

Library of Congress Cataloging-in-Publication Data

Pastor: a reader for ordained ministry / [edited by] William H. Willimon.
    p.   cm.
Includes bibliographical references and indexes.
  ISBN 0-687-09788-6 (pbk. : alk. paper)
  1. Pastoral theology.   2. Clergy—Office. I. Willimon, William H.
  BV4011.3 .P365 2002
253—dc21

2002011469

ISBN 13: 978-0-687-09788-3

08 09 10 11—10 9 8 7 6

MANUFACTURED IN THE UNITED STATES OF AMERICA

Contents

Introduction

Midway through his magisterial *Duties of the Clergy* (Book II, Ch. XX), St. Ambrose notes that it is a good thing for clergy to unite themselves to exemplary persons, and particularly important for younger clergy to seek out older, experienced "great and wise men." In commending wise mentors to his developing clergy, Ambrose is, on the whole, following the sensible advice of his model, Cicero. Ambrose's too heavy dependence upon Cicero's *De Officis* lends a certain tediousness to his *Duties*, only barely distinguishing it from conventional Roman manuals for would-be successful Roman civil servants. Young man, here is the way toward upward mobility in the empire.

Yet Ambrose does manage to write a uniquely Christian treatise on leadership. He cites Joshua, son of Nun, who "became so great, because his union with Moses was the means not only of instructing him in a knowledge of the law, but also of sanctifying him to receive grace." He also recalls Paul's mentoring of young Timothy and his collegial support of Barnabas, as well as the older examples of Elijah and Elisha. There really does seem to be something inherent in godly leadership that thrives upon the grace of good examples, wise mentors, fitting models of godly servants who preceded us, friends whom we know dearly, if only through their writing.

This book is an attempt to provide that sort of resource for today's clergy. Think of the readings here as a kind of conversation, across twenty centuries of ordained leadership, with (except for the selections written by the editor) some of our most distinguished mentors. I have made little attempt to be comprehensive or to do justice to the full historical sweep of writing about Christian ministry. This anthology is an unashamedly personal selection, but I hope not merely idiosyncratic. A grant from the Louisville Institute enabled me to poll a collection of pastors, seminary professors, and others on their favorite and most formative writings about ministry. Yet, finally, I chose the writings included here because I thought they were interesting to read, among the best that we clergy can produce, and because of their particular relevance for the contemporary practice of church leadership. My hope is that any pastor who rambles among these readings will find hope, correction, and refurbishment for the manifold tasks of pastoral leadership, will feel inspired by the good heritage of thought upon this most difficult yet noble of vocations. I also hope that anyone, regardless of vocation or commitment, might come away from encounter with this great cloud of witnesses convinced that some of the best thinking of which humanity is capable has come from the church's clergy. While this book is fully able to stand alone, to be read by itself with profit, it is designed as a companion piece to my book on church leadership, *Pastor: The Theology and Practice of Ordained Ministry*. This anthology represents a selection of the readings that played a role in the composition of that book. The readings are organized to follow the same progression of chapters as in *Pastor: The Theology and Practice of Ordained Ministry*.

Thanks to Ms. Jacquelyn Andrews and Mr. Dan Rhodes for their help in the preparation of this manuscript.

What treasure is committed to our care in our stewardship of the gospel, in our care for the Body of Christ, in our shepherding of God's people. Who among us pastors is worthy of the challenge? Let us be strengthened in our work, renewed in our vocation by the words of fellow workers, by the examples of the saints, by the lives of those who willingly speak words of encouragement to us today, who strengthen us for our ministry if we will willingly listen.

William H. Willimon
Duke University Chapel
Durham, North Carolina
Pentecost, 2002

CHAPTER ONE

Ordination

In almost any reform of the church, something is gained, but something may be lost as well. Martin Luther stood at the center of the Protestant Reformation in Germany. Luther's stress on the shared ministry of all Christians, the necessity for a biblically formed, learned pastorate, and his conviction of the centrality of justification by faith in the work of Jesus Christ, rather than our works, left an indelible stamp upon the Protestant pastoral ministry.

Yet there were losses in the continental Reformation. The Reformation's dissolution of the monasteries in Germany caused a grave crisis in the educational system. The monasteries had served as the school system for Europe. Now, with the demise of the monasteries, children were not being taught, particularly those children whom the church once prepared for the priesthood. The path to the priesthood had once provided talented youth a way out of poverty and into the prominent profession of the priesthood. Many parents now urged their children to take other paths to success.

Luther wrote a "sermon," a treatise actually, on the necessity of the church's selection of talented young people for service to the church. While stressing his famous "priesthood of all believers" principle, the notion that all the baptized share in the ministry of the church, Luther now felt the need for a strong stress upon the nobility of the pastoral vocation. He defends the "spiritual estate," the pastoral ministry, as the most noble of all vocations, as worthy as any profession a parent might urge upon a child. The result was one of the Great Reformer's most thoughtful and sustained commentaries on the Christian ministry.

The Nobility of the Ministry
Martin Luther (From "A Sermon on Keeping Children in School")

Dear friends, the common people appear to be quite indifferent to the matter of maintaining the schools. I see them withdrawing their children from instruction and turning them to the making of a living and to caring for their bellies. Besides, they either will not or cannot think what a horrible and un-Christian business this is and what great and murderous harm they are doing everywhere in so serving the devil. For this reason I have undertaken to give you this exhortation, on the chance that there may be some who still have at least a modicum of belief that there is a God in heaven and a hell prepared for unbelievers, and that by this exhortation they might be led to change their minds. (Actually, almost everybody is acting as if there were neither a God in heaven nor a devil in hell.) I propose, therefore, to take up the question of what is at stake in this matter in the way of gains and losses, first those that are spiritual or eternal, and then those that are temporal or worldly.

I hope, indeed, that believers, those who want to be called Christians, know very well that the spiritual estate[12] has been established and instituted by God, not with gold or silver but with the precious blood and bitter death of his only Son, our Lord Jesus Christ [I Pet. 1:18-19]. From his wounds indeed flow the sacraments[13] (they used to depict this on broadsides).[14] He paid dearly that men might everywhere have this office of preaching, baptizing, loosing, binding, giving the sacrament, comforting, warning, and exhorting with God's word, and whatever else belongs to the pastoral office. For this office not only helps to further and sustain this temporal life and all the worldly estates, but it also gives eternal life and delivers from sin and death, which is its proper and chief work. . . .

The estate I am thinking of is rather one which has the office of preaching and the service of the word and sacraments and which imparts the Spirit and salvation, blessings that cannot be attained by any amount of pomp and pageantry. It includes the work of pastors, teachers, preachers, lectors, priests (whom men call chaplains), sacristans, schoolmasters, and whatever other work belongs to these offices and persons. This estate the Scriptures highly exalt and praise. St. Paul calls them God's stewards and servants [I Cor.

---

12. *Der geistliche stand* refers to the clergy or the ministry.

13. In his *Lectures on the Gospel According to St. John* (Tractate 120), Augustine comments on how the Evangelist in John 19:34 significantly says that Jesus' side was not pierced "but 'opened,' that thereby, in a sense, the gate of life might be thrown open, from whence have flowed forth the sacraments of the Church." *PNF*[1] 7, 434.

14. Some of the one-page tracts or book pages frequently illustrated with woodcuts which Luther may have had in mind are suggested in WA 30[II], 527, n. 1, and *MA*[3] 5, 439, n. 266, 1. 21. The scene of Christ's blood dripping from his wounded feet into a sacramental chalice at the base of the cross was a common theme in art.

4:1]; bishops [Acts 20:28]; doctors, prophets [I Cor. 12:28]; also God's ambassadors to reconcile the world to God, II Corinthians 6 [5:20]. Joel calls them saviors.[16] In Psalm 68[17] David calls them kings and princes. Haggai [1:13] calls them angels,[18] and Malachi [2:7] says, "The lips of the priest keep the law, for he is an angel of the Lord of hosts." Christ himself gives them the same name, not only in Matthew 11 [:10] where he calls John the Baptist an angel, but also throughout the entire book of the Revelation to John.

This is why the ancients greatly avoided this estate.[19] Because of its great dignity and honor they so dreaded to take the office upon them that they had to be forced and driven into it. To be sure, there have been many since then who have praised this estate highly, though more because of the saying of mass than because of the preaching. This praise and glorification grew to the point where the office and estate of the priesthood (that is, of the sacrificing of the mass) was placed above Mary and the angels because the angels and Mary could not say mass but a priest could. . . .

He has not given you your children and the means to support them simply so that you may do with them as you please, or train them just to get ahead in the world. You have been earnestly commanded to raise them for God's service, or be completely rooted out—you, your children, and everything else, in which case everything you have done for them is condemned, as the first commandment says, "I visit the iniquities of the fathers upon the children to the third and fourth generation of those who hate me" [Exod. 20:5]. But how will you raise them for God's service if the office of preaching and the spiritual estate have fallen into oblivion?

And it is your fault. You could have done something about it. You could have helped to maintain them if you had allowed your

---

16. *Heilande*, which may have reference to Joel 2:23, where Luther followed the Vulgate (*doctorem justitiae*) in his 1545 German Bible by rendering the ambiguous Hebrew *hammoreh litsedaqah* ("early rain for your vindication" in the RSV) as *Lehrer zur gerechtigkeit* ("teachers unto righteousness"). WA, DB 11[II], 221.

17. Luther consistently understood the "kings" of Ps. 68:12 as "the host of those who bore the tidings" in the preceding verse. In his German Psalter he translated the verse, "The kings of the armies are friends with one another," and in a marginal gloss he noted that "[kings] are the apostles whose teaching is in harmony." WA, DB 10[I], 321-313.

18. Etymologically the term "angel" means "messenger." The Hebrew *malak* is translated both ways in German as in English.

19. Gregory of Nazianzus is an example. Cf. WA 30[II], 529, n. 1.

child to study. And where it is possible for you to do this but you fail to do so, where your child has the ability and the desire to learn but you stand in the way, then you—and mark this well!—you are guilty of the harm that is done when the spiritual estate disappears and neither God nor God's word remains in the world. To the extent that you are able you are bringing about its demise. You refuse to give one child—and would do the same if all the children in the world were yours. So far as you are concerned, the serving of God can just die out altogether.

It does not help your case to say, "My neighbor keeps his son in school, so I don't need to." For your neighbor can say the same thing, and so can all the neighbors. Meanwhile, where is God to get people for his spiritual office? You have someone you could give, but you refuse—as does your neighbor. The office simply goes down to destruction so far as you are concerned. But because you allow the office instituted and established by your God and so dearly won to go to ruin, because you are so horribly ungrateful as to let it be destroyed, you yourself will be accursed. You will have nothing but shame and misery both for yourself and for your children, or be so tormented in other ways that both you and they will be damned, not only here on earth but eternally in hell. This will happen so that you may learn that your children are not so wholly yours that you need give nothing of them to God. He too will have what is rightfully his—and they are more his than yours!

And lest you think I am being too severe with you in this matter, I shall lay before you a partial statement of the gains and losses you are effecting—for who can recount them all?—such that you will have to admit yourself that you indeed belong to the devil and rightly deserve to be damned eternally in hell if you acquiesce in this fault and do not amend your ways. On the other hand, you may rejoice and be glad from the heart if you find that you have been chosen by God to devote your means and labor to raising a son who will be a good Christian pastor, preacher, or schoolmaster, and thereby to raise for God a special servant, yes (as was said above), an angel of God, a true bishop before God, a savior of many people, a king and prince in the kingdom of Christ, a teacher of God's people, a light of the world—indeed, who can recount all the distinction and honor that a good and faithful pastor has in the eyes of God? There is no dearer treasure, no nobler thing on earth or in this life than a good and faithful pastor and preacher.

Just think, whatever good is accomplished by the preaching office and the care of souls is assuredly accomplished by your own son as he faithfully performs this office. For example, each day through him many souls are taught, converted, baptized, and brought to Christ and saved, and redeemed from sin, death, hell, and the devil. Through him they come to everlasting righteousness, to everlasting life and heaven, so that Daniel [12:3] says well that "those who teach others shall shine like the brightness of the firmament; and those who turn many to righteousness shall be like the stars for ever and ever." Because God's word and office, when it proceeds aright, must without ceasing do great things and work actual miracles, so your son must without ceasing do great miracles before God, such as raising the dead, driving out devils, making the blind to see, the deaf to hear, the lepers clean, and the dumb to speak [Matt. 11:5]. Though these things may not happen bodily, they do happen spiritually in the soul, where the miracles are even greater, as Christ says in John 14 [:12], "He who believes in me will also do the works that I do; and greater works than these will he do." If the single believer can accomplish these things working independently with individuals, how much more will the preacher accomplish working publicly with the whole company of people? It is not the man, though, that does it. It is his office, ordained by God for this purpose. That is what does it—that and the word of God which he teaches. He is only the instrument through which it is accomplished.

Now if he accomplishes such great things spiritually, it follows that he also does bodily works and miracles, or at least gets them started. For how does it happen that Christians will rise from the dead at the Last Day, and that all the deaf, blind, lame, and other sufferers of bodily ills must lay aside their ailments? How does it happen that their bodies will not only become healthy, sound, and beautiful, but even shine as bright and fair as the sun [Matt. 13:43], as Christ says? Is it not because here on earth, through God's word, they have been converted, become believers, been baptized and incorporated into Christ? . . .

A true pastor thus contributes to the well-being of men in body and soul, in property and honor. But beyond that see how he also serves God and what glorious worship and sacrifice he renders. For by his work and word there are maintained in this world the kingdom of God, the name and honor and glory of God, the true knowledge of God, the right faith and understanding of Christ, the fruits of the suffering and blood and death of Christ, the gifts and works and power of the Holy Spirit, the true and saving use of baptism and the sacrament, the right and pure teaching of the gospel, the right way of disciplining and crucifying the body, and much more. Who could ever adequately praise any one of these things? And what more can still be said? How much he accomplishes by battling against the devil, the wisdom of this world, and the imaginations of the flesh; how many victories he wins; how he puts down error and prevents heresy. For he must strive and fight against the gates of hell [Matt. 16:18] and overcome the devil. This too is not his own doing; it is accomplished by his office and his word. These are the innumerable and unspeakable works and miracles of the preaching office. In a word, if we would praise God to the uttermost, we must praise his word and preaching; for the office and the word are his.

Now even if you were a king, you should not think you are too good to give your son and to train him for this office and work, even at the cost of all that you have. Is not the money and the labor you expend on such a son so highly honored, so gloriously blessed, so profitably invested that it counts in God's sight as better than any kingdom or empire? A man ought to be willing to crawl on his hands and knees to the ends of the earth to be able to invest his money so gloriously well. Yet right there in your own house and on your own lap you have that in which you can make such an investment. Shame, shame, and shame again upon our blind and despicable ingratitude that we should fail to see what extraordinary service we could render to God, indeed, how distinguished we could be in his sight with just a little application of effort and our own money and property.

The sophists accuse us Lutherans of not teaching good works. Isn't that great! They know so much about good works! Are not these things we have been speaking of good works? What are all the works of the foundations and monasteries compared with these glorious miracles? They are like the cawing of jackdaws and ravens, though not as good. For the daws at least like to caw; they do so gladly. But the sophists take no pleasure in their croaking; they caw reluctantly, like the hoopoes and owls. Now if it was formerly the custom to think highly of new priests and their first masses, and if fathers and mothers and all their friends were glad that they had raised a son to be an idle, lazy, useless mass-priest or glutton[24] who puts God to shame with his blasphemous sacrifice of the mass and his wasted prayers and scandalizes and defrauds the world with his unchaste life, how much more should you rejoice if you have raised a son for this office of preaching in which you are sure that he serves God so gloriously, helps men so generously, and smites the devil in such knightly fashion? You have made of your son such a true and excellent sacrifice to God that the very angels must look upon it as a splendid miracle.

You ought also to know the harm that you are doing if you take the opposite course. If God has given you a child who has the ability and the talent for this office, and you do not train him for it but look only to the belly and to temporal livelihood, then take the list of things mentioned above and run over the good works and miracles noted there, and see what a pious hypocrite and unproductive weed[25] you are. For so far as it is up to you, you are depriving God of an angel, a servant, a king and prince in his kingdom; a savior and comforter of men in matters that pertain to body and soul, property and honor; a captain and a knight to fight against the devil. Thus you are making a place for the devil and advancing his kingdom so that he brings more souls into sin, death, and hell every day and keeps them there, and wins victories everywhere; the world remains in heresy, error, contention, war, and strife, and gets worse every day; the kingdom of God goes down to destruction, along with Christian faith, the fruits of the suffering and blood of Christ, the work of the Holy Spirit, the gospel, and all worship of God; and all devil worship and unbelief get the upper hand. All of this need not have happened and could have been prevented, things could even have been improved, if your son had been trained for this work and entered it.

Suppose God were to address you on your deathbed, or at the Last Judgment, and say, "I was hungry, thirsty, a stranger, naked, sick, imprisoned, and you rendered me no service. For in that you

---

24. *Messpfaffen oder fresspfaffen.*
25. *Kreutlein;* cf. WA 33, 162, n. 1.

have not done it to people on earth and to my kingdom or gospel, but have helped put them down and allowed men's souls to perish, you have done this to me. For you could have helped. I gave you children and material means for this purpose, but you wantonly allowed me and my kingdom and the souls of men to suffer want and pine away—and you thereby served the devil and his kingdom instead of me and my kingdom. Well, let him be your reward. Go with him now into the abyss of hell. You have not helped to build but to weaken and destroy my kingdom in heaven and on earth; but you have helped the devil to build and increase his hell. Live, therefore, in the house that you have built!" . . .

In saying this I do not mean to insist that every man must train his child for this office, for it is not necessary that all boys become pastors, preachers, and schoolmasters. It is well to know that the children of lords and other important people are not to be used for this work, for the world also needs heirs, people without whom the temporal authority would go to pieces.[27] I am speaking of the common people, who used to have their children educated for the sake of the livings and benefices but now keep them away from learning to earn a livelihood. Even though they need no heirs they keep their children out of school, regardless of whether the children have the ability and talent for these offices and could serve God in them without privation or hindrance. Boys of such ability ought to be kept at their studies, especially sons of the poor, for all the endowments and revenues of the foundations and monasteries are earmarked for this purpose. In addition, though, other boys as well ought to study, even those of lesser ability. They ought at least to read, write, and understand Latin, for we need not only highly learned doctors and masters of Holy Scripture but also ordinary pastors who will teach the gospel and the catechism[28] to the young and ignorant, and baptize and administer the sacrament. That they may be incapable of doing battle with heretics is unimportant. For a good building we need not only hewn facings but also backing stone. In like manner we must also have sacristans and other persons who serve and help in relation to the office of preaching and the word of God.

---

27. The temporal government which Luther knew best was the hereditary feudal lordship.

28. I.e., the Ten Commandments, the Creed, and the Lord's Prayer.

Even though a boy who has studied Latin should afterward learn a trade and become a craftsman, he still stands as a ready reserve in case he should be needed as a pastor or in some other service of the word. Neither will such knowledge hurt his capacity to earn a living. On the contrary, he can rule his house all the better because of it, and besides, he is prepared for the office of preacher or pastor if he should be needed there. It is especially easy in our day to train persons for teaching the gospel and the catechism because not only Holy Scripture but also knowledge of all kinds is so abundant,[29] what with so many books, so much reading, and, thank God, so much preaching that one can learn more now in three years than was formerly possible in twenty. Even women[30] and children can now learn from German books and sermons more about God and Christ—I am telling the truth!—than all the universities, foundations, monasteries, the whole papacy, and all the world used to know. Ordinary pastors, however, must be able to use Latin. They cannot do without it any more than scholars can do without Greek and Hebrew,[31] as St. Augustine says[32] and canon law even prescribes.[33]

But you say, "Suppose things turn out badly and my son becomes a heretic or a knave? As they say, 'The learned are

29. By this time Luther had already published his translation of the New Testament (1522), the Pentateuch (1523), Joshua–Esther (1524), Job–Song of Solomon (1524), Jonah (1526), Habakkuk (1526), Zechariah (1527), and Isaiah (1528). Complete Bibles translated by Protestants had appeared in German in 1529 at Zurich and Worms. Cf. *LW* 35, 227-229.

30. For instances of Luther's repeated advocacy of education for girls, see *LW* 45, 175, 188-189, 344 n. 12, 368-371, and *LW* 44, 206.

31. See Luther's fuller argument for the study of classical languages in his 1524 appeal *To the Councilmen of All Cities in Germany. LW* 45, 356-377 *passim.*

32. "Men who know the Latin language . . . have need of two others in order to understand the Sacred Scriptures. These are Hebrew and Greek, by which they may turn back to the originals if the infinite variances of Latin translators cause any uncertainty." *Christian Instruction (De doctrina Christiana)*, Book II, chap. 11. FC 4, 73: cf. *MPL* 34, 42.

33. The eleventh canon of the Council of Vienna (1312) directed that in the interests of scriptural exposition and world mission Greek, Hebrew, Syriac, and Arabic be taught at the principal universities of Paris, Oxford, Bologna, and Salamanca, as well as in the curriculum for curial studies—though not general studies—at Rome. Berthold Altaner, "Die Durchführung des Vienner Konzilsbeschlusses über die Errichtung von Lehrstühlen für orientalische Sprachen," *Zeitschrift für Kirchengeschichte*, LII (1933), 227. The text of the decree as altered and promulgated by Pope John XXII on October 25, 1317, is given in *Clementis papae V. Constitutiones*, lib. v, tit. I: *De Magistris, C. I. CIC* 2, 1179.

daft.' "[34] Well, you have to take that chance. Your diligence and labor will not be lost. God will have regard for your faithful service and count it as though it had turned out well. You simply have to take the chance as you would in any other occupation for which you might train your son. How was it with the good Abraham? His son Ishmael did not turn out well; neither did Isaac's son Esau, or Adam's son Cain. Should Abraham therefore have given up training his son Isaac, or Isaac his son Jacob, or Adam his son Abel for the service of God? . . .

Moreover, that you may not worry too much about where your son's living will come from if he gives himself to learning and to this divine office and ministry, God has not left you or forgotten you in this matter either, so you need not worry or lament. He has promised through St. Paul in I Corinthians 9 [:14] that "those who proclaim the gospel should get their living by the gospel"; and Christ himself says in Matthew, "The laborer deserves his wages; eat and drink what they have."[35] Under the Old Testament, so that his office of preaching might not perish, God chose and took the whole tribe of Levi, that is to say, one-twelfth of the whole nation of Israel, and gave them the tithe from the whole nation, besides the first-fruits, all kinds of sacrifices, their own cities and pasture lands,[36] fields and meadows, cattle, and all that goes with them. Under the New Testament, see how in former times emperors, kings, princes, and lords gave to this office rich possessions, which the foundations and monasteries now have in more abundance than even the kings and princes themselves. God will not and cannot fail those who serve him faithfully, for he has bound himself by the promise given in Hebrews 13 [:5], "I will never fail you nor forsake you."

Think, too, how many parishes, pulpits, schools, and sacristanships there are. Most of them are sufficiently provided for,[37] and vacancies are occurring every day. What does this mean except that God has provided kitchen and cellar for your son in advance? His living is ready for him before he needs it; he does not have to scrape it together for himself. When I was a young student I heard

---

34. *Die Gelehrten, die Verkehrten.*
35. Luke 10:7-8; cf. Matt. 10:10.
36. *Vorstedte;* cf. Num. 35:1-8.
37. I.e., by endowments.

it said that in Saxony there were (if I remember rightly) about eighteen hundred parishes.[38] If that is true, and every parish required at least two persons, a pastor and a sacristan (except that in the cities there are preachers, chaplains, assistants, schoolmasters, and helpers), then in this one principality about four thousand educated persons are needed, of whom about one-third die off every ten years. I would wager that in half of Germany today there are not four thousand pupils in the schools. Now I estimate that there are scarcely eight hundred pastors in Saxony; how many will that make for the whole of Germany? I would like to know where we are going to get pastors, schoolmasters, and sacristans three years from now. If we do nothing about this, and if the princes especially do not try to see that the boys' schools and the universities are properly maintained, there will be such a scarcity of men that we shall have to give three or four cities to one pastor and ten villages to one chaplain, if indeed we can get even that many men.

---

38. If the reference is limited to Electoral Saxony, Luther's memory—or information—could be wrong, for the 1528–1529 visitation disclosed that apart from Wittenberg there were only one hundred forty-five pastoral positions. C. A. H. Burckhardt, *Geschichte der sächsischen Kirchen- und Schulvisitation* (Leipzig: Grunow, 1879), pp. 30-36.

Martin Luther, "A Sermon on Keeping Children in School," Robert C. Schultz, ed. *Luther's Works*, Vol. 46 (Philadelphia: Fortress, 1967), pp. 219-34.

At an earlier point in her ministry, Barbara Brown Taylor was a parish pastor in a number of Episcopal churches in the Southeast. Pastors around the country have long valued her distinctive voice. Taylor is a master of words, a superb verbal craftsman, who writes from the perspective of someone who loves her vocation as priest and who speaks in a way that is always full of gospel hope and encouragement. Here, in a sermon on vocation, she offers a grace-filled word on the nature of the call of God upon our lives.

Vocation
Barbara Brown Taylor

Not too long ago I spoke with a recent college graduate about his desire to be ordained. He was an articulate Christian who had been active in campus ministry and deeply influenced by the Episcopal chaplain at his school. He was bright, committed, and knowledgeable about the faith, but as he talked I grew perplexed. He did not want to serve a church, did not think he would like being held accountable by a denominational body, and was not attracted to a ministry of the sacraments, although he did believe he would like to preach once a month or so.

"Then why do you want to be ordained?" I asked him. He thought a while and finally said, "For the identity, I guess. So I could sit down next to someone on a bus who looked troubled and ask them how they were without them thinking I'm trying to hustle them. So I could walk up to someone on the street and do the same thing. So I could be up front about what I believe, in public as well as in private. So I would have the credentials to be the kind of Christian I want to be." His honesty was both disarming and disheartening. God help the church if clergy are the only Christians with "credentials," and God help all those troubled people on the bus if they have to wait for an ordained person to come along before anyone speaks to them.

When God calls, people respond in a variety of ways. Some pursue ordination and others put pillows over their heads, but the vast majority seek to answer God by changing how they live their more or less ordinary lives. It can be a frustrating experience, because deciding what is called for means nothing less than deciding what it means to be a Christian in a post-Christian world. Is it a matter of changing who you are—becoming a kinder, more spiritual person? Or is it a matter of changing what you do—looking for a new job, becoming more involved at church, or witnessing to the neighbors? What does God want from us, and how can we comply?

In many ways, those who pursue ordination take the easy way out. They choose a prescribed role that seems to meet all the requirements, and take up full-time residence in the church. They forego the hard work of straddling two different worlds, while those they serve have no such luxury. Those in the pulpit may know where they belong, but the people in the pews hold dual citizenship. When they come together as the church, that is where they belong—in God's country, which is governed by love. But when they leave that place, they cross the border into another country governed by other, less forgiving laws—and they live there too.

One man I know describes his dilemma this way. "On Sunday morning," he says, "I walk into a world that is the way God meant it to be. People are considerate of one another. Strangers are welcomed. We pray for justice and peace. Our sins are forgiven. We all face in one direction, and we worship the same God. When it's over, I get in my car to drive home feeling so full of love it's unbelievable, but by the time I've gone twenty minutes down the road it has already begun to wear off. By Monday morning it's all gone, and I've got another whole week to wait until Sunday rolls around again."

It is not a new problem he describes. From the very beginning, being a Christian has meant being a sojourner in a strange land. The reversal in our own day is that for many people it is the church, and not the rest of the world, that is strange. As the moat between the two has widened, the old bridges have become obsolete, leaving commuters to paddle across by themselves as best they can.

What many Christians are missing in their lives is a sense of vocation. The word itself means a call or summons, so that having a vocation means more than having a job. It means answering a specific call; it means doing what one is meant to do. In religious language, it means participating in the work of God, something that few lay people believe they do. Immersed in the corporate worlds of business and finance, and in the domestic worlds of household and family, it is hard for them to see how their lives have anything to do with the life of God. From time to time they pay visits to their priests, confessing how they ache for more meaningful work. Lay people are doing their jobs, but are they doing the jobs they were born to do?

Somewhere along the way we have misplaced the ancient vision of the church as a priestly people—set apart for ministry in baptism, confirmed and strengthened in worship, made manifest in service to the world. That vision is a foreign one to many church members, who have learned from colloquial usage that "minister" means the ordained person in a congregation, while "lay person" means someone who does not engage in full-time ministry. Professionally speaking that is fair enough—ordained people make their livings in ministry, and lay people do not—but speaking ecclesiastically, it is a disaster. Language like that turns clergy into purveyors of religion and lay people into consumers, who shop around for the church that offers them the best product.

But affirming the ministry of every baptized Christian is not an idea that appeals to many lay people these days. It sounds like more work, and most of them have all the work they can do. It sounds like more responsibility, while most of them are staggering under loads that are already too heavy. I will never forget the woman who listened to my speech on the ministry of the laity as God's best hope for the world and said, "I'm sorry, but I don't want to be that important."

Like many of those who sit beside her at church, she hears the invitation to ministry as an invitation to *do* more—to lead the every member canvass, or cook supper for the homeless, or teach vacation church school. Or she hears the invitation to ministry as an invitation to *be* more—to be more generous, more loving, more religious. No one has ever introduced her to the idea that her ministry might involve being just who she already is and doing just what she already does, with one difference: namely, that she understand herself to be God's person in and for the world.

However simple it sounds, I suppose that invitation will always frighten people, if only because they have heard such hair-raising tales about what happens to God's representatives. Whether they are reading the Bible or the newspaper, the bottom line is the same: God's people draw fire. Meanwhile, however, their fear causes them to surrender their power, and what they are willing to lay down, someone else is always willing to pick up. Traditionally, it is the clergy who have filled that role, keeping the church neat by gathering up all the power the laity have dropped there. Part of it is their genuine if misguided desire to be helpful, but the rest of it is megalomania—their perverse notion that they are the only ones who can be trusted with the ministry of the church.

Almost five hundred years ago, a German monk named Martin Luther wrestled the same problem. In his day, clergy ruled the church like princes, selling salvation and getting fat off alms. They got away with it because they claimed a special relationship with God. They asserted the superiority of their own vocations and elected themselves to the highest offices of the church, until all that was left for the laity was to attend Mass as they might attend the theater, watching mutely as the clergy consumed communion all by themselves, and paying their dues on the way out.

In his address to the German nobles, Luther attacked this farce. He made careful distinction between a Christian's vocation and a Christian's office, suggesting that our offices are what we do for a living—teacher, shopkeeper, homemaker, priest—and that none of them is any dearer to the heart of God than another. In our offices we exercise the diversity of our gifts, playing our parts in the ongoing life of the world. Our offices are the "texts" of our lives, to use a dramatic term, but the "subtext" is the common vocation to which we are all called at baptism. Whatever our individual offices in the world, our mutual vocation is to serve God through them.

> Only look at your tools, your needle, your thimble, your beer barrel, your articles of trade, your scales, your measures, and you will find this saying written on them. You will not be able to look anywhere where it does not strike your eyes. None of the things with which you deal daily are too trifling to tell you this incessantly, if you are but willing to hear it; and there is no lack of such preaching, for you have as many preachers as there are transactions, commodities, tools and other implements in your house and estate, and they shout this to your face: "My dear, use me toward your neighbor as you would want him to act toward you with that which is his."[1]

---

1. Gustaf Wingren, *Luther on Vocation* (Philadelphia: Fortress Press, 1957), 72.

My office, then, is in the church. That is where I do what I do, and what I do makes me different from those among whom I serve. But my *vocation* is to be God's person in the world, and that makes me the same as those among whom I serve. What we have in common is our baptism, that turning point in each one of our lives when we were received into the household of God and charged to confess the faith of Christ crucified, proclaim his resurrection, and share in his eternal priesthood. That last phrase is crucial. Our baptisms are our ordinations, the moments at which we are set apart as God's people to share Christ's ministry, whether or not we ever wear clerical collars around our necks. The instant we rise dripping from the waters of baptism and the sign of the cross is made upon our foreheads, we are marked as Christ's own forever.

I have often wondered whether the church would be even smaller than it is if that cross were made not with water but with permanent ink—a nice deep purple, perhaps—so that all who bore Christ's mark bore it openly, visibly, for the rest of their lives. In many ways, I think, that is the chief difference between the ministry of the baptized and the ministry of the ordained. The ordained consent to be visible in a way that the baptized do not. They agree to let people look at them as they struggle with their own baptismal vows: to continue in the apostles' teaching and fellowship, to resist evil, to proclaim the good news of God in Christ, to seek and serve Christ in all persons, to strive for justice and peace among all people. Those are not the vows of the ordained, but the baptized, even though we do not seem to know how to honor them in the course of ordinary life on earth.

Perhaps we should revive Luther's vision of the priesthood of all believers, who are ordained by God at baptism to share Christ's ministry in the world—a body of people united by that one common vocation, which they pursue across the gamut of their offices in the world. It is a vision that requires a rich and disciplined imagination, because it is largely a matter of learning to see in a different way. To believe in one's own priesthood is to see the extraordinary dimensions of an ordinary life, to see the hand of God at work in the world and to see one's own hands as necessary to that work. Whether those hands are diapering an infant, assembling an automobile or balancing a corporate account, they are God's hands, claimed by God at baptism for the accomplishment of

God's will on earth. There are plenty who will decline the honor, finding it either too fearsome or too intrusive to be taken seriously, but those willing to accept the challenge will want to know more about what a priest does, exactly.

The first thing to say is that a priest is a representative person— a *parson*—who walks the shifting boundary between heaven and earth, representing God to humankind, representing humankind to God, and serving each in the other's name. It is not possible to exercise such priesthood without participating in Christ's own, which means there are no entrepreneurs in ministry, only partners. Pursuing that vocation, priests are likely to wear a hundred different hats—social worker, chauffeur, cook, financial advisor, community organizer, babysitter, philanthropist, marriage counselor, cheerleader, friend—but whatever hat they happen to be wearing at the time, priests remember that they wear it as God's person, for God's sake, in God's name.

Everything else a priest does comes to focus in worship, where all of God's ministers—the baptized ones and the ordained ones— approach God through the sacraments of word and table. In the early church, believers decided it was not practical for all of them to preside over community worship, so they elected different members of the body to officiate from week to week. Sometimes they drew lots, making it clear that the job had nothing to do with superiority. It was a representative function, whereby one member of the congregation stepped forward to do what everyone present was able to do. That person's ministry did not overshadow theirs, but affirmed it, so that what they did together in worship became a model for what they did after worship as they returned to their offices in the world.

In our own time, the lots are fixed. Through long and sometimes arduous processes, we choose certain people to lead us in worship, so that we become accustomed to hearing them from the pulpit and seeing them at the altar—so accustomed that it is easy to forget they are not the only ministers in the church. The ministry of the ordained is no substitute for the ministry of the baptized; it is a prototype, copied from Christ's own, that offers the whole people of God a pattern for seeking and responding to the Lord's presence in our midst.

While preaching and celebrating sacraments are discrete tasks, the two particular functions to which I was ordained, they are also metaphors for the whole church's understanding of life and faith. For me, to preach is first of all to immerse myself in the word of God, to look inside every sentence and underneath every phrase for the layers of meaning that have accumulated there over the centuries. It is to examine my own life and the life of the congregation with the same care, hunting the connections between the word on the page and the word at work in the world. It is to find my own words for bringing those connections to life, so that others can experience them for themselves. When that happens—when the act of preaching becomes a source of revelation for me as well as for those who listen to me—then the good news every sermon proclaims is that the God who acted is the God who acts, and that the Holy Spirit is alive and well in the world.

Understood in this way, preaching becomes something the whole community participates in, not only through their response to a particular sermon but also through identifying with the preacher. As they listen week after week, they are invited to see the world the way the preacher does—as the realm of God's activity—and to make connections between their Christian faith and their lives the same way they hear them made from the pulpit. If the preaching they hear is effective, it will not hand them sacks of wisdom and advice to take home and consume during the week, but invite them into the field to harvest those fruits for themselves, until they become preachers in their own right. Preaching is not something an ordained minister does for fifteen minutes on Sundays, but what the whole congregation does all week long; it is a way of approaching the world, and of gleaning God's presence there.

Likewise, the sacraments of the church embody a broad Christian understanding of life on earth: chiefly, that the most ordinary things in the world are signs of grace. The God who created them and called them good keeps on doing so. Through the sacraments, we are invited to understand that all the things of this world are good enough to bear the presence of God and to deepen the relationship between heaven and earth. To glimpse the holiness of ordinary bread or wine or oil or water is to begin to suspect that holiness may be hiding in other things as well. Holiness may be lurking inside a green leaf, a clay cup, a clean sheet, a freshly sawn board; it may be just below the surface of a key, a clock, a shiny stone. To draw a line around the seven sacraments for which the church has rites is to underestimate the grace of God and the holiness of the creation. According to the catechism, "God does not limit himself to these rites; they are patterns of countless ways by which God uses material things to reach out to us."

Sacraments not only hallow the stuff of the world; they also hallow our handling of that stuff. They give us something to look at, something to taste and smell, something to feel upon our skin and experience for ourselves. They give us something to do with our hands and with our bodies as well—walking up to receive communion, bending over the baptismal font, kneeling so that hands may be laid upon our heads. We may spend our whole lives learning what those sacraments mean, but the experience of them exceeds our understanding of them. Reaching out to handle God, it is we who are handled, gently but with powerful effect.

Several weeks ago I took communion to an elderly and beloved woman at her home. She sat heaped in her wheelchair as I turned the television tray between us into an altar: tiny chalice, tiny paten, and a yellow rose from the garden, all spread on an embossed white paper napkin. Because she was ninety-seven years old and all but blind, I suggested that she not bother with a prayer book. "I'll read all the lines," I said, "yours and mine too. You just join in on the parts you know." She nodded and we began, each of us delivering our lines on cue until I came to the Great Thanksgiving. Then, when I raised my hands, she raised hers too, the sleeves of her flowered gown falling down her bony arms as she lifted her gnarled fists into the air. We faced each other across the table, mirror images of one another.

"Holy and gracious Father," I began, "in your infinite love you made us for yourself. . . ."

"In your infinite love," she said slowly, tasting each word.

"And, when we had fallen into sin and become subject to evil and death," I went on, "you, in your mercy, sent Jesus Christ. . . ."

"In your mercy," she said, smiling as though someone she knew had just entered the room. When I realized she meant to say the whole prayer with me, I waited for her to catch up and we prayed it together, our voices looping through one another in an unstudied duet. I had thought they were my lines, but they turned out to be hers as well. No one had fooled her, all those years she sat watching someone else bless the bread and the wine. She knew she was a priest.

Barbara Brown Taylor, *The Preaching Life* (Boston, Mass.: Cowley Publications, 1993), pp. 25-34.

In the early 1980s, the World Council of Churches set at work to devise an ecumenical statement of shared beliefs and practices related to the three most controversial, at times both terribly divisive and wonderfully unifying, aspects of the Christian faith. After years of discussion and debate, the result was the publication of Baptism, Eucharist, and Ministry. *I include here most of the ministry paragraphs as essential for anyone who wants to understand what the church believes about its ministry. B.E.M., as it came to be known, treats all the biblical and historic bases for the ordained ministry. It begins its discussion of church leaders, as all such discussions ought to begin, with affirmations about the church. Pastors have no purpose other than that which is derived from the baptismal ministry of all Christians. The calling of priests and pastors is derivative of the calling of the whole people of God. Behind nearly every paragraph of B.E.M. is a hard-fought, carefully worded, honest declaration of the ecumenical agreement on the most important theological substance of the church. The resulting report does not make for scintillating reading. However, it is the most succinct, comprehensive, ecumenical statement that we have on the nature of Christian leadership.*

Baptism, Eucharist, and Ministry
Faith and Order Paper No. 111

I. The Calling of the Whole People of God

M1. In a broken world God calls the whole of humanity to become God's people. For this purpose God chose Israel and then spoke in a unique and decisive way in Jesus Christ, God's Son. Jesus made his own the nature, condition and cause of the whole human race, giving himself as a sacrifice for all. Jesus' life of service, his death and resurrection, are the foundation of a new community which is built up continually by the good news of the Gospel and the gifts of the sacraments. The Holy Spirit unites in a single body those who follow Jesus Christ and sends them as witnesses into the world. Belonging to the Church means living in communion with God through Jesus Christ in the Holy Spirit.

M2. The life of the Church is based on Christ's victory over the powers of evil and death, accomplished once for all. Christ offers forgiveness, invites to repentance and delivers from destruction. Through Christ, people are enabled to turn in praise to God and in service to their neighbors. In Christ they find the source of new life in freedom, mutual forgiveness and love. Through Christ their hearts and minds are directed to the consummation of the Kingdom where Christ's victory will become manifest and all things made new. God's purpose is that, in Jesus Christ, all people should share in this fellowship.

M3. The Church lives through the liberating and renewing power of the Holy Spirit. That the Holy Spirit was upon Jesus is evidenced in his baptism, and after the resurrection that same Spirit was given to those who believed in the Risen Lord in order to recreate them as the body of Christ. The Spirit calls people to faith, sanctifies them through many gifts, gives them strength to witness to the Gospel, and empowers them to serve in hope and love. The Spirit keeps the Church in the truth and guides it despite the frailty of its members.

M4. The Church is called to proclaim and prefigure the Kingdom of God. It accomplishes this by announcing the Gospel to the world and by its very existence as the body of Christ. In Jesus the Kingdom of God came among us. He offered salvation to sinners. He preached good news to the poor, release to the captives, recovery of sight to the blind, liberation to the oppressed (Luke 4:18).

Christ established a new access to the Father. Living in this communion with God, all members of the Church are called to confess their faith and to give account of their hope. They are to identify with the joys and sufferings of all people as they seek to witness in caring love. The members of Christ's body are to struggle with the oppressed towards that freedom and dignity promised with the coming of the Kingdom. This mission needs to be carried out in varying political, social and cultural contexts. In order to fulfil this mission faithfully, they will seek relevant forms of witness and service in each situation. In so doing they bring to the world a foretaste of the joy and glory of God's Kingdom.

M5. The Holy Spirit bestows on the community diverse and complementary gifts. These are for the common good of the whole people and are manifested in acts of service within the community and to the world. They may be gifts of communicating the Gospel in word and deed, gifts of healing, gifts of praying, gifts of teaching and learning, gifts of serving, gifts of guiding and following, gifts of inspiration and vision. All members are called to discover, with the help of the community, the gifts they have received and to use them for the building up of the Church and for the service of the world to which the Church is sent.

M6. Though the churches are agreed in their general understanding of the calling of the people of God, they differ in their understanding of how the life of the Church is to be ordered. In particular, there are differences concerning the place and forms of the ordained ministry. As they engage in the effort to overcome these differences, the churches need to work from the perspective of the calling of the whole people of God. A common answer needs to be found to the following question: How, according to the will of God and under the guidance of the Holy Spirit, is the life of the Church to be understood and ordered, so that the Gospel may be spread and the community built up in love?

II. The Church and the Ordained Ministry

M7. Differences in terminology are part of the matter under debate. In order to avoid confusion in the discussions on the ordained ministry in the Church, it is necessary to delineate clearly how various terms are used in the following paragraphs.

a) The word *charism* denotes the gifts bestowed by the Holy Spirit on any member of the body of Christ for the building up of the community and the fulfillment of its calling.

b) The word *ministry* in its broadest sense denotes service to which the whole people of God is called, whether as individuals, as a local community, or as the universal Church. Ministry or ministries can also denote the particular institutional forms which this service may take.

c) The term *ordained ministry* refers to persons who have received a charism and whom the church appoints for service by ordination through the invocation of the Spirit and the laying on of hands.

d) Many churches use the word *priest* to denote certain ordained ministers. Because this usage is not universal, this document will discuss the substantive questions in paragraph 17.

A. The Ordained Ministry

M8. In order to fulfil its mission, the Church needs persons who are publicly and continually responsible for pointing to its fundamental dependence on Jesus Christ, and thereby provide, within a multiplicity of gifts, a focus of its unity. The ministry of such persons, who since very early times have been ordained, is constitutive for the life and witness of the Church.

M9. The Church has never been without persons holding specific authority and responsibility. Jesus chose and sent the disciples to be witnesses of the Kingdom (Matt. 10:1-8). The Twelve were promised that they would "sit on thrones judging the tribes of Israel" (Luke 22:30). A particular role is attributed to the Twelve within the communities of the first generation. They are witnesses of the Lord's life and resurrection (Acts 1:21-26). They lead the community in prayer, teaching, the breaking of bread, proclamation and service (Acts 2:42-47; 6:2-6, etc.). The very existence of the Twelve and other apostles shows that, from the beginning, there were differentiated roles in the community.

M10. Jesus called the Twelve to be representatives of the renewed Israel. At that moment they represent the whole people of God and at the same time exercise a special role in the midst of that community. After the resurrection they are among the leaders of the community. It can be said that the apostles prefigure both the Church as a whole and the persons within it who are entrusted with the specific authority and responsibility. The role of the apostles as witnesses to the resurrection of Christ is unique and unrepeatable. There is therefore a difference between the apostles and the ordained ministers whose ministries are founded on theirs.

M11. As Christ chose and sent the apostles, Christ continues through the Holy Spirit to choose and call persons into the ordained ministry. As heralds and ambassadors, ordained ministers are representatives of Jesus Christ to the community, and proclaim his message of reconciliation. As leaders and teachers they call the community to submit to the authority of Jesus Christ, the teacher and prophet, in whom law and prophets were fulfilled. As pastors, under Jesus Christ the chief shepherd, they assemble and guide the dispersed people of God, in anticipation of the coming Kingdom.

M12. All members of the believing community, ordained and lay, are interrelated. On the one hand, the community needs ordained ministers. Their presence reminds the community of the divine initiative, and of the dependence of the Church on Jesus Christ, who is the source of its mission and the foundation of its unity. They serve to build up the community in Christ and to strengthen its witness. In them the Church seeks an example of holiness and loving concern. On the other hand, the ordained ministry has no existence apart from the community. Ordained ministers can fulfil their calling only in and for the community. They cannot dispense with the recognition, the support and the encouragement of the community.

M13. The chief responsibility of the ordained ministry is to assemble and build up the body of Christ by proclaiming and teaching the Word of God, by celebrating the sacraments, and by guiding the life of the community in its worship, its mission and its caring ministry.

M14. It is especially in the eucharistic celebration that the ordained ministry is the visible focus of the deep and all-embracing communion between Christ and the members of his body. In the celebration of the eucharist, Christ gathers, teaches and nourishes the Church. It is Christ who invites to the meal and who presides at it. In most churches this presidency is signified and represented by an ordained minister.

B. Ordained Ministry and Authority

M15. The authority of the ordained minister is rooted in Jesus Christ, who has received it from the Father (Matt. 28:18), and who confers it by the Holy Spirit through the act of ordination. This act takes place within a community which accords public recognition to a particular person. Because Jesus came as one who serves (Mark 10:45; Luke 22:27), to be set apart means to be consecrated to service. Since ordination is essentially a setting apart with prayer for the gift of the Holy Spirit, the authority of the ordained ministry is not to be understood as the possession of the ordained person but as a gift for the continuing edification of the body in and for which the minister has been ordained. Authority has the character of responsibility before God and is exercised with the cooperation of the whole community.

M16. Therefore, ordained ministers must not be autocrats or impersonal functionaries. Although called to exercise wise and loving leadership on the basis of the Word of God, they are bound to the faithful in interdependence and reciprocity. Only when they seek the response and acknowledgment of the community can their authority be protected from the distortions of isolation and domination. They manifest and exercise the authority of Christ in the way Christ himself revealed God's authority in the world, by committing their life to the community. Christ's authority is unique. "He spoke as one who has authority (*exousia*), not as the scribes" (Matt. 7:29). This authority is an authority governed by love for the "sheep who have no shepherd" (Matt. 9:36). It is confirmed by his life of service and, supremely, by his death and resurrection. Authority in the Church can only be authentic as it seeks to conform to this model.

C. Ordained Ministry and Priesthood

M17. Jesus Christ is the unique priest of the new covenant. Christ's life was given as a sacrifice for all. Derivatively, the Church as a whole can be described as a priesthood. All members are called to offer their being "as a living sacrifice" and to intercede for the Church and the salvation of the world. Ordained ministers are related, as are all Christians, both to the priesthood of Christ, and to the priesthood of the Church. But they may appropriately be called priests because they fulfil a particular priestly service by strengthening and building up the royal and prophetic priesthood of the faithful through word and sacraments, through their prayers of intercession, and through their pastoral guidance of the community.

D. The Ministry of Men and Women in the Church

M18. Where Christ is present, human barriers are being broken. The Church is called to convey to the world the image of a new humanity. There is in Christ no male or female (Gal. 3:28). Both women and men must discover together their contributions to the service of Christ in the Church. The Church must discover the ministry which can be provided by women as well as that which can be provided by men. A deeper understanding of the comprehensiveness of ministry which reflects the interdependence of men and women needs to be more widely manifested in the life of the Church.

Though they agree on this need, the churches draw different conclusions as to the admission of women to the ordained ministry. An increasing number of churches have decided that there is no biblical or theological reason against ordaining women, and many of them have subsequently proceeded to do so. Yet many churches hold that the tradition of the Church in this regard must not be changed.

III. The Forms of the Ordained Ministry

A. Bishops, Presbyters and Deacons

M19. The New Testament does not describe a single pattern of ministry which might serve as a blueprint or continuing norm for all future ministry in the Church. In the New Testament there appears rather a variety of forms which existed at different places and times. As the Holy Spirit continued to lead the Church in life, worship and mission, certain elements from this early variety were further developed and became settled into a more universal pattern of ministry. During the second and third centuries, a threefold pattern of bishop, presbyter and deacon became established as the pattern of ordained ministry throughout the Church. In succeeding centuries, the ministry by bishop, presbyter and deacon underwent considerable changes in its practical exercise. At some points of crisis in the history of the Church, the continuing functions of ministry were in some places and communities distributed according to structures other than the predominant threefold pattern. Sometimes appeal was made to the New Testament in justification of these other patterns. In other cases, the restructuring of ministry was held to lie within the competence of the Church as it adapted to changed circumstances.

M20. It is important to be aware of the changes the threefold ministry has undergone in the history of the Church. In the earliest instances, where threefold ministry is mentioned, the reference is to the local eucharistic community. The bishop was the leader of the community. He was ordained and installed to proclaim the Word and preside over the celebration of the eucharist. He was surrounded by a college of presbyters and by deacons who assisted in his tasks. In this context the bishop's ministry was a focus of unity within the whole community.

M21. Soon, however, the functions were modified. Bishops began increasingly to exercise *episkope* over several local communities at the same time. In the first generation, apostles had exercised *episkope* in the wider Church. Later Timothy and Titus are recorded to have fulfilled a function of *episkope* in a given area. Later again this apostolic task is carried out in a new way by the bishops. They provide a focus for unity in life and witness within areas comprising several eucharistic communities. As a consequence, presbyters and deacons are assigned new roles. The presbyters become the leaders of the local eucharistic community, and as assistants of the bishops, deacons receive responsibilities in the larger area.

M22. Although there is no single New Testament pattern, although the Spirit has many times led the Church to adapt its ministries to contextual needs, and although other forms of the ordained ministry have been blessed with the gifts of the Holy Spirit, nevertheless the threefold ministry of bishop, presbyter and deacon may serve today as an expression of the unity we seek and also as a means for achieving it. Historically, it is true to say, the threefold ministry became the generally accepted pattern in the Church of the early centuries and is still retained today by many churches. In the fulfillment of their mission and service the churches need people who in different ways express and perform the tasks of the ordained ministry in its diaconal, presbyteral and episcopal aspects and functions.

M23. The Church as the body of Christ and the eschatological people of God is constituted by the Holy Spirit through a diversity of gifts or ministries. Among these gifts a ministry of *episkope* is necessary to express and safeguard the unity of the body. Every church needs this ministry of unity in some form in order to be the

Church of God, the one body of Christ, a sign of the unity of all in the Kingdom.

M24. The threefold pattern stands evidently in need of reform. In some churches the collegial dimension of leadership in the eucharistic community has suffered diminution. In others, the function of deacons has been reduced to an assistant role in the celebration of the liturgy: they have ceased to fulfill any function with regard to the diaconal witness of the Church. In general, the relation of the presbyterate to the episcopal ministry has been discussed throughout the centuries, and the degree of the presbyter's participation in the episcopal ministry is still for many an unresolved question of far-reaching ecumenical importance. In some cases, churches which had not formally kept the threefold form have, in fact, maintained certain of its original patterns.

M25. The traditional threefold pattern thus raises question for all the churches. Churches maintaining the threefold pattern will need to ask how its potential can be fully developed for the most effective witness of the Church in this world. In this task churches not having the threefold pattern should also participate. They will further need to ask themselves whether the threefold pattern as developed does not have a powerful claim to be accepted by them.

B. Guiding Principles for the Exercise of the Ordained Ministry in the Church

M26. Three considerations are important in this respect. The ordained ministry should be exercised in a personal, collegial and communal way. It should be personal because the presence of Christ among his people can most effectively be pointed to by the person ordained to proclaim the Gospel and to call the community to serve the Lord in unity of life and witness. It should also be collegial, for there is need for a college of ordained ministers sharing in the common task of representing the concerns of the community. Finally, the intimate relationship between the ordained ministry and the community should find expression in a communal dimension where the exercise of the ordained ministry is rooted in the life of the community and requires the community's effective participation in the discovery of God's will and the guidance of the Spirit.

M27. The ordained ministry needs to be constitutionally or canonically ordered and exercised in the Church in such a way that each of these three dimensions can find adequate expression. At the level of the local eucharistic community there is need for an ordained minister acting within a collegial body. Strong emphasis should be placed on the active participation of all members in the life and the decision-making of the community. At the regional level there is again need for an ordained minister exercising a service of unity. The collegial and communal dimensions will find expression in regular representative synodal gatherings.

C. Functions of Bishops, Presbyters and Deacons

M28. What can then be said about the functions and even the titles of bishops, presbyters and deacons? A uniform answer to this question is not required for the mutual recognition of the ordained ministry. The following considerations on functions are, however, offered in a tentative way.

M29. Bishops preach the Word, preside at the sacraments, and administer discipline in such a way as to be representative pastoral ministers of oversight, continuity and unity in the Church. They have pastoral oversight of the area to which they are called. They serve the apostolicity and unity of the Church's teaching, worship and sacramental life. They have responsibility for leadership in the Church's mission. They relate the Christian community in their area to the wider Church, and the universal Church to their community. They, in communion with the presbyters and deacons and the whole community, are responsible for the orderly transfer of ministerial authority in the Church.

M30. Presbyters serve as pastoral ministers of Word and sacraments in a local eucharistic community. They are preachers and teachers of the faith, exercise pastoral care, and bear responsibility for the discipline of the congregation to the end that the world may believe and that the entire membership of the Church may be renewed, strengthened and equipped in ministry. Presbyters have particular responsibility for the preparation of members for Christian life and ministry.

M31. Deacons represent to the Church its calling as servant in the world. By struggling in Christ's name with the myriad needs of societies and persons, deacons exemplify the interdependence of worship and service in the Church's life. They exercise responsibility in the worship of the congregation: for example by reading the scriptures, preaching and leading the people in prayer. They help in the teaching of the congregation. They exercise a ministry of love within the community. They fulfil certain administrative tasks and may be elected to responsibilities for governance.

D. *Variety of Charisms*

M32. The community which lives in the power of the Spirit will be characterized by a variety of charisms. The Spirit is the giver of diverse gifts which enrich the life of the community. In order to enhance their effectiveness, the community will recognize publicly certain of these charisms. While some serve permanent needs in the life of the community, others will be temporary. Men and women in the communities of religious order fufil a service which is of particular importance for the life of the Church. The ordained ministry, which is itself a charism, must not become a hindrance for the variety of these charisms. On the contrary, it will help the community to discover the gifts bestowed on it by the Holy Spirit and will equip members of the body to serve in a variety of ways.

M33. In the history of the Church there have been times when the truth of the Gospel could only be preserved through prophetic and charismatic leaders. Often new impulses could find their way into the life of the Church only in unusual ways. At times reforms required a special ministry. The ordained ministers and the whole community will need to be attentive to the challenge of such special ministries.

IV. Succession in the Apostolic Tradition

A. *Apostolic Tradition in the Church*

M34. In the Creed, the Church confesses itself to be apostolic. The Church lives in continuity with the apostles and their proclamation. The same Lord who sent the apostles continues to be present in the Church. The Spirit keeps the Church in the apostolic tradition until the fulfillment of history in the Kingdom of God.

Apostolic tradition in the Church means continuity in the permanent characteristics of the Church of the apostles: witness to the apostolic faith, proclamation and fresh interpretation of the Gospel, celebration of baptism and the eucharist, the transmission of ministerial responsibilities, communion in prayer, love, joy and suffering, service to the sick and the needy, unity among the local churches and sharing the gifts which the Lord has given to each.

B. Succession of the Apostolic Ministry

M35. The primary manifestation of apostolic succession is to be found in the apostolic tradition of the Church as a whole. The succession is an expression of the permanence and, therefore, of the continuity of Christ's own mission in which the Church participates. Within the Church the ordained ministry has a particular task of preserving and actualizing the apostolic faith. The orderly transmission of the ordained ministry is therefore a powerful expression of the continuity of the Church throughout history; it also underlines the calling of the ordained minister as guardian of the faith. Where churches see little importance in orderly transmission, they should ask themselves whether they have not to change their conception of continuity in the apostolic tradition. On the other hand, where the ordained ministry does not adequately serve the proclamation of the apostolic faith, churches must ask themselves whether their ministerial structures are not in need of reform.

M36. Under the particular historical circumstances of the growing Church in the early centuries, the succession of bishop became one of the ways, together with the transmission of the Gospel and the life of the community, in which the apostolic tradition of the Church was expressed. This succession was understood as serving, symbolizing and guarding the continuity of the apostolic faith and communion.

M37. In churches which practice the succession through the episcopate, it is increasingly recognized that a continuity in apostolic faith, worship and mission has been preserved in churches which have not retained the form of historic episcopate. This recognition finds additional support in the fact that the reality and function of the episcopal ministry have been preserved in many of these churches, with or without the title "bishop." Ordination, for example, is always done in them by persons in whom the Church recognizes the authority to transmit the ministerial commission.

M38. These considerations do not diminish the importance of the episcopal ministry. On the contrary, they enable churches which have not retained the episcopate to appreciate the episcopal succession as a sign, though not a guarantee, of the continuity and unity of the Church. Today churches, including those engaged in union negotiations, are expressing willingness to accept episcopal succession as a sign of the apostolicity of the life of the whole Church. Yet, at the same time, they cannot accept any suggestion that the ministry exercised in their own tradition should be invalid until the moment that it enters into an existing line of episcopal succession. Their acceptance of the episcopal succession will best further the unity of the whole Church if it is part of a wider process by which the episcopal churches themselves also regain their lost unity.

V. Ordination

A. The Meaning of Ordination

M39. The Church ordains certain of its members for the ministry in the name of Christ by the invocation of the Spirit and the laying on of hands (I Tim. 4:14; II Tim. 1:6); in so doing it seeks to continue the mission of the apostles and to remain faithful to their teaching. The act of ordination by those who are appointed for this ministry attests the bond of the Church with Jesus Christ and the apostolic witness, recalling that it is the risen Lord who is the true ordainer and bestows the gift. In ordaining, the Church, under the inspiration of the Holy Spirit, provides for the faithful proclamation of the Gospel and humble service in the name of Christ. The laying on of hands is the sign of the gift of the Spirit, rendering visible the fact that the ministry was instituted in the revelation accomplished in Christ, and reminding the Church to look to him as the source of its commission. This ordination, however, can have different intentions according to the specific tasks of bishops, presbyters and deacons as indicated in the liturgies of ordination.

M40. Properly speaking, then, ordination denotes an action by God and the community by which the ordained are strengthened by the Spirit for their task and are upheld by the acknowledgment and prayers of the congregation.

B. The Act of Ordination

M41. A long and early Christian tradition places ordination in the context of worship and especially of the eucharist. Such a place for the service of ordination preserves the understanding of ordination as an act of the whole community, and not of a certain order within it or of the individual ordained. The act of ordination by the laying on of hands of those appointed to do so is at one and the same time invocation of the Holy Spirit (*epiklesis*); sacramental sign; acknowledgment of gifts and commitment.

M42. (a) Ordination is an invocation to God that the new minister be given the power of the Holy Spirit in the new relation which is established between this minister and the local Christian community and, by intention, the Church universal. The otherness of God's initiative, of which the ordained ministry is a sign, is here acknowledged in the act of ordination itself. "The Spirit blows where it wills" (John 3:3): the invocation of the Spirit implies the absolute dependence on God for the outcome of the Church's prayer. This means that the Spirit may set new forces in motion and open new possibilities "far more abundantly than all that we ask or think" (Eph. 3:20).

M43. (b) Ordination is a sign of the granting of this prayer by the Lord who gives the gift of the ordained ministry. Although the outcome of the Church's *epiklesis* depends on the freedom of God, the Church ordains in confidence that God, being faithful to his promise in Christ, enters sacramentally into contingent, historical forms of human relationship and uses them for his purpose. Ordination is a sign preformed in faith that the spiritual relationship signified is present in, with and through the words spoken, the gestures made and the forms employed.

M44. (c) Ordination is an acknowledgment by the Church of the gifts of the Spirit in the one ordained, and a commitment by both the Church and the ordinand to the new relationship. By receiving the new minister in the act of ordination, the congregation acknowledges the minister's gifts and commits itself to be open towards these gifts. Likewise those ordained offer their gifts to the Church and commit themselves to the burden and opportunity of new authority and responsibility. At the same time, they enter into a collegial relationship with other ordained ministers.

C. The Conditions for Ordination

M45. People are called in differing ways to the ordained ministry. There is a personal awareness of a call from the Lord to dedicate oneself to the ordained ministry. This call may be discerned through personal prayer and reflection, as well as through suggestion, example, encouragement, guidance coming from family, friends, the congregation, teachers, and other church authorities. This call must be authenticated by the Church's recognition of the gifts and graces of the particular person, both natural and spiritually given, needed for the ministry to be performed. God can use people both celibate and married for the ordained ministry.

M46. Ordained persons may be professional ministers in the sense that they receive their salaries from the church. The church may also ordain people who remain in other occupations or employment.

M47. Candidates for the ordained ministry need appropriate preparation through study of scripture and theology, prayer and spirituality, and through acquaintance with the social and human realities of the contemporary world. In some situations, this preparation may take a form other than that of prolonged academic study. The period of training will be one in which the candidate's call is tested, fostered and confirmed, or its understanding modified.

Baptism, Eucharist, and Ministry, **Faith and Order Paper No. 111 (Geneva: World Council of Churches, 1982).**

CHAPTER TWO

Ministry for the Twenty-first Century

His word moved America, his life and his death made him one of the church's noble martyrs. But before all that, Martin Luther King Jr. was a pastor, a preacher who knew what it was like to enter the pulpit on a weekly basis and proclaim the Word of God to the gathered flock. The most influential American orator of the twentieth century was one whose preaching skills where first honed within the tug and pull of a congregation.

My friend Richard Lischer wrote a wonderful book on the preaching of King, The Preacher King. *Working from King's unpublished sermons, recordings, and interviews with those to whom King was a pastor, Lischer rendered a portrait of the man whose words reformed the moral conscience of a nation. Today, King is best remembered for his words written from a Birmingham jail or spoken before the multitudes at the Lincoln Memorial. But before he spoke these words as a prophet, he was a pastor whose words were born in that weekly confrontation with scripture in the context of a vibrant congregation called Ebenezer. There King developed what Lischer calls, King's "Ebenezer Gospel."*

The Ebenezer Gospel
Richard Lischer

Not counting his days of student apprenticeship, Martin Luther King, Jr. served Ebenezer Baptist Church as its "co-pastor" for eight years and three months, just under one hundred months in all. He did not preach at Ebenezer every Sunday, but he spoke there often enough to establish what Paul (or any preacher) would have called "my gospel," an evolving, sometimes volatile, interpretation of God's will for Ebenezer and the world. The Ebenezer gospel is what the preacher King had to say to his people over the course of his one-hundred-month pastorate; it is his "message." It is important to gather the fragments of this gospel into a coherent whole because he carried a modified version of it into world history, thus making knowledge of the Ebenezer gospel essential to an understanding of his public message—his quest for justice, yearning for redemption, insistence on nonviolence, embrace of suffering, prophetic rage, and all else that emerged from his Sundays in Atlanta. King's Ebenezer sermons differ from his mass-meeting speeches and his civil addresses, but they are not inconsistent with them; they are the religious subtext for his sermon to the nation. The "first draft" of all that he said, achieved, and suffered from Montgomery to Memphis is present in the audiotape recordings and crudely typed transcripts of his Ebenezer gospel.

I

The bent of King's gospel follows the contours of the Christian story of redemption. It begins with the human condition, which is nothing other than the experience of one of life's many perplexities. The perplexity suggests a larger problem, the problem yields a sin, the sin opens onto a social concern (always related to race or war), the concern invites a generalization about "man" or "life," and the stage is set for the next phase of the message. Each of the following sentences represents a statement of the human predicament from a variety of sermons ranging from 1960 to 1968:

> Probably no admonition of Jesus has been more difficult to follow than the command to "love your enemies." . . .

> [Like James and John] we will discover that we too have those same basic desires for recognition, for importance, that same desire for attention. . . .

> Life is full of annoying interruptions. Things go smoothly for many days, and many years, often, and then our lives are interrupted. . . .

> I guess one of the great agonies of life is that we are constantly trying to finish that which is unfinishable.

> One of the great problems of life is that of dealing creatively with disappointment. Very few of us live to see our fondest hopes fulfilled.

There are some things that are as basic and structural in history [as sunrise and sunset] and if we don't know these things, we are in danger of destroying ourselves. . . .

[O]ne of the great tragedies of life is the fact that, after a while, most people lose the capacity to say "thank you."

Any attempt to "fix" the problem with our own resources only makes it worse. We invariably exaggerate or become overly reliant upon one of the possible solutions to the problem, which leads to another sin. In King's vocabulary "sin" is a disordered or one-sided attempt to solve a problem by taking it into our own hands and denying its true nature. Sin entails the denial of the transcendent character of our problems, which means that we fail to see them in the context of God's power to rectify them. In "Pride versus Humility," he concludes, "[T]herefore the sin can't be pardoned because you've lost the capacity of realizing the necessity of being pardoned," which, he adds pointedly, is the white southern Christian's problem. Life's interruptions, to cite a frequently recurring theme, may evoke the reactions of despair and fatalism, or they may cause us to lash out in anger toward others. In either case, it does not occur to us to transform these adversities into opportunities for service.

Our frustrations produce in us an internal civil war. We know what is good, but we always fail to do it. Instead of dealing creatively with the many forces that assail us, we nurture personal and social resentment. In our own community, those who are robbed of their civil rights practice other, more banal forms of robbery on one another: "The barbershop, the beauty shop, the card table, the telephone—[are] all centers and instruments of robbery."

What we do to one another is both a microcosm and a consequence of what has been done to us. The little robberies, petty hatreds, and daily insecurities in the Negro community reflect a larger evil: the greater robbery of our very selves by means of slavery and segregation, the gross hatred of one race for another, and the racist policies that produce only shame and self-hate in those upon whom they are perpetrated. The Negro finds himself living in a "triple ghetto" of poverty, race, and misery, forced to pay exorbitant rent for substandard housing, compelled to attend inadequate schools, plagued by low wages or unemployment. By the thousands, he says, Negro men face the embarrassment of not being able to be men because they can't support their children. "Out of embarrassment and out of frustration, they often turn to alcoholism or dope to try to run from it and escape its tragedies." There has been "no greater robbery" than the robbery of the stability of the Negro family. And what of those who escape the triple ghetto? Their response is often the mirror image of the poorer Negro's shame:

> [S]o often in the Negro middle class [as E. Franklin Frazier has said] you find a brother who is ashamed to identify with his relatives. He doesn't like to read poetry that's written by Negro poets, and Negro art doesn't have any meaning to him, and he doesn't like listening to Negro spirituals, because you see this reminds him of the fact that he has a slave and an African heritage. He doesn't want to be identified with that. So he goes and tries to identify with all of the values of the white middle class, and he's rejected by the white middle class, so he's left out there in the middle with no cultural roots. And he ends up hating himself and he tries to compensate for this through conspicuous consumption—Cadillac cars, fine houses, foreign mink coats. This is this brother's problem.

Even the universal sin of ingratitude assumes a special modality among the Negro middle class. Not only have Negroes been robbed of their cultural memory but those who have escaped the "triple ghetto" have forgotten the contributions of those who made their freedom possible. They enjoy the desegregated facilities and the better jobs, and take it for granted that Thurgood Marshall sits on the Supreme Court, but "[t]hey've forgotten the fact that some people have had to die in order for us to get these things." The black middle class enjoys a perverse partnership with white moderates, both of whom want the good life at the expense of the many who are left behind in "the stench of back waters."

The evil we see in ourselves and in society around us does not merely *remind* us of certain Christian doctrines. Our life in America enacts these doctrines, proves them, with painful empirical certainty. The entire process of humiliation by which Negroes are ensnared in evil and perpetrate it upon themselves King called "original sin." Original sin is not a bad habit but a pervasive "habit structure" that can be shattered only by God. Black shame and self-hatred, no less than white racism, are not merely psychologically unhealthy; they efface the more original condition of dignity, the image of God, in which all people were created. King comforts Ebenezer, "So if you are worried about your somebodyness, don't worry any longer because God fixed it a long time ago. He said, 'I'm making *all* my children in my image, and I will declare that every child of mine has dignity and every child of mine has worth.' " Race supremacy not only contradicts the Declaration of Independence but makes a mockery of the doctrine of creation in the image of God and violates God's continuing will for his creatures. In his 1966 sermon entitled "Who Are We?" King says, "Despite a man's tendency to live on low and degrading planes, something reminds him that he is not made for that." "This is my *Father's* world," he had heard his own father sing many times, to which King adds defiantly, "And God has not yet decided to turn this world over to George Wallace. Somewhere I read, 'The earth is the Lord's and the fullness thereof.' " Like race supremacy, American militarism is not only morally wrong; it is a modern exercise of idolatry, which is nothing less than the denial of the lordship of God above princes and nations. When Negroes and poor people languish in the captivity of poverty or serve as cannon fodder in senseless wars, they are not simply economically or politically disadvantaged but bound in the chains of sin that God means to break.

In the Ebenezer gospel, what the preacher introduces as a perplexity or a universal problem he skillfully correlates with Christian doctrine, thereby exposing its sinful dimension and its potential for redemption. Only after the preacher has elevated his topic to one of universal proportions does he draw it through the ashes of Negro life and history. In each sermon, that which presents itself as a problem to be solved or an interesting "truth" for disquisition, ends as an impassioned appeal for redemption. With Paul, the preacher cries, "Who will deliver us from this body of death?"

II

The answer rests on the character and history of God. In the civil addresses "God" sometimes appears as Jefferson's God, a shadowy guarantor of liberal values, but in the Ebenezer and black-church sermons God assumes his biblical identity as the creator of the world, the liberator of Israel, and the Father of Jesus Christ. It is inconceivable to the preacher that a God who created all people in his own image could have created some "more equal" than others or would sanction the systematic exploitation of one race by another. The sermons do not engage the twisted hermeneutics of the white racist preachers, like the Texas Baptist who proclaimed God "the original segregationist," nor do they attempt to prove racial equality on the basis of the doctrine of creation or the character of God, but in the Bible's own spirit of defiance, the sermons assume the created equality of all.

It goes without arguing that God wills to liberate Negroes from captivity in America because that is the kind of God we have. That is his demonstrated character. We have already explored King's reliance on the Exodus and shown how its dynamic as a "setting free" and a "coming through" informs so many of his sermons. Unlike the static and inactive God of deism, who appears in the civil addresses but rarely in the sermons, the God of Ebenezer is relentless in his forward motion. In a 1963 sermon King declares, "Whenever God speaks, he says, 'Go forward!' " Although the preacher sometimes invests history with a forward tilt or a moral bent, his Ebenezer gospel makes it clear that it is the God of Israel, not inevitable laws, who is the motor of deliverance. With the character of God's relentlessness King establishes one of several links between the deity of the Old and New Testaments, for the father of Jesus "is a seeking God" who never quits searching for the lost. A parent who loses a child doesn't say, "Oh well, I've got four more," but he or she continues to seek and to love the prodigal, even the child in prison.

The most prominent characteristic of the New Testament's revelation of God, however, is his love. Whatever hopeful laws are discernible in the universe are due to the Creator's loving character. Like the pulsating life of the universe, "God's love is unceasing and eternal. Love is not a single act of God but an abiding part of his nature." The preacher observes, "You cannot say that man 'is' love but only 'man loves or men love,' but they also hate. Only 'God' and 'love' are joined by 'is.' " ...

Although King had been trained in liberal, personalistic Christology, when he addressed his own congregation he preached as evangelical a message—as "sweet" a Jesus—as could be found in any black congregation. When it came to Jesus, Negro Christianity cared as little about the liberal "laws" of Jesus' personhood as it did about the orthodox formulas for his divinity. Instead of dwelling on the metaphysical proportions of Jesus' divinity and humanity, by which orthodoxy thought to safeguard the uniqueness of Christ, the Negro church simply showered its Lord with glory and praise. Now, long after the Greek formulations have lost their significance to many Christians, the hallelujahs and Yes Lords continue to ring out in the African-American church. The effusions King heard from his father on the Lily of the Valley and the Bright Morning Star he repeated many times in the Ebenezer pulpit. In a 1967 sermon he merges his voice with a couple of gospel songs in the praise of the Lord:

> Thank you Lord, thank you Jesus,
> For you brought me from a mighty,
>   mighty long way. . . .
> How I got over. And I just want to thank
> you Lord for bringing me over.

In telling what this Jesus could do for the believer—what church doctrine calls "soteriology"—King's rendering attained its evangelical peak. It was another matter altogether when he spoke of the transformation of society, for then he evoked the Pillar of Fire of the Exodus God and the angry God of the Prophets. The Jesus of Ebenezer was the Savior of troubled individuals. There is nothing in King of the old Greek theology of Jesus as the head, the vanguard, of the human race, nor of Nat Turner's Jesus the Liberator, who came to cast fire upon the earth. Jesus' role in the Movement was to be the supernatural partner in Negro suffering, to model a nonviolent response toward racist oppression, and to console the preacher in his moments of discouragement. This is not to say that Jesus played a marginal role at Ebenezer. He is everywhere in King's sermons, for true to their Baptist roots, the Ebenezer sermons portray a Jesus who alone is able to rescue the individual from sin and transport him to eternal life.

> I know he is a-ble to raise us up
> when we are down,

his Daddy sang.

> Are you torn within
> And somehow beaten from without?
>   Cry, "God is able" . . .
> Are you giving up on your journey?
>   Why? God is able!

the son proclaimed.

Whenever we are threatened with the sins of personal disintegration, such as sexual immorality, dope, or despair, we find rescue in the Savior. Jesus doesn't merely forgive sins but he has the power to change sinners, to do for us what we are unable to do for ourselves. The sermons are quiet on the substitutionary Atonement of Jesus on the cross, and they say little about the necessity of the Negro's unmerited suffering—much less than his public utterances. It may be that face-to-face with his segregated brothers and sisters he could not speak these words. In the later sermons, King makes it clear that if anyone will bear the sins of all and die for them, it will be the preacher. Although the sermons make little of Jesus' vicarious Atonement, they do not express reliance on human goodness to effect change. The intricacies of the Atonement were never a concern to the traditional Negro pulpit, but God's exclusive power to transform lives was its stock and trade. The uneducated Negro preacher reminded his rural Macon County flock, "He make an ugly person look pretty well. Can't he make you *pretty*, so to speak?" The sophisticated Atlantan draws on the same tradition in the following set piece:

> "You may be a dope addict,
>   But I can deal with dope addicts . . .
> You may be an alcoholic,
>   but I can deal with alcoholics . . .
> You may be engaging in sexual promiscuity,
>   but I can make you a faithful husband," says Christ.

> "Come unto me, just as you are,
>   and accept your acceptance."
> . . . I know Christ:
> He can change the lying man
>   into a truth-telling man.
> He can change a dishonest woman
>   into an honest woman.
> He can change a prostitute
>   into a woman of honor.

Again, a 1963 sermon promises, " 'If any man is in Christ,' " says Paul, " 'he is a new creation. The old has passed away, the new has come.' " What does this mean for the Ebenezer Christian?

> The things I used to do,
>   I don't do them now.
> The places I used to go,
>   I don't go there now.
> The thoughts I used to think,
>   I don't think them now,
>   because God through Christ
>   has put his hands on me.

"I know Christ," the preacher repeatedly testifies. "And I tell you this morning that one of the great glories of the gospel is that Christ has transformed so many nameless prodigals." "I recommend him to you this morning, because I know from my own experience that He can make a way out of no way."

King's celebrations of God constituted the climax of his sermons, which is perhaps the element most characteristic of the African-American sermon. This is the gospel, the distinctive genius of Christian speech, and the very thing that is unfailingly eliminated from his printed sermons and that he himself apparently could not *say* to predominantly white congregations. He could not say it because the nature of his gospel, which was the Ebenezer gospel, required the shared articulation of a people's suffering and hope, and that he could not find at Saint John the Divine or the National Cathedral. What remains in his printed and white-church sermons is the residue of psychology and borrowed moralisms for which the preachers of his generation were well approved.

III

The message of Jesus Christ demands a response of the hearer's whole life. Although Ebenezer was a verbally responsive congregation, its co-pastor did not measure the effectiveness of his message by the emotions it aroused on Sunday morning. Churches that were satisfied with getting people "happy" in worship but had no social mission he frequently called "entertainment centers." King's Baptist tradition put great store in the congregation's response to the spoken word, but King himself never "begged" for a verbal response or even subtly suggested it. What he had in mind was a far more nuanced spiritual and behavioral change.

That response begins with repentance and ends in commitment to others, particularly to the struggle for racial freedom. Although he occasionally called Ebenezer to repentance, King usually reserved his most radical religious language, his appeals for repentance or his exhortations to be "born again," to the political sphere. To be sure, Ebenezer must be "transformed by the renewing of its mind," he said, but the evil from which it turns is not as savage or pervasive as white racism.

Whatever change that occurs will take place in the believer's partnership with Christ. In personal matters as well as the Civil Rights Movement, reliance on our own activism is as big an error as supine resignation. God works through us, and his agency includes our hard work and commitment. "Do we want peace in this world?" King asked. "Man can not do it by himself. And God is not going to do it by himself. But let us cooperate with him. . . ." In his early years, the preacher tended to warn against human self-sufficiency; in his middle and later years, he became increasingly infuriated with those who used God's all-sufficiency as an excuse not to march or commit themselves to the struggle.

At Ebenezer, King modeled a spirituality that abolished the traditional distinctions between belief and action. Much traditional theology, including his own Baptist heritage, isolated "faith" and "love" as successive moments in the life of the believer. In King's vocabulary the two are inseparably joined. There can be no discussion of faith as the intellectual or spiritual preparation for love, or of love as the inevitable response to faith. Faith assumes two modalities at the same time: trust and love.

Faith has an "in-spite-of" quality that always contradicts prevailing conditions. When Job's wife counsels him to despair of God's favor, Job colloquially responds, "Honey, I'm sorry, but my faith is deeper than that." The preacher confesses to being a terrible swimmer because he couldn't relax in the water—until he learned the "dead man's float." God will carry us if we lie back and ride his wave to freedom. Almost canceling the metaphor, he adds, "We can't do it alone. God will not do it alone. But let's go all out on it and protest a little bit and He will change this thing and make America a better nation."

Floating is something like accepting. Using Paul Tillich's formula for faith, "accept your acceptance by God," to which Ebenezer was enormously responsive, King patiently explained the difference between grace and works. He reminds Ebenezer (as if they needed reminding) of the many organizations and clubs with closed memberships. But God's acceptance is not like getting into a fraternity "where they will paddle you a bit to get you in to see if you can pass the test." Not at all, for God specializes in hopeless cases and failed projects. "No matter what your marks were in school, come on just as you are." Only the preacher King could fuse Paul Tillich and the pathos of an evangelical hymn: "Faith is accepting the fact that you are already accepted. And this is why we sing 'Just As I Am.' Christ will take you, if you will just have faith and accept your acceptance. No matter who you are. . . . That's all it takes."

Floating and acceptance finally lead to freedom from fear. The preacher knows that some in his own congregation have refrained from joining the Movement because of fear. He can address their fear because he has experienced it himself. He has also experienced the supernatural relief that possesses one who has been set free from this most elemental bondage. On the basis of his call-experience in the kitchen, the preacher declares himself to have been forever liberated from fear, but he cannot help but notice how fear continues to rob the Movement of white and black support. He exhorts his hearers to stand up against unjust laws, the way the three men in the fiery furnace defied Nebuchadnezzar, the way Julian Bond has "dared to speak his mind" in Georgia. In his sermon on Julian Bond he recounts a poignant meeting with a Duke Divinity School student, a white man, who had been convinced by King's speech but sorrowfully confessed, "[I]f I even talked about brotherhood from my pulpit, they would kick me out."

The definitive form of faith is love. Perfect love casts out fear. The ubiquity of love in King's sermons has already been remarked upon. In the heat of the Movement, theological ethicist James Sellers attacked King's doctrine of love as a theological mistake, and soon after, but on different grounds, the black nationalists derided it as a political betrayal. The main point of Sellers's criticism was that traditionally (by which he meant "in Niebuhr") love is the goal of life, and justice is the means to the goal. To "sloganize love as a technique" places love in the midst of conflict, coercion, and all manner of morally ambiguous situations where it cannot possibly remain true to its own character as disinterested *agape*. To carry out a protest "in love," nonviolently, requires that each person involved in the protest be possessed by that love, which necessitates an absurdly idealistic view of ordinary people. King's belief in the power of love, said Sellers, depends on his belief in the goodness of humanity, both black and white. A more realistic and theologically responsible alternative would be to follow Calvin's notion of "forced and extorted righteousness" and admit that God's righteousness in society takes other forms beside love. Sellers's article, which appeared in *Theology Today* in 1962, complemented the more savage political critique of love to which King was subjected for the rest of his life.

For all their repetitiveness and disorganization, the Ebenezer sermons reveal what a solid theologian and pastor King was. Although he did not have the leisure to publish an academic theology of the Civil Rights Movement, the sermons show that he well understood the grounds on which he was repudiating the position represented by his critics. Sellers's argument never quite touched earth and, perhaps because of the abstract tendencies of most formal theology, it never got around to confronting the sociopolitical alternatives to King's teaching on love.

Against Sellers' criticisms, King in fact did *not* exhort his members to love on the basis of the laws of the universe or the goodness of humanity but on the basis of the revealed nature of God. God created the universe and continues to preserve it out of love. If there is any doubt about the character of God's love, one need only look to the cross of Jesus for clarification, for the cross is "God's photograph." In the Incarnation, God saw fit to plunge Jesus into a politically ambiguous situation, subjected him to suffering, and finally took his life. Jesus' ministry and crucifixion have become the paradigm for the Christian's life in society. "I have long since learned that being a follower of Jesus Christ means taking up the cross," he said in 1967. We are conditioned to expect success and personal fulfillment; our preachers like to preach "nice little soothing sermons on how to relax and how to be happy" or "go ye into all the world and keep your blood pressure down and I will make you a well-adjusted personality." But "[m]y Bible tells me that Good Friday comes before Easter," and the cross is not a piece of jewelry you wear but something you die on.

In this 1967 sermon the preacher is not merely musing on his own fate but pastorally attempting to explicate the meaning of the cross for daily life. The cross may take the form of the "death of the budget of your church," the loss of a job for the sake of principle, or the loneliness of a life without friends. To restrict the cross to the realm of personal spirituality or to the end of history, after all the nasty battles for justice have been fought, makes a mockery of the Incarnation. It also ignores the *teaching* of Jesus on nonviolence in the Sermon on the Mount and restricts it to personal relations. In fact, it was Reinhold Niebuhr who remarked, "We may be able to put God back in nature by a little serious thought, but we cannot put God back in society without much cross-bearing." Immersed in a conflict whose meaning was not yet historically defined, King was trying to do precisely what Niebuhr and the Lutherans were unable to accomplish: to provide a Christological foundation for civil society from which the love of Jesus had been banished by theological rationalizations.

King's agenda did not blind him to the uses of love as a political tactic, nor did it dull his appreciation of the law. No African American worked harder for the passage of civil rights *laws* in the 1960s, and no one labored under fewer illusions about life in a society ruled by love than Martin Luther King. Scores of times he repeated the maxim, "The law can't make a man love me, but it can restrain him from lynching me." Six weeks before he died, struggling with a case of laryngitis, he explained how laws help avert paternalism by putting all citizens on an equal footing. But this was a sermon on the Parable of the Good Samaritan, and even though King had preached this same text to Ebenezer many times before, on this Sunday he found something new to say. Two years earlier he had focused on the *robbery* of the black man's dignity; today he said ("hoping that my voice will hold up") that he would discuss the difference between law and love. Of course, stronger laws are necessary to combat housing discrimination and acts of violence against blacks. Even though "you can't legislate morality" the law can change people's habits and "pretty soon they adjust." "So I['m] not underestimating the enforceable obligations," he explained. "They are real, and they are necessary."

But the point of the parable and of King's own mission is that if "genuine integration, in terms of genuine person-to-person relations, genuine inter-group relations, [and] mutual acceptance" is to become a reality, it will occur when people are "obedient to the *unenforceable.*" Integration "really will not come through the law" until the white person accepts the black person as a brother or sister. Just as the Samaritan's behavior surpassed the demands of the law, so must the white race be prepared to exceed the provisions of civil rights legislation. Only then shall we have integration—not the tokenism with which too many are satisfied but integration as "true spiritual affinity" between the races. It is important to remember that in terms of the development of King's thinking, this is an extremely late sermon, spoken in his life's eleventh hour. Furthermore, it is an old sermon whose text and structure he could have repeated at Ebenezer with impunity, but he chose instead to reshape it and fill it with material reflective of his final thinking on love.

King not only preached love but modeled it for his congregation. Sellers criticized King's doctrine for the unreasonable demands it placed on its practitioners—they must be transformed by the love of Jesus in the very practice of it—which was precisely King's spiritual aim and the aim of any serious expositor of God's love. The practice of love is self-validating. Although tactics have their place in social change, ultimately the Christian does what is right not merely to avoid hell or to gain entrance into heaven. "You must love, ultimately, because it's lovely to love. You must be just," he chides Ebenezer, "because it's right to be just."

The pastor knew that his own congregation as well as his national followers were having a hard time with his doctrine of nonviolent love. Even his father had proclaimed from Ebenezer's pulpit, "I'm not ready for the dogs to be turned loose on me. The dogs and somebody else gonna get *hit* if they turn 'em loose on me." The son responded with pastoral direction for his people. He reminds them that those we find most hateful and irritating need our love and can be healed by it. Therefore, don't respond to racists by cursing them or calling them "crackers" when they call you, "niggers." . . .

. . . As prowar sentiments grew throughout the nation, King's radical love became more prophetic and personalized. Finally, in a 1967 sermon he burst out with, "I ain't goin' to study war no more. And you know what? I don't care who doesn't like what I say about it." Likewise, as the pressures for violence increased among segments of the black community, King's insistence on love grew with passionate intensity. At the close of a pedestrian discourse to Ebenezer entitled "Levels of Love," the preacher suddenly reached through the veil that occasionally descends between pulpit and pew and confessed, "I say I love you. I would rather die than hate you."

No one in the Ebenezer congregation would have been persuaded to love by a single sermon, any more than the preacher King had discovered love in any one moment of his life. The movement from repentance to commitment occurs over time, and King repeatedly stresses that it is a movement, not an instantaneous change. In King's vocabulary, salvation does not await the believer at the end of the journey but is the journey itself. Both preaching and salvation are cumulative activities. Early and late in his Ebenezer pastorate King presented salvation as a long and uncertain road: "In this earthly life we never get there totally. It's always a process and never an achievement. But you know what *really* being good is? It's being on the right road." . . .

IV

But what, if anything, lay at the road's end? True to his focus on the way, King saved up little for the end of the struggle. While he appreciated the sustaining role played by the Negro preachers who preceded him, he discarded their vivid portrayals of the afterlife in favor of his own predictions of social transformation. He often said, "It's wonderful to talk about the New Jerusalem. One day we will have to start talking about the New Atlanta. . . . [A]ny preacher who isn't concerned about this isn't preaching the true gospel." His favorite sermon, "The Three Dimensions of a Complete Life," was a psychological and moral interpretation of the Heavenly City's dimensions given in the Apocalypse. Although he occasionally spoke of death as "the door that leads us into life eternal" or of those who have died (the three little girls in Birmingham) as "home today with God," he customarily rendered the future with the imagery of a transfigured society.

In his early sermons he borrowed the idealist Josiah Royce's phrase "the Beloved Community" to evoke the period of social harmony and universal brotherhood that would follow the current social struggle. The Beloved Community corresponds roughly to Karl Marx's postdialectical "Kingdom of Freedom," characterized by the full exercise of individual talents within the community of the whole. What neither thinker provided was a political or economic plan for the transition from class struggle to social coherence. As John Cartwright has observed, King placed less emphasis on a specific blueprint for the future than he did on the qualities that persons must acquire in order to hasten the coming of the new community—in other words, he was a preacher and not an economist.

As King's social idealism was succeeded by more realistic appraisals of human evil, references to the Beloved Community gradually disappeared from his sermons, their place taken by the theological symbol "the Kingdom of God." On the basis of King's published writings and utterances, scholars have debated the question of the kingdom's this-worldly as opposed to other-worldly character, but they have not commented on the radical conversion implicit in the shift from the humanism of the "Community" to the theology of the "Kingdom." The former carries overtones of utopian idealism; the latter acknowledges God's claim upon all human achievements.

In the Ebenezer sermons the symbol "Kingdom of God" represents God's hidden but dynamic role in the transfiguration of earthly relationships, cities, and institutions. In an early published sermon King sketches a few historical possibilities for the manifestation of the kingdom: "And though the Kingdom of God may remain *not yet* as a universal reality in history, in the present it may exist in such isolated forms as in judgment, in personal devotion, and in some group life. 'The Kingdom of God is in the midst of you.' " The image of the kingdom in this passage, like that of the early chapters of the New Testament Gospels, is one of a quietly germinating presence. In his later sermons the kingdom constitutes a rupture in the "old order"; it subjects current laws and institutions to the judgment of God, a picture that corresponds to the violence of the later chapters in the Gospels. According to King's gospel, the last judgment of God is being realized ahead of time in the turmoil of contemporary events. When governors and state legislatures make policies that contradict the law of God, they are arrogating to themselves an authority that belongs only to God. But "God is still in control. And God has not yet turned over this universe to Lester Maddox and Lurleen Wallace." Four years earlier he had said at the funeral for the three children, "God is the Supreme Court beyond which there is no appeal." In his later sermons, the preacher realizes that it is not sufficient to witness to these false authorities, but the evil they represent must be defeated before "we begin in our little way to build God's kingdom right here."

Nowhere is the present reality of the kingdom given greater force than in his 1966 sermon on "the acceptable year of the Lord." On the basis of Isaiah's prophecy, Jesus strode into his hometown synagogue and announced that his ministry was the fulfillment of God's promise to Isaiah. The Bible's prophetic and messianic utterances are often nested in concrete historical circumstances, such as the return of exiles or the beginning of Jesus' ministry, but they quickly transcend local occurrences and reveal God's universal lordship. In the Bible, what originates as a prediction of David's kingship is eventually celebrated as God's rule over all nations; Jesus' prediction of local persecutions (as in Mark 13) by the end of the chapter has escalated to catastrophes of cosmic significance.

King's sermonic performance of "The Acceptable Year" follows the biblical pattern, for he begins by locating the kingdom in the midst of his congregation's experience of history: "You know the acceptable year of the Lord is the year that is acceptable to God because it fulfills the demands of his kingdom. Some people reading this passage feel that it's talking about some period beyond history, but I say to you this morning that the acceptable year of God can be *this* year." He continues with a set piece whose rhetorical form is as explosively eschatological as its content:

> The acceptable year of the Lord is any year
> when men decide to do right. . . .
> The acceptable year of the Lord is any year
> when men will stop throwing away the precious
> lives that God has given them in riotous living.
> The acceptable year of the Lord is that year
> when people in Alabama will stop killing civil
> rights workers. . . .

The piece continues with a survey of contemporary history and international relations until the preacher suddenly removes his blinders and envisions the whole world beneath the lordship of God. He does this by reciting a series of Bible passages in an ascending and ever-widening order of universality concluding at the highest emotional peak:

> The acceptable year of the Lord is that year
> when every knee shall bow and every tongue
> confess the name of *Jesus*, and everywhere
> men will cry, "Hallelujah! Hallelujah!"
> The kingdom of this world has become the kingdom
> of our Lord and of his Christ, and he shall
> reign forever and ever. "Hallelujah! Hallelujah!"
> [tumult]

If the world is really being governed by God, and if that governance will one day be made plain, then the most appropriate Christian stance in the world is one of hope. A war rages between hope and despair in the preacher's own heart and in the lives of discouraged people everywhere. The vision of God's imminent triumph lends resources to hope. Hope does not come to the Christian as easily as optimism, for it is surrounded by the evidences of its foolishness. Yet, to those with eyes to see, "what is hoped for is in some sense already present" in the witness of those who love peace and are willing to work for it. Like faith and love, hope belongs to the Christian's journey through life. . . .

V

. . . There was a time when King was able to speak of the church as an undifferentiated body of Christians and even to lament the existence of a white and black church. There was a time when he viewed the Civil Rights Movement, especially the Selma campaign, as a movement representing the whole church and as the catalyst for an ecumenical awakening in America. However, when the white churches had an opportunity to prove themselves, they failed.

He frequently told how he had expected the support of the white ministers, if not the congregations, in the Montgomery struggle, only to have his hopes dashed. The cause of freedom for God's people has been repeatedly stymied by pious men of God and their congregations. He frequently complained to Ebenezer of the outrageous hypocrisy of the white congregations—such as the Baptist church that sent money to Africa but fired its pastor for allowing a black man to sing in the choir; such as the churches that emphasize the aesthetics of the liturgy above the demands of the prophets; such as the Dutch Reformed Church in South Africa that sanctions apartheid; such as the churches that crusade to keep the county dry but remain "wet" when it comes to prejudice; such as the good southern Christians who participate in bombings and lynchings.

> [D]o you know that [the] folk [who] are lynching them are often big deacons in Baptist churches and stewards in Methodist churches, feeling that by killing and murdering and lynching another human being they were doing the will of the almighty God? *The most vicious oppressors of the Negro today are probably in church.* [Governor] Ross Barnette teaches Sunday School in a Methodist church in Mississippi. Mr. Wallace of Alabama taught Sunday School for years.

The "white preachers" are no better than their lay members. "[T]hey can look at racial injustice and never open their mouths against it." King could only conclude that "we are no better than strangers" to those Christians "even though we sing the same hymns in worship of the same God."

Nor did he spare the complacency of his own African Baptist church. Even among the membership of Ebenezer there were influential voices raised against his activities, but they were few and ineffectual. Ebenezer's parent-church organization, however, the National Baptist Convention, led by the autocratic Joseph H. Jackson, did not support King's demonstrations or violations of the law. King's dream of harnessing the Civil Rights Movement to the enormous train of the National Baptist Convention was dashed at the denomination's convention in 1960 when delegates rejected the King-backed challenge to Jackson's presidency and stripped King of his official position in the organization. From that time onward, he stepped up his criticism of the other-worldly, individualistic nature of the black Baptist churches that had spurned him.

One type of black church "burns up" in mindless emotionalism while another "freezes up" in bourgeois dignity. The latter group does not understand the American paradox, that the first step to becoming fully American is to celebrate one's own distinctiveness. Its members are "ashamed that their ancestral home was Africa." Its preacher "preaches a nice little essay on Sunday. . . . And they don't sing Negro spirituals and gospel songs because that reminds them of their heritage. So they are, you know, they are busy trying to be ashamed that they are black." King was concerned that many black congregations were not providing measurable support to the Movement, but even more concerned that they were not living up to their unique messianic assignment in America. They had been refined in the furnaces of slavery and segregation for a purpose, and now the proving of that purpose had begun. How would they respond? "This," he cried out to Ebenezer with evangelical and historical urgency, "is your great opportunity."

In the later sermons King's criticisms of the Negro church receded into the background, as another model of the black church assumed greater definition. In his earlier period of accommodation, King practiced a rhetoric of balance in which his assessment of the church consistently mirrored black with white failures—for example, black otherworldliness appears as a reflection of white secularity, and so forth. But the moral bankruptcy of the white churches and the downright evil of many of their leaders upset the balance both in King's rhetoric and his theology, and the black church finally emerges in all its splendid *contrast* to the churches around it. The black church serves as an agent of redemption because it continues to live as a "colony of heaven" in an alien world. Unlike the white church, it continues to enact the Christian story and has not rationalized away the harder demands of the prophets and Jesus. It still understands that the church is called to heal the brokenhearted, preach deliverance to the captives, and to announce the acceptable year of the Lord. Because of the evil it has caused or sanctioned, the white church has defaulted on its task and is no longer worthy to bear the name "church." King was willing to acknowledge a spiritual *ecclesia*, a germ of authenticity, in the white church, but little more.

Instead of understanding the black church as the mirror-image of the white, King interpreted its mission as an extension of the early church, which defined itself *over against* its pagan environment. The early church, King reminded his hearers in 1967, refused to fight wars, engaged in civil disobedience, accepted persecution, and knew how to suffer. Like Martin Luther, who made suffering one of the "marks" of the church, King asserted that the greatest strength of the black church is its willingness to suffer on behalf of the entire nation in order to bring about reconciliation. "I am grateful to God," King wrote in 1967, "that, through the influence of the Negro church, the way of nonviolence became an integral part of our struggle." What is also clear from his comments on the church is how fully King broke with civil religion and eventually with his rhetorical strategy of identification. By differentiating the black from the white church and identifying the latter as the oppressor-church, he effectively eliminated the illusion of commonality between all Christians and demolished the theological facade of the white churches.

In the crucible of the Movement and weekly preaching, theology retained its importance for King, as he continued to believe in the power of ideas to shape social behavior, but theology assumed a sense of immediacy—and danger—that it had not possessed at Crozer or Boston. The safe interval between theory and practice had disappeared. In his sermons to Ebenezer about suffering, commitment, and the witness of believers, King was redefining the contemporary church. In his emerging theology, the black church would no longer appear as a footnote to mainline Protestantism, for that god had failed. Instead, the black-church experience would become the new criterion of faithfulness against which all theology and practice must be measured.

VI

The final element in the Ebenezer sermons and one, like the gospel climax, that never appears in King's printed or white-church sermons, is the invitation. In many black and evangelical churches the sermon concludes with an exhortation to accept the preacher's offer of salvation. This is followed by a final appeal or invitation for the hearers to come to the altar as an expression of their conversion to Christ. The conclusions of King's sermons follow this two-step process. His concluding words usually take the form of an offer whose theme and imagery are closely related to the main topic of the sermon. By the sermon's end, however, the complications and ambiguities of life in a racist society are set aside, as the preacher offers nothing less saluatory or more complex than a personal relationship with Jesus. As one listens to King speak such words Sunday after Sunday, one senses that these conclusions are not merely preacher-formulas for him but represent expressions of his own settled peace with his vocation. He appears to derive immense satisfaction from them, perhaps because they are "pure" gospel, pure grace, which, when it is verbally applied to discour aged people, is something like anointing a wound with healing oils. For example, in his 1966 sermon on the seeking God entitled "The God of the Lost," the preacher concludes with the following offer:

> And that is it this morning, my friends. Somebody here is lost. Somebody here is away from the fold this morning. God is searching. God is still seeking. And the beauty of our gospel, the beauty of our religion, is that when you are found, heaven rejoices. . . . This is it. God is still seeking and searching for someone here.

> "Softly and tenderly, Jesus is calling,
>   Calling for you and for me."

> There is a voice saying, "Come home, come home. Ye who are
> weary, come home. You've been out of the fold a long time. It's
> terrible to be lost out there! Come on back home."

In the 1963 sermon in which he compared faith to the "dead-man's float," he concludes on the same theme: "This is a magnificent time. . . . Just throw your all out on the divine. He will hold you up. You can't sink. You don't need to struggle any longer. God will hold you up." Then with the choir singing softly in the background, he implores his hearers, "Wherever you are, will you come this morning? Wherever you are."

Out in Macon County in the 1940s, William Pipes recorded the country preacher's concluding invitation, "Won't He take care of you, chillun? Be consolation for you? My, my Lord! I done tried! I know He *do* take care of you, preserve your soul, and den what I like bout You, carry you home. Here rain wouldn't fall on you. Beautiful land. Gwine to sing and open de doors of the church." King's Ebenezer maintained the traditional "We open the doors of the church now," and invited worshippers to come forward to join the church by baptism (in the evening service), by profession of faith, or for "watch care" (for sojourning students carrying a letter of recommendation). But the general tenor of the invitations indicates that their main purpose was to encourage repentance and conversion in the seeker. "This is the time to make your decision," King cries. As a worshipper comes forward, he exalts, "God, be thank[ed] for this young man. Is there another who will come this morning? Is there another?" On a sweltering Sunday in July 1963, with the organ playing softly in the background, he intoned, "We open the doors of the church now. Someone here this morning needs to make a decision for Christ. . . . Who this morning, wherever you are, whether you're in the main sanctuary, or whether you're downstairs in the first unit of the church, whether you're in the balcony, come now and take that step." The choir begins singing, *Where He Leads Me*, and King, speaking above the choir continues, "Who this morning will take that step?" until he too begins singing in makeshift bass harmony with the choir. As people file forward, he is pleased to report, "There's another this morning, there's another. Where he leads me . . ." and the preacher is humming, then singing once again. . . .

If the conclusions show anything about Martin Luther King, Jr., they demonstrate the appropriateness of his role as a Christian civil rights leader whose political stance and rhetorical performance were deeply informed by the church's gospel. These invitations, as well as the Ebenezer gospel as a whole, reveal the springs of his religious appeal to America: to repent of its racist and militarist sin; to honor the provisions of its covenant with the divine Being; to discipline its life according to the demands of brotherhood; to embrace the higher Power who makes new life possible; and to anticipate with joy the physical and spiritual transfiguration of the nation. The invitations in particular, with their emphasis on decision, had their counterparts in the religiously charged atmosphere of the mass meetings in Negro churches throughout the nation. There King translated the personal and religious altar calls of Ebenezer into corporate and political appeals for racial solidarity.

Richard Lischer, *The Preacher King: Martin Luther King, Jr. and the Word That Moved America* (New York: Oxford, 1997), pp. 221-42.

CHAPTER THREE

The Pastor as Priest

In 1976, minding my own business and that of the church in a small parish in South Carolina, I was invited to come to Duke Divinity School to teach Liturgy and Worship to mostly United Methodist seminarians. Upon entering seminary teaching, I discovered that most of my students were not too interested in matters liturgical. Many of them were suspicious of liturgical studies as being antiquarian, irrelevant, "high church" fussiness that had little to do with their future as pastors in a Free Church, low church, Protestant denomination.

In my efforts to entice them toward an interest in the liturgy, I created a course, "Worship as Pastoral Care," in which I attempted to wed the study of worship with a subject of greater interest to them—pastoral care. Combining the insights of psychology with the demands of liturgical leadership, I sought to lure my seminary students toward a fresh consideration of the liturgy as our principal opportunity for pastoral care. This led me to some thoughts about how the pastor's liturgical leadership of a congregation is also revelation of the pastor's ability to shoulder the responsibilities of priestly leadership.

Liturgy and Leadership: Priest and Pastor
William H. Willimon

. . . Why, when a pastor is before more people in Sunday morning worship than at any other time in the week, do we mumble through vague, poorly constructed, almost inaudible prayers; slouch around the altar as if we were fixing a washing machine rather than making Eucharist; chatter incessantly about nothing throughout the entire service, and, in general, appear to go to great lengths to give people the impression that we are doing nothing of any consequence, leading them nowhere of any great importance, and dealing with material of no particular significance?

Our casualness with the Holy, our sloppiness with the liturgy, is not missed by lay persons. When I talk with laity about worship, they continually express bafflement at why their pastors seem to invest themselves within every other pastoral activity besides the leadership of public worship—the one pastoral activity every pastor is expected to be able to do and the activity the lay persons themselves continue, in every study I have seen, to rank at the top, or at least near the top, of all pastoral activities. I have also found that many ministers, no less than their parishioners, are baffled by their own devaluing of and lack of investment within worship. What is the source of our timidity, hesitance, avoidance, sloppiness, and general lack of attention to the Sunday morning gatherings of our people?

Undoubtedly, the sources of this problem are complex and multifaceted, related to our perception of ourselves as individual pastors, our understanding of the church and its ministry, our evaluation of our individual strengths and weaknesses, our assessment of our people's expectations, and a host of other psychosocial-theological factors. . . .

But I suspect that problems with the pastoral leadership of the liturgy may have deeper roots. While it is important, very important, for each pastor to adequately articulate a sound liturgical theology, to know something of the history of the liturgy, and to have some practical skills in how to lead worship; even knowledge and skills do not appear to be enough. Why is it, I have had to ask myself of late, too many of my fellow pastors know all the "facts" of worship, show personal gifts and abilities in their activities outside of worship that should make them excellent worship leaders and yet still seem unable to lead worship? One suspects questions of ministerial identity, role confusion, and authority may be at the root of the problem.[1] In other words, a major source of the problem

---

1. Ronald Sleeth, in inquiring into the possible motives behind recent attempts to detract from the importance of preaching (in spite of a large amount of data that suggests its continued centrality), suspects the preacher's self-doubts may be the source of doubts about preaching:

"Many clergymen today within the Church are questioning the preaching office under the guise of its ineffectiveness communicatively or its authoritarian theological claims when the real problem is the preaching office in relation to their own being. . . . Preaching reveals their own internality, and this can be a terrible threat. They are not sure of their own being and are terrified by the resultant insecurities of faith and personality that such exposure as preaching unveils. . . . They do not want to preach for they fear the revelation of their innermost selves."
Ronald E. Sleeth, "The Crisis in Preaching," *Perkins Journal*, vol. 30 (Summer, 1977), p. 11.

for many pastors is inadequate understanding and experience of ordination. . . .

Ministry as a Function of Community

In recent discussion of the ordained ministry, I sense confusion stemming from fuzzy definitions of the "priesthood of believers" principle, based upon the "royal priesthood" image that is applied to God's people in I Peter 2:9. . . . While all Christians share Christ's high priestly ministry to the world by virtue of their "ordination" at baptism . . . , this does not mean that there is no need or any basis for the development of the role of the ordained priesthood. While we Protestants affirm the "priesthood of all believers" in the sense that I Peter speaks of it, we do not thereby claim that this eliminates the need for an ordained ministerial office. I am unimpressed with much recent thought on ministry which wrongly attempts to support the ministry of the laity ("the priesthood of all believers") by detracting from the need for an ordained ministry. In fact, one reason few lay persons feel like "priests" to one another and to the world is that they so rarely see or receive "priesting" from their pastor. I have yet to see a dynamic, committed church with a vibrant lay ministry that is not led and challenged by the dynamic, committed, vibrant ministry of some pastor who knows that his or her ordained ministry is the essential sign and focus for the shared ministry of all Christians within that congregation. And it makes no difference whether that ordained person is called priest, pastor, or preacher.

The theology of ordination has at its heart "the simple fact that priests (pope, bishops) are and function as officials of the Christian community."[2] All our pious accretions, talk about a special aura of holiness, shamanism, alleged virtues and skills, and undue

---

2. George McCauley, S.J., *The God of the Group* (Niles, Illinois: Argus Communications, 1975), p. 84. I am deeply indebted to Father McCauley's book for helping me to organize my thoughts on ordination. While I approach the subject somewhat anthropologically and therefore functionally, as does Father McCauley, I believe that my conclusions are not at odds with historical and theological scholarship on the subject. For an excellent survey of that scholarship, see Bernard Cooke, *Ministry to Word and Sacrament* (Philadelphia: Fortress Press, 1976), mentioned in chap. 1.

reverence for the community's ordained representatives are only distractions from the simple fact that the ordained ministry is a function of the Christian community. An ordained minister is an official of the community, a representative, a designated leader. With my Protestant heritage, I recognize that an ordained minister should be, must be, called by God. That call from God should be personal, experiential, and received and responded to with some degree of specificity. I know of no good pastor who cannot point to some time in life in which he or she was led to say yes. But with Calvin, I recognize a "twofold call" to the presbyterate. God calls us, and the church calls us. While the explication of and reflection upon God's call to the priesthood is a worthy subject for study, here I wish to emphasize the call of the community, because I sense that it is the currently neglected aspect of our ministerial identity. An ordained minister is an official of the community. It does not advance our understanding of the ordained minister's role to say that it is God's action in and through the minister that is the central factor in his or her functioning. God is involved in the ministry of all Christians. It does not help to claim that the minister's training and expertise are the central factors in his or her functioning. It can be readily demonstrated that the clergy's current attempt to claim "professional" status and expertise are not particularly relevant to either the historical claims for ministry or to the community's current perceptions of what it needs from its ministers.

No, the central matter is in the office, in the officialness of the ordained minister's activities. To put it bluntly, there is no difference when a priest baptizes, preaches, forgives, blesses, prays, counsels, or supports compared to when any other Christian does these things—save in the officialness of the action. The difference is only in the official character of the ordained minister. The Service of Ordination, in whatever tradition it occurs and whatever form it takes, is simply, but also most significantly, the conferring by the community of that official character upon certain designated individuals. God may have designated the persons *a priori* to the community's recognition. But without that community authorization, all individual claims for officialness are unrecognized and therefore invalidated.

I choose to speak of the ordained minister by the rather mundane term *official* in order to lay out, in as stark a manner as possible, the Christian community as the source of our authorization as priests. To speak of the priesthood in an "official," functional way runs counter to the humanly unrealistic and theologically unfounded expectations some of us have of our priests. Some of us have claimed that priests are different from the run of "average" Christians in a spiritual sense. This alleged "specialness" has taken many forms of late. Henri Nouwen speaks romantically of "the Wounded Healer" as if suffering and empathetic sensitivity were somehow the peculiar domain of the priest. Urban Holmes speaks mysteriously of "sacramental persons" who, "not only in word but in their very person, embody the Christ" thereby incarnating "the expectancy of the transcendent with the immanence of the personal."[3] Talk of this kind betrays a kind of insecurity on the part of the clergy and their self-appointed defenders, a fear that if we speak of the clergy as "officials" of the Christian community, we will do away with some "essential" quality that somehow makes them "special." We act as if officialness alone were not enough, not exciting enough for leadership, not dramatic enough to deserve the lifetime call of God. . . .

While the call to skilled competence and mastery of certain exclusive disciplines of the clerical "profession" has an appeal, particularly as a way of legitimizing Christian ministry before the goals and standards of the secular world, one strongly suspects that the call to professionalism represents a rather questionable attempt on the part of the clergy at self-legitimization and self-justification by using currently popular secular standards of efficiency and competence. This is troubling, not only because it tends to be at odds with historic, theological bases for the ordained ministry in its new claim for "specialness" by virtue of certain skills and abilities *apart from* the community's bidding and authorization, but also because it succumbs to a pragmatic, utilitarian, self-serving position that is today the greatest tragedy of two of our

---

3. Henri Nouwen, *The Wounded Healer: Ministry in Contemporary Society* (Garden City, N.Y.: Doubleday, 1972); Urban T. Holmes, *The Future Shape of Ministry* (New York: The Seabury Press, 1971), pp. 27, 31. In a recent book on ministry, Holmes goes on to claim special intuitive, imaginative powers for the clergy, *Ministry and Imagination* (New York: The Seabury Press, 1976), chap. 9. See also Holmes, *The Priest in Community* (New York: The Seabury Press, 1978).

major "professions"—medicine and law. The very "professional-ism" doctors and lawyers so jealously guard has removed both of these professions from the community and the people who need their services the most and has contributed to a producer-consumer mentality the clergy would do well to avoid. Richard Neuhaus makes a helpful distinction in his criticism of the professional model for ministry: Anthropologists, in their study of so-called primitive societies, sometimes distinguish between the role of the magician and the role of the priest. Magicians offer certain expertise to a clientele. Priests participate in a community. You go to a magician—in our society he may be called doctor or lawyer—with a particular problem to be fixed. You *belong* to a community of which the priest is an agent of the community's identity and ministry.[6] The call to the Christian ordained ministry is a call to the priesthood of the community, not to the performance of magic. The priest lives to serve, not to be served. . . .

Officials are neither desirable nor necessary for any community except for the realization of the community's purposes, the pursuit of communal goals. All groups designate leaders, in all manner of formal and informal ways, not to make leaders but to make a group. Leadership is not an optional matter for a group. . . .

. . . The pastor is the one who is charged with seeing—in all aspects of pastoral care—individual lives within the context of the whole; to bear the sometimes heavy burden of the community's tradition; to note the presence of inequality, division, and diversity; to create the conditions necessary for consensus; to foster a climate where reconciliation can occur; to judge the potentially demonic aspects of our "togetherness"; to ask whether the community we seek and attain is a specifically *Christian* community; to distinguish between his or her personal preferences and what community cohesion, maintenance, and critique require.[9]

Admittedly, others in the community may do all these things and may even do them better. But it is particularly significant when an ordained minister does these things because that is the priest's job. Yes, his job. Charism, skill, good looks, sensitivity, intelligence, may make the priest better at the job, but none of these character-

---

6. Richard John Neuhaus, "Freedom for Ministry," *The Christian Century* (February 2-9, 1977), p. 86.

9. McCauley, *God of the Group*, p. 87.

istics is the origin, source, or rationale for the job. Members of the community recognize the community dimension, the concern for the Body in its past, present, and future state as the job of the priest. Their recognition gives significance to what the priest does. They also recognize that the community dimension is placed upon the shoulders of the official on a standing basis, as the priest's specific concentration and burden. Whatever community-building skills or perceptivity others in the community may have is not acknowledged by the community in the same way as those of the pastor. This is the pastor's job. He is expected to care for the community by virtue of the office. The pastor is authorized, however inarticulately or haphazardly, by the community in this job—with no disrespect for the competence of others.

Without that authorization, the job of priest or pastor is impossible. If the pastor neglects his community-forming role, assumes that someone else can do it, and gets sidetracked into being a counselor of individuals, a changer of society in general, an independent biblical scholar, or some other similarly individualized task, sooner or later the pastor will be driven back to the communal dimension. If not, the pastor will never discover his or her uniqueness and identity as priest.[10] Because of its officialness, one cannot become priest by private fiat. People who are confused into thinking that the call to the priesthood is simply a call by God addressed to an individual conscience are invariably disappointed when the community fails to recognize their officialness. Failing to receive the official authorization of the community, they may seek official standing in some subgroup of the community where they can lead those of similar ideological persuasion. But this ends in cliques, sects, or faddish partisan movements that are invariably less than the fullness of Christian community.[11]

Admittedly, the presence of the priest or pastor does not guarantee community. But his or her presence does guarantee a visible, personal reminder that community is desirable and that common concerns are paramount to individual ones. The very presence of

---

10. Earlier, Gibson Winter noted how pastoral counseling's fondness for one-to-one caring relationships often obscured the pastoral function of the church as a fellowship and turned clergy away from their community-building function. "Pastoral Counseling or Pastoral Care," *Pastoral Psychology*, vol. 8 (February, 1957), pp. 16-22.

11. McCauley, *God of the Group*, p. 88.

the priest is a testimony, an invitation to community. Other fellow Christians may chiefly concern themselves with their own struggle as individual Christians. The priest cannot indulge in such individualized concern. He is a community person by virtue of his ordination. Through the priest, people come to see their individual religious striving as membership in a community, as common enterprise, interrelationship, mutuality, as continuous with the struggle of saints in the past, and linked with other Christians who "at all times and places" have called upon the name of the Lord. . . .

The burden of the ordained ministry (and it is always more burden than privilege) is that priests and pastors have the vantage point from whence to get a firsthand, official view of the lack of community, the difficulties of community, and the separateness within the community they serve. Most pastors have nagging doubts about what they are doing in the midst of an apparent noncommunity so full of division. Those doubts may be a sign that the pastor is about his or her business, standing in the middle of the tension between our rugged individualism and Christ's call to community.

But if a priest or pastor doubts the *desirability* of community or the *possibility* of community, then that is another matter. In the face of that kind of doubt, the priest will attempt to obtain self-fulfillment through control of others or through false prestige or worldly power, falling into paternalism and authoritarianism and thereby assisting the laity in avoiding their responsibility for community. Or the preacher will abandon the community's book (Bible) and take his text from some other source that is more vague and less prone to judge the limits of our self-conceived "gospel." Or the pastor will attempt self-justification by putting impossible leadership demands upon himself, thinking that he must be a super-Christian, a superempathizer, a superdoer of good works, a paragon of faith and virtue, a better practitioner of the priestly arts than the laity ("super apostles," Paul called them in II Cor. 11:5 NEB, RSV). In so doing, the pastor not only diverts people's vision from the Body but also sets himself up for becoming the scapegoat for the people's failures at community. After all, since their pastor has helped them to dispose of both God and the community, who else do they have to blame?

The Service of Ordination is that rite of the church that sets apart some people for the crucial yet modest function of helping the community to gather and then to be edified. All Services of Ordination are clear in their statement and demonstration that they are creating an official of the community. They will invariably claim the presence and work of God in the ordination. But that presence and work is not for the creation of some larger-than-life Christian or some mysterious guru. It is for the purpose of community formation. . . . The laying on of hands, a historic gesture symbolizing the transference of power, the gift of the Holy Spirit, and the commissioning of someone by the community, are part of every ordination rite. The candidate for ordination may be asked some questions about the facts of the faith and his or her own personal predisposition toward those facts. The candidate may have gone through some process of education and skill acquisition. But the sacramental, symbolic focus of the Service of Ordination is always upon the laying on of hands as a sign of the bestowal of officialness by the community of faith.

In most rites of ordination, the symbols of that officialness will be presented to the ordinand. A stole, an ancient Roman symbol of rank which came to symbolize the yoking of the priest to Christ and his church will be placed around the person's shoulders. A Bible, the church's book, the repository of the church's tradition, will be presented. A eucharistic chalice and paten will then be given to the new priest. These will be the priest's tools of the trade in the work of community formation and edification. The new pastor is now equipped, by virtue of the community's designation, to identify the Lord's people by baptism, to be host at the Lord's Table, to wait upon the Lord's people, and thereby to help form them into the Lord's Body. Through the rite, the church proclaims the source and the purpose of its ordained ministry.

"Take thou authority to preach the Word and administer the sacraments," the bishop says to the ordinand as he or she is presented with the Bible. These words are both command and promise. The new priest may boldly take authority because authority has been so boldly given. The command is to "take." While the community's gift of officialness is prior to the candidate's reception of the gift, unless the ordinand assumes the new role that is being given, then the community's offer of officialness is void of meaning. The promise is this: When one dares to take the community's offer of authority, one will be confirmed by God in the fruits one's ministry yields.

Within the seminary, in working with future candidates for ordination, I have often noted reluctance to "take thou authority." Students will sometimes speak of their humble desire for the church to "treat me like anybody else," to "respect me as an individual person." These wishes, they will come to see, are not possible to grant. "Anybody else" and "individual persons" will be of little help to the community in its task of becoming the Body. In some of our current fuzzy thinking about the "ministry of the laity" and the need for pastors to "just be themselves," I suspect that a subtle evasion of the command and the promise of ordination may be at work. We ministers sometimes wish to God that we could be "just one of the boys—or girls" so we should not have to bear the burden of being a community person. Our desire to be like anybody else may stem, not from our egalitarian humility but rather from our stubborn, self-centered pride that recognizes the threat of linking our personhood to the community's will. Some of our agonized doubts about our own lack of ability and our unsuitability for the demands of ministry may be rooted in our inability to accept the gift of officialness when it is offered to us. Our doubts about ourselves as ministers may stem, not so much from our doubts about our own personal attributes (for, as we have said, personal attributes are secondary considerations in ordination; the community's attributes are primary) but rather from our doubts about the ability of the community to bestow authority and the ability of God to empower and form community through us.

These doubts and misgivings about the validity and efficacy of our officialness will invariably be expressed in our leadership of the community's worship. For in the leadership of worship, the community function of the priest is revealed most clearly, the source of the priest's officialness is affirmed most strongly, and a pastor's self-understanding will be laid bare for all to see. Lay persons are correct in assuming that their pastor's leadership of worship is the primary and revelatory pastoral activity. They know enough to sense that if the pastor cannot be helpful to them in the leadership of the community's worship, the pastor will not be of much help to them elsewhere. If the pastor cannot be of service as the presence of Christ's community-wide vision, then the pastor will be unhelpful in their fulfillment of their individual vocations to become members of the community-wide vision.

Some Practical Observations on Pastoral Leadership of the Liturgy

Some time ago I was seated next to a woman at a dinner party who, in the course of the evening's conversation, told me that her congregation had just been sent a new pastor. "How do you like him?" I asked.

"Oh, he is wonderful," she replied enthusiastically. "He gives the best benedictions."

I confessed that I heard many compliments of ministers' abilities, but that was a compliment I had never heard. I asked her to explain.

"Well, we had never thought much about benedictions. Perhaps we had never really had one. But the first Sunday he was with us, at the conclusion of the worship service, rather than rush back to the door to greet everyone, he stayed at the front and said something like: 'Now I am going to bless you. I want you all to look at me and receive my blessing because you may really need it next week.' We all watched as he raised both hands high above his head, stretching out as if to embrace us, looking at each one of us, and almost like a father, blessing us in the name of the Father, and of the Son, and of the Holy Spirit. His benedictions have become the highlight of each Sunday as far as I am concerned."

In a way, I think that woman's testimony says all that I wanted to say here. Her testimony on the helpfulness of her pastor's blessing reminded me of a fine essay Paul Pruyser wrote a few years ago on "The Master Hand: Psychological Notes on Pastoral Blessing."[13] Pruyser noted the potential usefulness of this ancient gesture as a means through which to "dedicate the individual to the divine providence." Pruyser was disturbed at the halfhearted way in which many pastors pronounce benedictions within the worship service and speculated on the possible reasons pastors avoid this

---

13. Paul W. Pruyser, "The Master Hand: Psychological Notes on Pastoral Blessing," William B. Oglesby, Jr., ed., *The New Shape of Pastoral Theology: Essays in Honor of Seward Hiltner* (Nashville: Abingdon, 1969), pp. 352-65.

powerful symbol of providence. First he noted that the decay in the performance of pastoral benedictions coincided with the erosion of the classical theological doctrine of providence. Was this erosion due to poor theological instruction on providence, or due to poor demonstration of divine providence through the pastoral blessing? Perhaps people found it difficult to conceive of divine providence because they had never experienced that providence through another human being—their pastor.

Another possible reason . . . lay in the pastors' own conflicts concerning their professional identity:

> When worship leaders perform sloppily in their liturgical work, they are obviously not attributing a high professional value to this part of their activities. And when they perform badly in benedictions, the unspoken messages to the congregation are that: (1) benedictions are rather meaningless, (2) the pastor does not deem the people worthy of receiving them, (3) the pastor himself has long given up thought of providence, or (4) the pastor refuses to shoulder the shepherd's role.[14]

The poor performance of significant liturgical gestures like the benediction, indicates that the pastor may have let his own misgivings about his ability to bless overcome the community's authorization of the pastor as the one to whom is given the power to bless. By refusing to bless, the pastor shows insensitivity to or lack of knowledge about the needs of people. The pastor also shows that he or she may be so consumed by his or her own conflict about authorization and competence, or need for self-fulfillment and self-understanding that the pastor cannot respond to the needs of others. Ordination reminds us that the pastor blesses not because he or she has answered all inner questions about divine providence, not because the pastor does it better than anyone else in the community might do it, and not because the pastor may feel the personal need at that moment to do it but because the community has bestowed upon the pastor the job of doing it.

In fact, as Pruyser goes on to suggest, by merely attempting to do the job of blessing right, the pastor may find that his or her own

---

14. Ibid., p. 361.

doubts and misgivings are assuaged by the very action of the performance itself. Liturgical gestures are psycho-dynamically so important and are so closely tied to the inner emotions, that performing the proper motion may very likely stimulate the corresponding emotion. In blessing, the pastor may be blessed. But whether or not the pastor is blessed (an entirely secondary matter to the pastor's job), it is important for the pastor to get out of the way, so to speak, and be willing to function for the community that is always in need of such blessing. I suppose this is what C. S. Lewis was thinking about when he complained somewhere, "The modern habit of doing ceremonial things unceremoniously is no proof of humility; rather it proves the offender's inability to forget himself in the rite, and his readiness to spoil for everyone else the proper pleasure of ritual." . . .

In our current fear of authoritarianism we have developed a phobia of authority. The political "hero" of my student days was Eugene McCarthy, the ultimate in the nonleader. McCarthy represented the very antithesis of what we saw in the authoritarian style of Lyndon Johnson. But leadership ills will not be cured by having no leaders. If some styles of leadership are inadequate and the self-understanding of some leaders is faulty, then such things can be changed. But we must have leaders. We must learn to exercise legitimately given authority without being authoritarian.

Oddly enough, sometimes there is a kind of incipient clericalism behind our efforts to appear to be nonleaders of the community's worship. By demonstrating our own crisis of identity through our fumbling leadership, our determined effort to appear to be "just one of the boys" who is obviously uncomfortable with this "holy man" image, we call attention to ourselves as if our own self-image were the central issue in ministry. The congregation is saved from having to worship and meet God by our turning the service into a display of our self-doubts, authority questions, and loudly proclaimed sense of inadequacy. The preacher is still the center of the show, a paradigm not of one who is servant of the Word and an official of the community at worship, but one who subtly dominates worship with his or her own personality struggles. . . .

... When the priest dares to boldly and expectantly lead God's people before the throne of grace, I have confidence that such shepherding will not go unrewarded. The people will be blessed through the pastor's leading—perhaps not cured, not improved, or not fully healed. They will be blessed. That blessing will be reward enough for the one who has faithfully led.

William H. Willimon, *Worship as Pastoral Care* (Nashville: Abingdon, 1979), pp. 196–218.

After the Second Vatican Council, countless parish priests found themselves within a Catholic Church that was so transformed as to seem almost a different church—particularly in the Sunday liturgy. New liturgies required new understandings of pastoral leadership. Robert W. Hovda, himself a priest, authored a manual for those who preside in the liturgy, Strong, Loving and Wise. *Here Hovda recalled priests to the most prominent pastoral task—leading the assembly in the Christian liturgy. He presented a supremely practical pastoral theology, in which such matters as posture, gesture, eye contact, and facial expression became significant aspects of pastoral leadership, signs of the unique way that pastors lead when they lead the liturgy.*

Liturgical Celebration
Robert W. Hovda

Because the church is ministerial, the entire church is minister, and all specific ministerial functions depend on the church, a time of ecclesial rediscovery is also a time of ministerial rediscovery. All ministries, including those of bishops and presbyters, are undergoing a rethinking and reshaping, a radical critique. All this is essential, good, healthy for the churches as it is for the ministries. A manual on presiding can note these developments, as we have in earlier sections, but cannot give it the attention it must have. That attention depends on many essential studies now under way or in prospect.

It is not surprising that these developments should shake up the clergy and make the best of them—those most sensitive to the baptismal dignity of Christians and to the distance which now exists between ordained ministers and the rest of the church—uneasy in their presiding function. Perhaps the most important thing we can say in this manual is that it is not the function of presiding in liturgy that has created this distance, this inflation of the clergy and their separation from the churches. And it does not solve the problem to abdicate the presiding function.

One is tempted to sympathize with anyone who reacts against clericalism in any way, even if the reaction is clumsy, ill-considered and ineffectual. However, one should not sympathize with priests or other clergy who seem to think that refusing to preside is a contribution to the reformation of ministries.

. . . When a liturgical presider drops out of sight whenever the service does not require some vocal activity, or looks apologetic or ill at ease whenever it does, that person deprives everyone in the assembly of something that is essential to good liturgical experience.

Unlike a meeting of the Society of Friends, which has its own genius, sacramental liturgy requires specific ministerial functions, the most essential among them being the ministry of the congregation and the second most essential being that of the presider. Unless one is willing to accept the presider's role and do it as well as one can, one should not accept episcopal or presbyteral ordination. . . .

. . . A liturgical celebration needs a presider who is present to, visible to, in touch with the entire assembly at all times in the course of a service of public worship. That person is the assembly's servant as well as the servant of any other ministers required by the particular rite. One's service, in this case, is not a question of self assertion but of leadership. To abdicate this leadership is to fail to serve the community.

Personal Attention

Physical presence is only the beginning of a presence, but it is a sine qua non. The presider must be present to the assembly as a warm body—that's why the chair is important even when the presider is not actively leading at a particular moment. But liturgical presence that remains merely spatial is disastrous, as all Christians know from experience.

Personal attention throughout the celebration is one of the primary characteristics of a good presence. This means at the very least that one is "together," and is trying to stay together. The constitutive elements of this personal attention are probably many and complex, but it is certain that one cannot manifest it unless one feels that what one is doing is worth doing.

Faith is involved fundamentally, and an extraordinary conviction about the centrality of liturgy in the life of faith, a conviction about the moments of celebration as faith-life orientation. Unless one has discovered a necessary relation between faith and happiness in one's own life, it cannot be reflected or communicated. And if liturgy is felt (no matter how subconsciously) to be a packaged talisman, a thing, rather than a community's praising action, one's presiding will do more harm than good.

Personal attention in the whole and in each part of celebration is, like all the other elements of presence, communicated by the voice, the eyes, facial expressions, gestures, body postures and movements, the way one handles material objects, and so on. . . . [B]ut the feeling that the presider is together and is attending to the persons of the assembly, the ritual action and the objects employed in it is a critical ingredient of a good experience for all.

Personal Peace

Separation and distinction of these elements is a theoretical exercise, because they all go together, but it is necessary in a manual of this sort. If the presider is together and capable of focusing attention, he/she also needs a peace that comes, not from an absence of the doubting that always accompanies faith, but from facing doubts and reaching a daily resolution and commitment.

No doubt it is very honest and open and vulnerable and all those good things to stand before a congregation week after week testifying to one's anguish and uncertainty. It is also extremely inappropriate in liturgy and an abject failure in service or ministry. One's presence, then, becomes a burden on the assembly rather than a facilitating leadership.

We cannot ask less of the presider than we ask of other members of the faith community. Now that our baptismal consciousness has been raised a bit (or is in the process of being raised) and we see Lent and Easter as an annual reinitiation and recommitment for all Christians, we are beginning to realize that a personal commitment is our entry to the eucharistic assembly. The presider's commitment is of the essence. When no commitment can be summoned— and this can happen to clergy as well as to anybody else—the church should remain supportive and encouraging to that person, but its liturgies should not be made victims. A stiff upper lip is insufficient for the presider's task.

Personal peace is not apathy nor is it comfort in a rut. It is an active resolution of real human conflicts. It belongs to life, not to death. It is a work of struggle, not a yielding to rest. And what a service it is to an assembly of struggling believers, who bear daily in their bodies, the world-kingdom tension, the cross! It is a presence that everyone can feel.

Being Oneself

At one time—a time this author remembers well—it was popularly considered desirable for the one presiding to be as anonymous as possible. The less of oneself that showed through, the better. The ideal was pretty much an obliteration of self in liturgical celebration, if that isn't putting it too crudely. . . .

The trouble with that effort (to be other than oneself) is its futility and costliness. We can't escape ourselves at any time, especially when we are exercising a function of leadership. Only the one who recognizes the futility of the effort to be anonymous and is without illusions will be effective in minimizing individual idiosyncrasies and peculiarities for the sake of the social event. And the costliness of anonymity is a matter of experience: the "sacred alias" that was responsible for so many past and present problems, e.g., "pulpit tone," mechanical performance, failure to summon one's talents, and other manifestations of phony or unreal behavior.

Part of one's service to the assembly as presider is to be willing to present oneself to the whole group, consenting to be a focal point in the action, being in constant communication with the other ministers and the entire assembly through eye contact, gesture, body posture and movement, as well as word. The self-centered person, the ecclesiastical prince, the person who is out for privileges and status is opaque in this role. If, however, the presider is close to and part of the lives of all in the faith community, one of the people, clearly the servant of all, then there is the possibility of being transparent to the presence and action of the Lord. But it is a transparency that is accomplished, not with an anonymous persona, but with oneself.

Liturgy is something that persons of faith do in community. And they have to bring their real selves and their whole selves and their true selves to it. Surely they step out on the "threshold" of their daily lives and roles and categories to play at being sisters and brothers, daughters and sons of God—stripped of everything enslaving or divisive—but they can do this only as themselves.

So, when one functions as a presider or other minister, it is the whole person, the real person, the true person, the full and complete person who functions. It is you the church has chosen for this task. It is you God calls through the church. God wants no sacred alias, no pulpit tone, nor does the church.

Of course the personal nature of the presider's presence was always evident in liturgy, but more as a reluctant concession to humanity than as a desirable and valuable gift. Now we see it positively as a gift, a gift to be disciplined by the social and formal and ritual nature of the occasion, but a gift nonetheless.

The Other Ministers

To preside is to work with and facilitate and direct or conduct not only a congregation's action but also a number of other ministers: choral and instrumental musicians, readers, ushers, acolytes and others. One's service to the other ministers is chiefly to facilitate a team-making process, by attending to the value and the specific contribution of each and by choreographing or orchestrating their ritual interaction.

Working with the same team of other ministers week after week is very helpful to the presider's growth and performance. One must balance this value with the desirability of opening ministries to as many as possible in the faith community who have talent, training and desire for them. In most places, it should be possible to have a presider working with the same team of ministers for at least a month or a season at a time.

This practice enables members of the team to become sensitive to one another's unspoken cues, to move together more easily, to give full attention to the one or more of their number who are actively functioning at any given moment. The presider thus learns to conduct the group by simple glances and gestures, rather than by agitated whispers and scurrying about. The presider's presence to the other ministers is their focus and stable point of reference throughout the action.

Efficiency Versus Liturgy

Few things threaten one's effectiveness as a presider and the presence one has to establish as much as the lust for efficiency. Preceding pages have spoken of the importance of art, beauty, contemplation in celebration, and have described the play character of liturgy. But the work ethic and a compulsion to get things done as quickly, cheaply and with as little inconvenience as possible is never far below the surface in American church life.

This is not simply a matter of style, though it enters into every aspect of one's style. The whole presence of the presider is affected by one's approach to the words as well as to the action. If what counts for a person is getting the words said with the least expenditure of energy, that comes through as a negative experience for everyone in the assembly. If what counts is getting the actions performed with the least expenditure of energy, that, too, comes through as a totally negative experience.

Better use ten words and treat them lovingly and speak them meaningfully and savor them tenderly than ratatatat a thousand. Better use one gesture and make it a real picture, make it big and broad and smooth, than try to signify anything with a hundred muscular spasms. Do not hurry. Do not abbreviate. Do not shortchange. Do not condense. Do not telescope. Do not "reduce to essentials" in the sense of "getting everything in" no matter what the cost or speed.

The usual excuse for this elephant-in-a-china-shop approach to rites is time. Many Christians, as a matter of fact, *are* time conscious during liturgical celebrations . . . because they are having a bad experience. If people are having a good experience, they stop looking at their watches, they have no interest in their watches. It does not occur to people who are having a good experience to wonder about the time.

But the presence of a presider who is conscious of time and unconscious of the value of the persons and things dealt with in the ritual action is enough to glue anybody's eyes to the second hand. Such a one communicates impatience and haste and lack of concern as the carrier of a contagious disease spreads its malevolence.

Hovda, Robert W., *Strong, Loving and Wise* **(Collegeville, Minn.: The Liturgical Press, 1976), pp. 53-59.**

CHAPTER FOUR

The Priest as Pastor

As pastor, writer, and James M. Houston Professor of Spiritual Theology Emeritus at Regent College, Eugene H. Peterson has ministered to the ministers. Peterson combines a generous evangelical theology with heartfelt concern for pastors and their plight, all served up with truthfulness, honesty, and his loving way with the language. In The Message *he rendered the Bible into contemporary English, as he did in most of his sermons as a pastor. His* The Contemplative Pastor *was an eloquent rebuke to secularized, worldly conceptions of the pastoral ministry that infected many pastors in the late twentieth century. In this selection, Peterson works a theme that he engaged in many books and articles—the unique quality of pastoral leadership, the countercultural, theologically rooted basis for ministry that is a rebuke to all utilitarian, purely pragmatic views of ministry. The pastor, Peterson is bold to say, is wonderfully, faithfully "unnecessary."*

On Being Unnecessary
Eugene H. Peterson

The gospel of Jesus Christ is profoundly countercultural. "I came to cast fire upon the earth," said Jesus; "and would that it were already kindled!" (Luke 12:49).

There are powerful cultural forces determined to turn Jesus into a kindly, wandering peasant sage, teaching us how to live well, dispensing homespun wisdom, arousing our desire for God, whetting our appetite for higher truths—all of which are good things. These same forces are similarly determined to turn us, the church's pastors and leaders, into kindly religious figures, men and women who provide guidance through difficult times, who dole out inspiration and good cheer on a weekly schedule, who provide smiling reassurance that "God's in his heaven . . . ," and keep our congregations busy at tasks that bolster their self-esteem—also good things.

And if they don't turn us into merely nice people, they turn us into replicas of our cultural leaders, seeking after power and influence and prestige. These insistent voices drum away at us, telling us pastors to go out and compete against the successful executives and entertainers who have made it to the top, so that we can put our churches on the map and make it big in the world.

In such a culture, it is continuously difficult to cultivate an everyday identity that derives from the crucified and risen Jesus Christ. No matter how many crosses we hang around our necks, paste on our bumpers, and place on our churches, the radical life of repentance and baptism is mighty hard to sustain.

But the Christian is a witness to a new reality that is entirely counter to the culture. The Christian faith is a proclamation that God's kingdom has arrived in Jesus, a proclamation that puts the world at risk. What Jesus himself proclaimed and we bear witness to is the truth that the sin-soaked, self-centered world is doomed.

Pastors are in charge of keeping the distinction between the world's lies and the gospel's truth clear. Not only pastors, of course—every baptized Christian is part of this—but pastors are placed in a strategic, countercultural position. Our place in society is, in some ways, unique: no one else occupies this exact niche that looks so inoffensive but is in fact so dangerous to the status quo. We are committed to keeping the proclamation alive and to looking after *souls* in a soul-denying, soul-trivializing age.

But it isn't easy. Powerful forces, both subtle and obvious, attempt either to domesticate pastors to serve the culture as it is or to seduce us into using our position to become powerful and important on the world's terms. And so we need all the help we can get to maintain our gospel identity. . . .

The leading premise is that pastors are "unnecessary," but unnecessary in a defined sense. I don't mean worthless or irrelevant or shiftless. I mean unnecessary in three ways in which we often are assumed to be necessary:

1. We are unnecessary to what the *culture* presumes is important: as paragons of goodness and niceness. Culture has a fairly high

regard for pastors as custodians of moral order. We are viewed as persons who provide a background of social stability, who are useful in times of crisis and serve as symbols of meaning and purpose. But we are not necessary in any of those ways.

Several years ago, I was invited to the Pentagon to meet with the chaplains of the various services—Army, Navy, Air Force, Marines—to talk about their difficult position. We'd been in a peacetime mode for a number of years, and the Pentagon was trying to cut back on budgeting for chaplains. Chaplains weren't high-profile, necessary figures. And these chaplains had called on me to come and try to convince their superiors that they were necessary, that they had to be there. They were being used in all sorts of programs—drug counseling, marriage counseling. They were finding all sorts of ways to keep their jobs, and none of them had to do with anything they thought they had signed up to be chaplains for. In the middle of all of this—and I wasn't much help to them, for I was thinking about what I'm talking to you about—they told me that in wartime, on the front, every captain, every colonel, every leader of a force *demands* to have a chaplain. When the bullets are flying and the bombs are exploding, they want a chaplain right there. Chaplains are important, everybody knows they are important. They are life-and-death people. But in peacetime, who needs a chaplain? And in the course of all this, one of the men slammed down his fist and said, "What we need is a war!"

Three weeks later, the Gulf War broke out and their jobs were assured.

2. We are also unnecessary to what *we ourselves* feel is essential: as the linchpin holding a congregation together. Some of us have been reared with an idea that being a pastor is the apex of ministry—we hold the highest position in the hierarchy of those who serve in Jesus' name. We are entrusted with the Word of God and the souls of men and women—no one else occupies this privileged position quite like we do. We come to take ourselves very seriously indeed. But we are not necessary in these self-important ways. None of us is indispensable. Mordecai's message to Esther puts us in our place: "if you keep silence at such a time as this, relief and deliverance will rise for the Jews from another quarter . . ." (Esther 4:14). We have important work to do, but if we don't do it God can always find someone else—and probably not a pastor.

3. And we are unnecessary to what *congregations* insist that we must do and be: as the experts who help them stay ahead of the competition. Congregations want pastors who will lead them in the world of religious competition and provide a safe alternative to the world's ways. They want pastors who *lead*. They want pastors the way the Israelites wanted a king—to make hash of the Philistines. Congregations get their ideas of what makes a pastor from the culture, not from the Scriptures: they want a winner; they want their needs met; they want to be part of something zesty and glamorous.

I am in conversation right now with a dozen or so men and women who are prepared to be pastors and who are waiting to be called by a congregation. And I am having the depressing experience of reading congregational descriptions of what these churches want in a pastor. With hardly an exception they don't want pastors at all—they want managers of their religious company. They want a pastor they can follow so they won't have to bother with following Jesus anymore. . . .

Vows—Putting in Protection

I just recently celebrated the fortieth year of my ordination into the gospel ministry. Through these forty years, I have spent much time trying to stay honest, prayerful, and biblical as I have served Jesus in this role. I have been dismayed by the widespread defection of many of my friends into officiating over Baal shrines and Ashteroth groves—this incredible revival of old Canaanite religion on the North American continent. You would have thought that men and women who had their heads full of Elijah and Isaiah and Jeremiah would have been proof against a religion that was designed to meet the needs of people as the people understood them, appealing to their pride, nurturing their greed, and providing escapist fantasies that incapacitate them from faithful and committed relationships and work. But we look around us—yes, and within us—and realize that there is not much correspondence between those fierce prophets and what is being put on display these days as the successful pastor. . . .

As I approached this fortieth anniversary of my ordination, I had occasion to go back and revisit the eight vows I took at the time.

One of them, the sixth vow, struck me as being generic to all pastors, and I want to use it now to give focus to the spirit that infuses these Pastoral Epistles, and what we are doing here. Here's the vow: *Will you, in your own life, seek to follow the Lord Jesus Christ, love your neighbors, and work for the reconciliation of the world?*

Sixty miles or so from Vancouver, up the sunshine coast, there is a mountain popular among rock climbers—the Stalamus Chief. It presents itself as a vertical slab of smooth granite, two thousand feet high. It looks like a sheet of glass. On summer days, rock climbers are spread out in varying levels of ascent up and down its face. Occasionally, climbers spend the night in hammocks (they call it bivouacking), hanging like cocoons attached to barn siding. It always strikes me as a mighty dangerous way to have fun.

I am fascinated by the sight and, when in the vicinity, pull off the road and watch for awhile with my binoculars. It is not the action that holds my attention, for there is certainly not much in the way of action up there. The climbers move slowly, cautiously, every move tested, calculated. There is no spontaneity in this sport, no thrills. Except perhaps the ultimate thrill of not falling—not dying. Maybe what grips my attention is death, the risk of death—life dangling by a thread.

Still, dangerous as it is, I know that it is not as dangerous as it looks. Looking from the valley floor with my naked eye the climbers appear to be improbably exempt from gravity. But with my binoculars, I can see that each climber is equipped with ropes and carabiners and pitons (or chocks, wedges, and camming devices). The pitons, sturdy pegs constructed from a light metal, are basic. My two sons are both rock climbers, and I have listened to them plan their ascents. They spend as much or more time planning their climbs as in the actual climbing. They meticulously plot their route and then, as they climb, put in what they call "protection"—pitons hammered into small crevices in the rock face, with attached ropes that will arrest a quick descent to death. Rock climbers who fail to put in protection have short climbing careers.

Recently, while watching several of these climbers, it suddenly struck me that my ordination vows had functioned for the past forty years as pitons, pegs driven firmly into the vertical rock face (stretching between heaven and earth) on which Christian ministry is played out. Vows are pegs, protection against moods and weather, miscalculation and fatigue. Vision and call, risk and inspiration are what we are most aware of and what others see when we become pastors or take up leadership positions in the church, but if there is no "protection" the chances of survival are slim. And so we take vows. Various churches and denominations have different ways of wording them, but they all amount to about the same thing: protection.

Here again is the one that I want to hold up for examination: *Will you, in your own life, seek to follow the Lord Jesus Christ, love your neighbors, and work for the reconciliation of the world?*

Eugene H. Peterson, in Marva J. Dawn and Eugene H. Peterson, *The Unnecessary Pastor: Rediscovering the Call*, Peter Santucci, ed. (Grand Rapids, Mich.: Wm. B. Eerdmans, 2000), pp. 1-13.

Richard Lischer, newly minted University of London Ph.D. in hand, found himself and his family hung out to dry at a forlorn Lutheran parish in southern Illinois, somewhere from here to eternity. Open Secrets *is Lischer's honest yet gracious memoir of his first pastoral assignment. He looks back from Duke Divinity School, where he has taught homiletics for many years, upon a little church amid the corn- and soybean fields where he learned the secret of being a pastor.*

"When you pull up to your first church," he writes, "it's a moment of truth, like the first glimpse of a spouse in an arranged marriage." In many ways, Lischer's first glimpse of the parish was grim. The doors of his little church were painted a "sickly salmon." The cross atop the peeling steeple was missing an arm.

And yet here was where the twenty-eight-year-old pastor found the church, and the church found him. Here is where he discovered, to his surprise, the real presence of Christ, the church, reflected in the stumbling celebration of the sacraments, shining through the dullness of everyday parish life. In the daily liturgy of life within the parish, a young pastor experiences an epiphany. These folk gathered at a place called New Cana, despite themselves and their pastor, really are a miraculous sign of water made into wine, the glorious Word become flesh in the middle of a cornfield.

The Real Presence
Richard Lischer

From the very first week in New Cana, my preparation for worship began at the Sacred Burning Barrel. There was no garbage pickup in our part of the county, just as there was no newspaper or, for the first year, home mail delivery (to say nothing of pizza), which meant that we burned our own trash in a big rusty barrel at the southwest corner of the property. My wife and I playfully invested this lonely but beautiful place with transcendent meaning and a holy name. If God showed up on the Plain of Midian in a burning bush, why not here in a creosote-stained trash barrel? At first it was a joke between us, but soon we were vying with one another to see who got to burn the trash while the other minded the baby.

I don't know what Tracy thought about when she stood in the freezing cold before the flames and watched the sun setting behind the heath-like Brush. I made the experience a time of preparation, when I reflected on the events of the past week and planned my Sunday sermon. As time went on, I began praying for individual parishioners at the Sacred Burning Barrel.

On my first Sunday morning I was taken aback by a ghastly sight in the sacristy. A dying man was sprawled on a chaise lounge in the center of the room. He was white as snow and as cold to the touch. His total hairlessness, I was soon to learn, was the result of an experimental drug therapy. He was dressed in a cassock, surplice, and stole. A hymnal lay open across his lap.

Erich Martin was the former pastor of the church. He was so weakened by cancer that he couldn't sit in a pew. He worshiped in the sacristy with the door to the chancel wide open. From his lounge chair he could also keep an eye on me, and from anywhere in the chancel I had him in view. Since no one could see him but me, he constituted my private audience of one, a second congregation. Whenever I stood in the pulpit during those first months, Erich was a barely living blur to my right. If I was tempted, as preachers occasionally are, to replace the proclamation of the gospel with affable chatter, the presence of a liturgically vested, dying man in a chaise lounge never failed to dissuade.

Long after he was gone, I could not step into the pulpit without instinctively checking the sacristy door. Although Erich never played the lovable, crusty old mentor toward me, his presence, at first intimidating, grew to be a source of reassurance. If we are "surrounded by so great a cloud of witnesses," as the Book of Hebrews promises, here at least was one I could keep my eye on.

The old academy system of education had forged Erich with a discipline that was foreign to me. I never met a person so utterly controlled by the patterns and duties of the ministry as he. Even among farmers, who are not famous for their introspective nature, I never met anyone less absorbed in himself or driven by a personal agenda than Erich. Unlike the therapeutically trained cleric, Erich did not compulsively insist on being a friend or a pal to his parishioners. He was not, as one of my friends says of Protestant ministers in general, "a quivering mass of availability." He did not personalize his every act of ministry. Unlike ministers who make a career of getting along with people, Erich's approach was to do his duty, and to let the duties symbolize something larger and more important than his own personality.

Erich had been seasoned by many years of ministry in India, where he and his wife had lost a son to malaria. New Cana was just another mission field to him. No one who has buried a child in Jabalpur can be beaten by a little loneliness or a few stubborn farmers in Illinois.

No doubt owing to his background as a missionary, Erich's practice had been to refuse his paycheck until the monthly mission allotment had been paid. He never made an issue of it, but in a small town word gets around. It was solely due to his example that in good years and in bad an ingrown rural congregation gave away one half its income. Everyone respected him, but if someone were to ask, "Did you like Pastor Martin?" they would say, "*Like?*" then look quizzically at one another and reframe the question.

With Erich a constant presence to my right, I was physically linked to the authority of tradition. But I soon recognized other fixed positions in our small-town sociogram. Most of the older generation sat on the pulpit side of the church; their grown children and families sat on the other side of the aisle. This probably represented a vestige of the old days when the men and women sat on opposite sides of the church. Most people clustered to the center of the church, which might have been a memory of the enormous pot-bellied stove that once sat in the center aisle, around which parishioners would toast one side of their bodies and freeze the other while the whole room slowly filled with smoke. Only the young teens, giggling and elbowing one another like hockey players, sat in the first couple rows. Their position represented their first adventurous separation from their parents.

Leonard and June Semanns always sat in the fourth row on the lectern side. Buster Island and (when she came) Beulah, along with the smiling Max, Angela, and the lank-haired Lacy, usually sat farther back by the window. Buster, his neck bulging out of a filthy dress shirt with loosened tie, sweat popping through his flattop, was always hoping to catch a little breeze on steamy summer days. Lacy, for all his surliness toward anyone in authority, tended his little sister more like a young father than an older brother. She responded by laying her head on his shoulder with theatrical sighs of fatigue.

The ushers usually began the service standing officiously at the rear in the tiny narthex, but as the hour wore on they would *slyly* inch their way backward out the door for a smoke. Even the reclusive Henry Dire had his appointed spot. He sat in the darkest corner of the sacristy and pretended to monitor the PA system, which, as everyone knew, didn't work. Each member had a place in this congregation and, in summer, everyone swung a fan provided by Metz's ("Be-in-Time-for-Eternity") Mortuary of Cherry Grove.

Ernie Semanns was once a trustee whose responsibilities dictated that he and his family sit in the front row on the lectern side, from which position he could easily exit if the toilets flooded the downstairs hall, as they frequently did, or if any other physical calamity occurred. For example, one Sunday early in my ministry, a little girl threw up onto the dark wooden floor in front of her pew. I was about two minutes into my sermon at the time and decided to demonstrate my professionalism by continuing to preach. A trustee (not Ernie, by the way) immediately sprang up to attend to the stiffening puke. He surveyed it and within minutes returned to the scene pushing a bucket on wheels with rollers and a mop. The wheels and rollers squeaked noisily. I found it possible to preach through this distraction, and after a few minutes of squishing, mopping, and squeaking, he and the vomit were gone.

Several moments later, however, as I moved persuasively into my next point, the trustee returned to the scene of the mishap, this time with a can of scented air freshener. *Psss-psss-psss.* Pause. *Psss-psss-psss.* And for good measure: *Psss.* Suddenly the whole church smelled like an alpine forest gone slightly off. That was the first time I heard laughter in the church.

Ernie and Darlene had had one child, a son who was enrolled in the agriculture program at Carbondale and would some day make the family farm a success. One night Ernie junior was killed in a wreck out where 140 T's into the hard road. I had heard the story from several parishioners. "He died on the road, Pastor," Leonard had said in the formulaic pattern that everyone in New Cana seemed to use:

Took forever to get an am-bu-lance.
We're on our own out here.
He was a good boy
 but hell on wheels.
He died on the road.

It took Ernie and Darlene a long time to come back to church, and when they did Darlene spent most of her time helping in the nursery, counting offerings in the parish hall, or preparing coffee in the kitchen. Ernie took up residence in the last pew on the lectern side, as far removed from the word of God as is physically possible, and never moved. He became an expatriate in his own church while his old pew remained empty.

Early on I noticed a young stranger to the community who sat in the back row on the pulpit side. Every Sunday she wore the same floor-length, Aquarian dress with (I could only imagine) beaded anklets and sandals. From a distance of sixty feet, all I could make out was long, dark brown hair and powerful, Mongolian cheekbones. That was all I knew of her in those first few weeks, for she always vanished between stanzas of the final hymn. My mystery woman invariably arrived late and left before anyone could greet her, though I never actually saw her walk out. Why did she come? What did she have in common with the farmers? The best I could do was arc my voice toward the back pew in order to include her in the sermon and liturgy.

Within the physical pattern of our worship several movable parts stood out, like Elmer Branson's uncanny ability to pop up like a cheerleader a split second before the entire congregation for the *Gloria*. Like eighty-year-old Lydia Semanns's practice of kneeling at her pew on the hardwood floor after receiving communion. What made the practice even more remarkable was that she kneeled with her back to the altar, head bowed, with her hands folded on the seat of the pew.

When I asked forty-five-year-old Leonard why he thought she did that, he replied, "Well, *we all* did that fifty years ago for confession. Must've been the peculur'ist sight to the preacher: hunert'n fifty *backs* facing him as he got us ready to confess our sins."

"Why did *you* stop?" I asked, getting into the swing of his corporate sense of identity.

A shrug. "Hard to say. Maybe we don't *feel* that sinful anymore. Ha!"

"When did it stop?"

Another shrug. "Couldn't tell ya."

Because Erich had been sick so long, the elders, and others appointed by the elders, had assumed helping roles in the worship service, which was an irregular practice in our pastor-centered tradition. Elders distributed the wafers in communion, and other laypeople read the lessons. The elders seemed to think that the new pastor would want to reclaim control of the service. They were pleasantly surprised when I showed no interest in asserting my clerical rights.

It was the practice in our churches for the pastor to place the wafer into the opened mouth and onto the tongue of the communicant. The elders were uncomfortable performing this intimate sacramental act. Instead, they placed the wafer into the cupped hands of each recipient. They were clearly nervous whenever it was their turn to touch the bread.

Our elders had the thickest and most heavily muscled fingers I have ever seen. How they got a wedding ring over such enormous knuckles I can't imagine. Gnarled and callused hands, textured by manure and industrial grit in equal parts, gingerly pressed the Bread of Life into the uplifted palms of their neighbors, cousins, and parents. In a patriarchal church, the daintiness with which their monstrous hands handled the sacrament, like little girls laying a tea table, was our nearest brush with the femininity of God. Their role in the ritual reinforced our church's teaching on the "real presence." I was trained to believe that Jesus was really *there* in the bread and wine, but now I saw him with my own eyes in poor Erich to my right and in the calluses and knuckles of the servers.

Body of Christ. Body of Christ, they said robotically. They meant the body of Jesus, to be sure, but also the body of believers. All of us. Paul warned his readers in Corinth to "discern the body," which means to see Jesus' body in a new way. Not as a miracle of physics occurring in the elements, but as a miracle of community in which atoms of solitude are re-created into new families and friends. Christianity is a body religion. I had only begun to discern it.

I took such pleasure in lifting the chalice—"the way the Catholics do it!" someone said—when I came to the words, "Do this as often as you drink it, in remembrance of me." Because, when the light was filtering through our art-glass windows or flooding through the open doors in back, I could just see the whole congregation reflected in the silver cup. And in the congregation, the whole church.

Richard Lischer, *Open Secrets: A Spiritual Journey Through a Country Church* (New York: Doubleday, 2001), pp. 65-71.

CHAPTER FIVE

The Pastor as Interpreter of Scripture

Master preacher and lifelong teacher of preachers at Erskine, Princeton, and Candler seminaries, Tom Long typifies the best of contemporary homiletics. Whereas much of late twentieth-century homiletics focused upon what Long has called "the turn to the listener," concerning itself with the limits of the contemporary hearers of sermons, Long keeps close to the theological rationale for Christian preaching. Christian preachers receive a hearing when they have something interesting to say. Preaching is powerful, not primarily because the preacher has a pleasing personality or a charming voice but because the preacher has witnessed something, namely, the advent of God in Jesus Christ, that demands to be told. Thus Long speaks of the preacher as witness, someone who testifies to something that has been seen and heard, an event not of the preacher's personal devising, good news. To preachers who are overly troubled by their lack of homiletical skill and talent, Long implies that when the messenger is grasped by a significant message, the messenger will find the means to speak it.

Preaching as Bearing Witness
Thomas G. Long

Seeing the preacher as a witness is not a new idea. It has deep roots in the Bible, appearing in such passages as Acts 20:24, where Paul is reported to have said, "I do not account my life of any value nor as precious to myself, if only I may accomplish my course and the ministry which I received from the Lord Jesus, to witness to the gospel of the grace of God." The New Testament concept of witness grows out of Old Testament precedents. Consider the following passage from Isaiah 43:8-13:

Bring forth the people who are blind, yet have eyes,
 who are deaf, yet have ears!
Let all the nations gather together,
 and let the peoples assemble.
Who among them can declare this,
 and show us the former things?
Let them bring their witnesses to justify them,
 and let them hear and say, It is true.
"You are my witnesses," says the LORD,
 "and my servant whom I have chosen,
that you may know and believe me
 and understand that I am He.
Before me no god was formed,
 nor shall there be any after me.
I, I am the LORD,
 and besides me there is no savior.
I declared and saved and proclaimed,
 when there was no strange god among you;
 and you are my witnesses," says the LORD.
"I am God, and also henceforth I am He;
 there is none who can deliver from my hand;
 I work and who can hinder it?"

Commenting on this passage in an important essay, Paul Ricoeur identified four claims about the witness made by this text:[35]

1. The witness is not a volunteer, not just anyone who comes forward to give testimony, but only the one who is *sent* to testify.

2. The testimony of the witness is not about the global meaning of human experience but about God's claim upon life. It is Yahweh who is witnessed to in the testimony.

3. The purpose of the testimony is proclamation to all peoples. It is on behalf of the people, for their belief and understanding, that the testimony is made.

4. The testimony is not merely one of words but rather demands a total engagement of speech and action. The whole life of the witness is bound up in the testimony.

---

35. Paul Ricoeur, "The Hermeneutics of Testimony," in *Essays on Biblical Interpretation*, ed. Lewis S. Mudge (Philadelphia: Fortress Press, 1980), p. 131.

One can quickly see the relationship between preaching and the idea of witness, and in this light it may seem curious that the witness image has not been more prominent in homiletical literature. There are reasons for this, however. To begin with, the terms "witnessing" and "giving a testimony" have often been associated with some of the more aggressive forms of evangelism. Homileticians have sniffed the odor of manipulation around these words and thus have stayed far away from them. As such, "witness" is a good word that has gotten into some trouble through no fault of its own.

More significantly, homileticians have not been greatly attracted to the witness image because it seems out of place. Witness is a legal term; a witness appears in the courtroom as part of a trial. An aura of law and judgment surrounds the witness idea, and this appears to be at odds with the grace and freedom associated with preaching the gospel. It is important to keep in mind, though, that the image implies that the preacher is the one bearing witness, not the lawmaker, the police officer, or the judge, and in that light it is precisely the lawcourt origin of the witness metaphor that gives it power as an image for the preacher.

Consider what happens in a court trial. The trial is conducted in a public place because what happens is a public matter. A trial is designed to get at the truth, and the people have a vested interest in the truth. In order to get at the truth, a witness is brought to the stand to testify. Now this witness is in every way one of the people, but he or she is placed on the stand because of two credentials: The witness has seen something, and the witness is willing to tell the truth about it—the whole truth and nothing but the truth. In one sense, the personal characteristics of the witness do not matter. The court is interested in the truth and in justice, not in the witness per se. In another sense, however, the character of the witness is crucial. If the witness lies—bears false witness—the ability of the people to discover the truth will receive a grievous blow. "False testimony," writes Ricoeur, "is a lie in the heart of the witness. This perverse intention is so fatal to the exercise of justice and to the entire order of discourse that all codes of morality place it very high in the scale of vices."[36]

---

36. Ibid., pp. 128-129.

The court has access to the truth only through the witness. It seeks the truth, but it must look for it in testimony of the witness. The very life of the witness, then, is bound up into the testimony. The witness cannot claim to be removed, objectively pointing to the evidence. What the witness believes to be true is a part of the evidence, and when the truth told by the witness is despised by the people, the witness may suffer, or even be killed, as a result of the testimony. It is no coincidence that the New Testament word for "witness" is *martyr*.

What happens to our understanding of preaching when this image of witness is taken as a guide?

1. The witness image emphasizes the authority of the preacher in a new way. The preacher as witness is not authoritative because of rank or power but rather because of what the preacher has seen and heard. When the preacher prepares a sermon by wrestling with a biblical text, the preacher is not merely gathering information about that text. The preacher is listening for a voice, looking for a presence, hoping for the claim of God to be encountered through the text. Until this happens, there is nothing for the preacher to say. When it happens, the preacher becomes a witness to what has been seen and heard through the scripture, and the preacher's authority grows out of this seeing and hearing.

Does this mean that the preacher is authoritative because the preacher has more Christian experience than the people in the pews? No, of course not. There may well be many in the congregation whose faith is richer, more mature, and more tested than the preacher's. In addition, there will probably be people in the congregation who have more education or more common sense, who have a firmer grasp of human nature, or maybe even know more Bible and theology than does the preacher. To call the preacher an authority does not mean that the preacher is wiser than others. What it does mean is that the preacher is the one whom the congregation sends on their behalf, week after week, to the scripture. The church knows that its life depends upon hearing the truth of God's promise and claim through the scripture, and it has set the preacher apart for the crucial activity of going to the scripture to listen for that truth. The authority of the preacher, then, is the authority of ordination, the authority of being identified by the faithful community as the one called to preach and the one who has been prayerfully set apart for this ministry, the authority that comes from being "sworn in" as a witness.

Accordingly, the church prepares and trains its ministers, including sending them to seminaries, not because ministers are better or smarter than other Christians, but because the church needs workers equipped to help the church to know the truth and to live in its light. If the preacher is to be the one sent to listen for God's truth in the Bible, the preacher not only must be willing to listen to the Bible but also must know how to listen. If the preacher is to be sent on behalf of the congregation, the preacher must also know how to listen to *them*. These activities require a right spirit, but they also require special preparation. Seminary training does not equip one to be a professor in the church but, rather, a trustworthy witness. An unreliable witness does not make the truth any less true, but the community's quest to encounter the truth is undeniably damaged by false or unreliable witnesses.

2. The witness image embodies a way of approaching the Bible. Witnesses testify to events, and the event to which the preacher testifies is the encounter between God and ourselves. This event is the same one proclaimed in Isaiah, "that you may know and believe me and understand that I am [God]." One of the essential ways that we come to "know" God is through the scripture, not because the Bible speculates about the nature of God in a metaphysical sense but because the Bible is itself the faithful witness to the interactions of God with the whole creation. We come to know God as the central "character" in the story, as a "Person" in relationship with human beings, as One who creates, judges, saves, loves, destroys, builds, forgives, and renews. "The primary focus [of the Bible] is not on God's being in itself," claims Lindbeck, "for that is not what the text is about, but on how life is to be lived and reality construed in the light of God's character as an agent as this is depicted in the stories of Israel and of Jesus."[37]

We go to scripture, then, not to glean a set of facts about God or the faith that can then be announced whenever and wherever, but to encounter a Presence, to hear God's voice speaking to us ever anew, calling us in the midst of the situations in which we find ourselves to be God's faithful people. The picture of the preacher

---

37. [George A.] Lindbeck, *The Nature of Doctrine* [*: Religion and Theology in a Post-Liberal Age* (Philadelphia, Pa.: Fortress, 1984)], p. 121.

sitting alone in the study, working with a biblical text in preparation for the sermon, is misleading. It is not the preacher who goes to the scripture; it is the church that goes to the scripture by means of the preacher. The preacher is a member of the community, set apart by them and sent to the scripture to search, to study, and to listen obediently on their behalf.

So, the preacher goes to the scripture, but not alone. The preacher goes on behalf of the faithful community and, in a sense, on behalf of the world. Their questions and needs are in the preacher's mind and heart. The preacher explores the scripture, faithfully expecting to discover the truth of God's claim there and always willing to be surprised by it. Those who have sent the preacher have questions and concerns, and sometimes the text will speak directly to those questions. The text may, however, call those questions into question. The truth found there may resolve a problem, and then again it may deepen that problem. The truth found there may generate a religious experience, but it may also create the experience of God's absence. Whatever needs of church and world have been brought to the text by the preacher, when the claims of God through the scripture are seen and heard, the preacher turns back toward those who wait—and tells the truth.

3. The witness image carries with it guidance about the rhetorical form of preaching. The witness is not called upon to testify in the abstract but to find just those words and patterns that can convey the event the witness has heard and seen. One can even say that the truth to which the witness testifies seeks its own verbal form, and the responsibility of the witness is to allow that form to emerge. Most often the witness is invited to "tell your story"; thus the prominence given to narrative in the storytelling image is also implied in the image of witness. On other occasions, though, the truth will demand another form. Preaching, in other words, will assume a variety of rhetorical styles, not as ornaments but as governed by the truth to which they correspond. The shape of the witness's sermon should fit the character of the testimony.

4. The witness is not a neutral observer. The truth is larger than the witness's own experience of it, and the witness is always testifying to a gospel larger than the preacher's personal faith, but the witness preacher *has* experienced it at some depth and is thereby involved in it. This is especially true of the New Testament concept

of witness, in which witnessing takes on an acted as well as a verbal form. The witness often testifies to hard truths, unpopular truths, and sometimes at great risk. As Paul Ricoeur has commented, "This profession [of a witness] implies a total engagement not only of words but of acts, and, in the extreme, in the sacrifice of a life."[38]

The witness is also not a neutral observer in the sense that where one stands influences what one sees. The location of the witness, in other words, is critical, and the preacher as witness is one who stands in and with a particular community of faith, deeply involved in the concrete struggles of that community to find meaning, to seek justice, and to be faithful to the gospel. If the community of faith to which the witness belongs and from which the witness comes is urban or rural, black or Asian, rich or poor, powerless or powerful, these circumstances firmly shape the character of the preaching. We have recognized, through the work of liberation and feminist theologians among others, that a "disinterested" reading of the gospel is neither possible nor desirable. Effective preaching has an invested local flavor because the preacher as witness participates in the mission of a specific community of faith, goes to the scripture on behalf of that community, and hears a particular word for them on this day and in this place.

5. The witness image also underscores the ecclesiastical and liturgical setting of preaching. Though it is not always apparent, the worship of the church is a dramatic enactment of a great and cosmic trial in which the justice of God is poised against all the powers that spoil creation and enslave human life. In this trial Christ is the one true and faithful witness. "For this I was born, and for this I have come into the world, to bear witness to the truth" (John 18:37). All human testimony is authentic only to the extent that it remains faithful to the witness of Christ. "You also are witnesses, because you have been with me from the beginning" (John 15:27).

"It is only with the day of the Lord," writes Richard Fenn, "that all accusation ends, and the trial is over." He goes on: "It is for that reason on the Lord's Day that the people of God celebrate a mock

---

38. Ricoeur, "The Hermeneutics of Testimony," p. 131.

trial, in which the law is read, confession and testimony obtained, and the verdict once again given as it was once before all time."[39]

"I give thanks to God always for you," wrote Paul to the Corinthians, speaking of the relationship between witness and the life of the Christian community, "because of the grace of God which was given you in Christ Jesus, that in every way you were enriched in him with all speech and all knowledge—even as the testimony to Christ was confirmed among you" (1 Cor. 1:4-5).

---

39. Richard K. Fenn, *Liturgies and Trials* (New York: Pilgrim Press), p. 27.

Thomas G. Long, *The Witness of Preaching* (Louisville, Ky.: Westminster John Knox Press, 1989), 42-47.

The Christian faith is an acoustical, auditory affair. Everything rests upon, begins with, comes to birth with that fateful phrase, "God said." Eugene Peterson attempts to ground all Christian spirituality in Scripture. Here he writes for all Christians, but his words seem to be of particular relevance for pastors. Those of us whom the church calls to read, to teach, to preach and to help the church embody Scripture too easily forget, in our daily dealings with the Sacred Text, that Scripture is "square one" for this faith. We are people of the Book. One of the most essential, peculiar qualities of Christians is an ability to read, a willingness to listen, an eagerness to submit our lives to this text called Sacred Scripture. Peterson not only does this through exhortation, by linkage with insights from child development, but also by demonstrating creative biblical interpretation of a segment of the book of Job.

Back to Square One: God Said
(The Witness of Holy Scripture)
Eugene Peterson

I

The characteristic element of Square One is this: God Said. There is, of course, much else, too. As we step into Square One the entire sweep of heaven and earth opens up before us. We are not capable of handling it all at once. It's best to take it in small bits and pieces. A story here, a prayer there, a song, a dream. Words are our primary tools for getting our bearings in the world—most of which we can't see, most of which we'll never touch—large, expanding, mysterious existence that is so much larger, more intricate, more real even, than we are.

We learn the word "ball," and by means of the word acquire the ability to experience the reality of the tennis ball even after it rolls under the dry sink and [we] cannot see it. As we add words to our working vocabulary, we become conversant with more and more reality. The absolutely indispensable word that we learn at Square One is God. We learn the word "God" and acquire the ability to experience everything that is beyond us as connectedly real and personally congenial. We don't learn this immediately, suddenly, absolutely; there are misunderstandings, superstitions, twists and turns in the imagination, advances and regressions. But we learn it. Everybody learns it. "For that which can be known about God is plain to them, because God has shown it to them. Ever since the creation of the world his invisible nature, namely, his eternal power and deity, has been clearly perceived in the things that have been made" (Rom. 1:19-20). The unknown takes precedence over the known. That which we can't see accounts for what we can see. And this mysterious unknown, unseen, is purposeful and personal: God.

Purposeful. For there is coherence and design and plan previous to my experience of life.

Personal. For there is something or other that connects with me that is more me than I am: God is more than I am, not less. Not just more powerful or more wise, but more *person*, more of whatever it is that makes me capable of thinking, believing, loving, hoping, trusting—all these great invisibles that I become aware of at Square One.

God. There is no single term that is as common and indispensable to human beings. There is no language in which the word does not occur. There is hardly a moment in our lives when the word does not figure in some way or other in the way we account for ourselves and the world around us—whether through denial, or modification, or blasphemy, or adoration. God.

In scientific theory and philosophy "the criterion of simplicity is crucial."[1] Richard Swinburne is the Nolloth Professor of the Christian Religion at Oxford University. He is one of our premier contemporary defenders of the Christian faith. A central thrust of his work revolves around this criterion of simplicity. The world, no matter from which direction you approach it, from the scientific or the religious, is amazingly diverse, with millions of details to be accounted for. Anyone can come up with a Rube Goldberg theory that explains by the most complicated mental machinery some aspect of what is going on. Much philosophical work consists of just such intellectual monstrosities. But the most convincing and useful theory is the simplest—the theory that uses the simplest vocabulary and fewest variables that leads us to expect the diverse phenomena that form the evidence which we face. Richard Swinburne wrote a trilogy of books that applied this criterion of simplicity to the word "God."[2] What he has done, in effect, is

---

1. Richard Swinburne, "The Vocation of a Natural Theologian," in *Philosophers Who Believe*, ed. Kelly James Clark (Downers Grove, IL: InterVarsity, 1993), p. 184.

2. The books in order are *The Coherence of Theism, The Existence of God,* and *Faith and Reason.*

account for all the material that our scientific and philosophical studies come up with, and account for it with the simple profundity of "God." He has returned us to our first insights and basic experiences of object permanence.

Professor Richard Swinburne and my grandson Andrew tell me the same thing and in virtually the same language to return us to Square One.

II

But you will notice that I am using the verb "return" and not "bring." We were there once, but chances are we are there no longer.

Square One is the place at which we realize that there is a huge world that we have not yet seen, an incredible creation that we cannot account for, a complex reality that is not defined or controlled by our experience of it. There is more—far more. Our experience, while authentic enough, is not encompassing. There is far more that we don't know than what we do know. We are enveloped, to use one of the classic phrases in our tradition, in "the cloud of unknowing."

There is something wonderfully exhilarating about this, the sense of space and time, of mystery and beauty. We become explorers, adventurers, knights errant.

But there is also something seriously disappointing, the realization that we are not at the center of the universe. In an infantile state— and this is true regardless of our chronological age—we have the perception that we are the center of everything. Our needs take precedence over everything, absolutely everything. Our appetites, our welfare, our comfort. We are as gods and goddesses, worshiped and adored and served.

Then we arrive at Square One and are told that we must wait our turn, or that our behavior is quite despicable and we must go to our room, or that we must share our toys with our sisters. There is a lot more going on than you and me. We experience finitude.

And we don't like it. For anyone who has had a taste of glory as a sovereign queen, as an almighty king, it is quite a come-down to be treated as a brat with bad manners. For anyone who has acquired enough money to be able to demand and pay for any conceivable whim, it is a shock to be told to walk away from it and start keeping company with a homeless and jobless itinerant preacher (Mark 10:17-31). For anyone who through long disciplined study has mastered an important body of knowledge, it is an impertinent insult to be assigned nursing care to a victim of random street violence (Luke 10:25-37).

When we first arrive at Square One, we are breathless before the unguessed splendors of infinity, stretching out endlessly. That is wonderful. And then we begin to realize the corollary, if there is such a thing as infinity, I am not it. I am finite. If there is God then there is no room for me as god.

The virtually unanimous response to this realization is some form or other of either narcissism or prometheanism. Narcissism is the attempt to retreat from Square One back into the spiritual sovereignty of self. Forget infinity. Forget mystery. Cultivate the wonderful self. It might be a small world, but it is my world, totally mine.

Prometheanism is the attempt to detour around Square One into the spirituality of infinity, get a handle on it, get control of it, and make something of it. All that spirituality sitting around idle needs managing. Prometheanism is practical. Prometheanism is entrepreneurial. Prometheanism is energetic and ambitious. Prometheanism wants to put all that power and beauty to good use.

Most of us, most of the time, can be found to be practising some variation on narcissism or prometheanism. It goes without saying then that most spirituality is a combination of narcissism and prometheanism, with the proportions carefully customized to suit our personal temperaments and circumstances.

And that is why I use the word "return"—it's *back* to Square One, back to the place of wonder, the realization of infinity, the worship of God.

The primary way in which we counter our stubborn propensities to narcissism and prometheanism is by cultivating humility. Learning to be just ourselves, keeping close to the ground, practising the *human*, getting our fingers in the *humus*, the rich, loamy, garden dirt out of which we have been fashioned.

And then listen.

III

Because returning to Square One is not only the return to a realization of God, but also to listening to what God says. God *said*. Did you listen? Do you listen?

Listening is linked, not only lexically (*akouo* and *hupakouo*), but spiritually to obedience, to response. "The hearing of man represents correspondence to the revelation of the Word, and in biblical religion it is thus the essential form in which this divine revelation is appropriated."[3]

Language is the primary means we have of acquiring "object permanence." The discovery that there is a word "ball" that refers to that round green fuzzy object that rolled under the dry sink, is a key to dealing with the reality of "things unseen." Words attest to the reality and distinctiveness of people and things and events that are outside the realm of my sensory experience. As I develop facility in words, my world expands; before long I am inhabiting remote centuries, dealing with faraway continents, having conversations with men and women in the cemeteries.

So it is not surprising that God, who is "far beyond what we can ask or think" should deal with us by means of language. God speaks. For Christians, basic spirituality is not only a noun, *God*, but also a verb, *Said* (or *Says*).

My purpose right now is not to argue this—it has been skillfully and competently reasoned and argued by our best Christian minds, some of them my colleagues here at Regent. What I want is simply to call your attention to the obvious, the accepted, the basic: when we go back to Square One, we listen, for God speaks.

And we do need reminding. For just as the realization of the world of Spirit that centers in the person and power of God frequently results in a proliferation of spiritualities that attempt to become or use God, so the acquisition of language that enables response and participation in the world of Spirit then results in spiritual talk that bypasses God.

Most, but certainly not all, of the spiritual talk that goes on in and out of Christian churches is of this kind. It is not listening to

---

3. G. Kittel, ed., *Theological Dictionary of the New Testament* (Grand Rapids: Eerdmans, 1964), vol. 1, p. 216.

God; it is not answering God; it is not believing in the Word of God. It is chatter.

Sometimes very interesting chatter. Often it is fascinating chatter. But it is *our* commentary on *our* experience with the spiritual, not a proclamation of *God's* address to us from the world of Spirit. We give witness, we testify endlessly—but more often than not we are talking about ourselves, not God. It is not proclamation, which is the basic form which language about God takes, but gossip.

* * *

The Book of Job is our classic exposé of this kind of thing. Job is back to Square One: God Said. But the noun, God, and the verb, Said, are separated in the Book of Job by a lot of spiritual talk that has nothing to do with God. Job has no question but that he is dealing with God. He is faced with mystery—none of the familiar ways of accounting for life work any more. He is confronted with unknowing. He will be satisfied by nothing less than God speaking to him, a God who tells him what's what, a God who reveals. And God does speak, "out of the whirlwind," and Job is satisfied. God does not answer his questions, does not explain the mystery—but he speaks. And that is enough. It is always enough.

But most of the text of Job is taken up with the spiritual talk of Job's religious advisors, Eliphaz, Bildad, Zophar, and Elihu. Almost all of what they say is true. But at the same time, almost nothing of what they say is true. None of it is a participation in listening to and answering God. One of the most arresting of the speeches is that of Eliphaz. It is his first speech, and he supports what he has to say by documenting it with the authority of spiritual experience. Eliphaz tells Job that he must have sinned, otherwise he would not be suffering. It's a logical, cause-effect spiritual universe that we live in. There is no mystery. There are answers to everything. But Eliphaz is not all logic—he attempts to give authority for his speech by testifying to a supernatural experience.

> A word came to me in secret,
> A mere whisper of a word, but I heard it clearly.
> It came in a dream that disturbed my sleep
> after I had fallen into a deep, deep sleep;

> Dread confronted me, and Terror,
> I was scared to death, trembled from head to foot.
> A ghost glided right in front of me,
> the hair of my head stood straight up.
> It stood there, but I couldn't tell what it was,
> a blur ... and then I heard a muffled voice.
>
> 4:12-16 (my trans.)

After an experience like that, you might think there would be some profound revelation to impart. But, no, it is more of the same—the conventional wisdom that Eliphaz could have picked up at some Babylonian shrine or Egyptian temple.

> Can mere mortals be more righteous than God?
> Can humans be more pure than their maker?
> Why, God doesn't even trust his own servants,
> doesn't even laud his angels,
> So how much less these bodies composed of mud,
> fragile as a moth?
> These bodies of ours can be unmade in no time at all
> and no one even notice—gone without a trace.
> Someone pulls the plug and that's it,
> we die and are never the wiser for it.
>
> 4:17-21 (my trans.)

Later on Eliphaz again attempts to give spiritual authority to his worn-out banalities by referring to "the vision I had" (15:17).

Job is not impressed. He is not impressed by the supernatural. He wants God. And he wants the God who speaks; he doesn't want to hear Eliphaz talk about his experience with a ghost. He has no interest in Eliphaz's stories about spooky whispers and blurs in the middle of the night; he wants to hear God speak. The Word of God.

When God speaks through his prophets he does so clearly. Isaiah is nothing if not clear: "I heard the voice of the Lord saying, 'Whom shall I send, ... Go, and say to this people ...' " (Isa. 6:8-9). Jeremiah is nothing if not clear: "Now the Word of the Lord came to me saying, 'Before I formed you in the womb I knew you. . . . I have set you this day over nations and over kingdoms, to pluck up and to break down, to destroy and to overthrow, to build and to plant' " (Jer. 1:4-10). Ezekiel is nothing if not clear: "And he said to me, 'Son of man, stand upon your feet, and I will speak with you.' And when he spoke to me, the Spirit entered into me and set me upon my feet; and I heard him speaking to me. And he said to me, 'Son of man, I send you to the people of Israel, to a nation of rebels . . .' " (Ezek. 2:1-3). "The prophets experienced the word in unequivocal terms; it was placed directly in their mouths as an oracle for public proclamation."[4]

And Eliphaz is nothing if not vague: ". . . a mere whisper of a word . . . a ghost glided in front of me . . . a blur . . . a muffled voice" (Job 4:12-16). "For Eliphaz the word steals in through the back door furtive, indistinct, and faint. Its origin and author are unknown. It is simply identified as a word, a passing sound, a noise in the night."[5]

This kind of stuff is the plague of spiritualities of all times and all places. The bizarre, the enigmatic, the pretentiously exotic. There is no suggestion here that Eliphaz is a fraud, that the experience itself is not real. But it is put before us in such a way that we realize that it is not significant. All these testimonies of brushes with the supernatural, descriptions of mystical states and heightened consciousness—not significant. All these techniques offered to us by which we can be in tune with the voices, feel the vibrations, hear the harmonies—not significant.

I am not suggesting that all this is sheer fraud and fantasy. The experiences might very well be real enough. There is nothing in Job to suggest that Eliphaz was a fraud. He may very well have had this supernatural experience that gave him goose bumps.

What I am saying is that it is not significant. Eliphaz was the Shirley McLaine of ancient Edom.

Christian spirituality is not impressed with the supernatural. Supernatural is neither here nor there for those of us who are standing at Square One, getting ourselves oriented, coming to terms with our human finitude, getting a glimpse of God's infinitude.

We are immersed in a world of Spirit, and so why wouldn't we have spiritual experience? But such experience does not confer

4. Norman C. Hable, *The Book of Job* (Philadelphia: Westminster Press, 1985), p. 126.
5. Habel, *The Book of Job*, p. 127.

authority upon *our* counsel or *our* character. The return to Square One is not only a return to God, but to God *Said*. For not only is there God, there is God's Word.

Christian spirituality does not begin with us talking about our experience; it begins with listening to God call us, heal us, forgive us.

This is hard to get into our heads. We talk habitually to ourselves and about ourselves. We don't listen. If we do listen to each other it is almost always with the purpose of getting something we can use in our turn. Much of our listening is a form of politeness, courteously waiting our turn to talk about ourselves. But in relation to God especially we must break the habit and let him speak to us. God not only is; God *Says*.

Christian spirituality, in addition to being an attentive spirituality, is a listening spirituality.

* * * *

Words are our primary tools for getting our bearing in a world, most of which we can't see, most of which we'll never touch—this large, expanding, mysterious existence that is so much larger, more intricate, more real even, than we are.

When Andrew learned the word "ball," he had a means for dealing with an object he couldn't see. When I learn the word "God" I am able to deal with a person I cannot see. God uses words to train us in object permanence.

But now I want to amend the phrase, from *object* permanence to *subject* permanence. For God is not an object that I deal with, but a subject who speaks to and addresses me. It is in learning to listen to God speak that I become familiar with and participate in basic spirituality.

There is an interesting detail here that I want to note. I said earlier that when we get to Square One we do not leave biology and embrace spirituality. Our physical senses do not become less important; they become more important because we are not limited by them. When we discover that God reveals himself by word, we are back in the realm of the sensory again—a word is spoken by a mouth/lips/tongue/throat; it is heard by ears, or in the case of the written word, seen with eyes. But once the word is uttered and heard, or written and read, it enters into us in such a way that it transcends the sensory. A word is (or can be) a revelation from one interior to another. What is inside me can get inside you—the word does it. Which is why language is the major bridge from basic biology to basic spirituality.

And why Christian spirituality insists on listening.

By God's grace, God's Word is also written. And that makes Holy Scripture the text for Christian spirituality. Holy Scripture is the listening post for listening to God's Word.

IV

Something remarkable takes place when we return to Square One, to the place of adoration and listening—a terrific infusion of energy within us; a release of adrenaline in our souls which becomes obedience. The reason is that the word that God speaks is the kind of word that makes things happen. When God speaks it is not in order to give us information on the economy so that we will know how to do our financial planning. When God speaks it is not as a fortune teller, looking into our personal future and satisfying curiosity regarding our romantic prospects or the best horse to bet on. No, when God speaks it is not in explanation of all the things that we have not been able to find answers to from our parents or in books or from reading tea leaves. God's Word is not, in essence, information or gossip or explanation. God's Word makes things happen—he makes something happen in us. The imperative is a primary verb form in Holy Scripture: "Let there be light . . . Go . . . Come . . . Repent . . . Believe . . . Be still . . . Be healed . . . Get up . . . Ask . . . Love . . . Pray. . . ."

And the intended consequence of the imperative is obedience. I love the Psalm phrase, "I will *run* in the way of thy commandments, when thou givest me understanding" (Ps. 119:32). Yes, *run*. Square One, with its attentiveness and listening, is that place of understanding—we know who we are and where we are . . . and who God is and where he is. At that place and in that condition, there is an inward gathering and concentration of energy that on signal from God's imperative expresses itself in, precisely, obedience—*running* in the way of God's commandments. For there is nothing grudging or hangdog or foot dragging in the biblical narrations of obedience.

St. Mark gives us a sharply etched detail of this aspect of God's Word when he tells the story of the healing of Bartimaeus at Jericho, the city where a millennium earlier Jesus' namesake, Joshua (in Greek, "Jesus"), signaled the acts of salvation and deliverance that launched the campaign that turned the promises of God into actual possession of the land. Jesus returns to Jericho to launch his final campaign—going up to Jerusalem against the forces of darkness and then, by means of crucifixion and resurrection, taking possession of the country of salvation. Jericho is a Square One kind of place.

Here's the detail: as Jesus starts out, Bartimaeus is sitting beside the roadside begging. He hears that it's Jesus and calls out for help, for mercy—persistently. Jesus hears him, stops, and calls for him. When Bartimaeus receives the summons there is not a moment of hesitation—he leaps to his feet and goes to Jesus (Mark 10:50). The verb "leaps" (*anapedesas*)—this is its only occurrence in the New Testament—catches our attention. Bartimaeus *jumps up*. Like a sprinter at the signal of a starting pistol, he explodes from his place and is off and running. Yes, "I will run in the way of thy commandments, when thou givest me understanding." Bartimaeus is at Square One, poised and ready; and so when Jesus speaks the word of invitation, *God's Word* no less, Bartimaeus at Square One is a rocket launched.

For Square One is not a place where we sit around discussing what to do next. It is not an oasis of repose from the strenuous business of pilgrimage. It is not a return to inaction when the action gets too much for us. It is the place to which we return so that our faith is God-initiated, our discipleship is Christ-defined, our obedience is Spirit-infused.

Eugen Rosenstock-Huessy, whom I honor as one of the wonderful, if maverick, teachers on the spirituality of language and life in our century, took as his life motto: *Respondeo etsi mutabor,* "I respond although I will be changed!"[6] For when we return to Square One where we hear God's Word, the obedience which follows will certainly change our lives. Repentance and commitment,

---

6. Quoted in *Judaism Despite Christianity*, ed. Eugen Rosenstock-Huessy (University, AL: University of Alabama Press, 1969), p. 4.

belief and faithfulness—all the energy-filled actions that are initiated at Square One, do not run in the ruts of our willful habits and routines, but are transformative: they take us with Jesus to Jerusalem and the cross and the resurrection.

We do not progress in the Christian life by becoming more competent, more knowledgeable, more virtuous, or more energetic. We do not advance in the Christian life by acquiring expertise. Each day, and many times each day, we return to Square One: God Said. We are constantly being "thrown back on the start and always opening up afresh."[7] We are always beginners. We begin again. We hear Jesus say, "Unless you turn and become like children, you will never enter the kingdom of heaven" (Matt. 18:3). And so we become as little children. We return to the condition in which we acquired subject permanence, God said. We go back to Square One. We adore and we listen.

* * * *

I want to simplify your lives. When others are telling you to read more, I want to tell you to read less; when others are telling you to do more, I want to tell you to do less. The world does not need more of you; it needs more of God. Your friends do not need more of you; they need more of God. And you don't need more of you; you need more of God.

The Christian life consists in what God does for us, not what we do for God; the Christian life consists in what God says to us, not what we say about God. We also, of course, do things and say things; but if we do not return to Square One each time we act, each time we speak, beginning from God and God's Word, we will soon be found to be practicing a spirituality that has little or nothing to do with God. And so it is necessary, if we are going to truly live a Christian life, and not just use the word Christian to disguise our narcissistic and promethean attempts at a spirituality without worshiping God and without being addressed by God, it is necessary to return to Square One and adore God and listen to God. Given our sin-damaged memories that render us vulnerable to every latest edition of journalistic spirituality, daily re-orientation in the

---

7. Karl Barth, *Church Dogmatics*, I/I (Edinburgh: T. and T. Clark, 1936), p. 15.

truth revealed in Jesus and attested in Scripture is required. And given our ancient predisposition for reducing every scrap of divine revelation that we come across into a piece of moral/spiritual technology that we can use to get on in the world, and eventually to get on without God, a daily return to a condition of not-knowing and non-achievement is required. We have proven, time and again, that we are not to be trusted in these matters. We need to return to Square One for a fresh start as often as every morning, noon, and night.

Eugene H. Peterson, *Subversive Spirituality* (Grand Rapids, Mich.: Wm. B. Eerdmans, 1997), pp. 19-31.

CHAPTER SIX

The Pastor as Preacher

Chrysostom, "the golden tongued," expended more effort on preaching than on any other pastoral task in his Six Books on the Priesthood. *If he had an exceedingly high view of clergy, he reserved his very highest regard for preaching. Perhaps because his was an age of intense doctrinal controversy, Chrysostom portrays the proclamation of the Word as a kind of war, a fierce struggle in which temptations to sin abound, those who ought to hear refuse to listen, and the preacher enters the pulpit itching for a fight. Eventually, Chrysostom's preaching got him exiled when, in a sermon in Constantinople, he rebuked the empress.*

In contrast to, say, Aristotle, whose Rhetoric *worried much about the interests and abilities of listeners, Chrysostom regards his listeners with disdainful suspicion. Preachers would do well, according to this master homoletician, to worry more about their own character and motives, than to concern themselves with the fickle acclamation or contempt of their congregations. The sermon's hearers are a resistant, rebellious, deceitful lot whose superficial applause has destroyed many a preacher. Throughout his treatise on ministry, Chrysostom repeatedly stresses the need for the pastor to cultivate contempt for both the praise and the criticism of the congregation, nowhere more than when he treats the task of preaching. In a time when many urge us preachers to fashion our preaching and teaching to the limitations and interests of our hearers—many of whom are unformed, uninformed, and who judge our preaching on the basis of mere entertainment—Chrysostom recalls us to a high view of preaching, strongly attached to the orthodox faith, wonderfully free from that "savage monster," "popular esteem."*

Temptations of the Teacher
St. Chrysostom (trans. by Graham Neville)

I have given sufficient proof of the experience needed by the teacher in contending for the truth. I have one thing more to add to this, a cause of untold dangers: or rather, I will not blame the thing itself so much as those who do not know how to use it properly; in itself it conduces to salvation and to many benefits, when it happens to be handled by earnest, good men. And what is it? It is the great toil expended upon sermons delivered publicly to the congregation.

In the first place, most of those who are under authority refuse to treat preachers as their instructors. They rise above the status of disciples and assume that of spectators sitting in judgement on secular speech-making. In their case the audience is divided, and some side with one speaker and others side with another. So in church they divide and become partisans, some of this preacher and some of that, listening to their words with favour or dislike. And this is not the only difficulty; there is another, no less serious. If it happens that a preacher weaves among his own words a proportion of other men's flowers, he falls into worse disgrace than a common thief. And often when he has borrowed nothing at all, he suffers on bare suspicion the fate of a convicted felon. But why mention the work of others? He is not allowed to repeat his own compositions too soon. For most people usually listen to a preacher for pleasure, not profit, like adjudicators of a play or concert. The power of eloquence, which we rejected just now, is more requisite in a church than when professors of rhetoric are made to contend against each other!

Here, too, a man needs a loftiness of mind far beyond my own littleness of spirit, if he is to correct this disorderly and unprofitable delight of ordinary people, and to divert their attention to something more useful, so that church people will follow and defer to him and not that he will be governed by their desires. It is impossible to acquire this power except by these two qualities: contempt of praise and the force of eloquence. If either is lacking, the one left is made useless through divorce from the other. If a preacher despises praise, yet does not produce the kind of teaching which is "with grace, seasoned with salt,"[1] he is despised by the people and gets no advantage from his sublimity. And if he manages this side of things perfectly well, but is a slave to the sound of applause, again an equal damage threatens both him and the people, because

---

1. Col. 4:6.

through his passion for praise he aims to speak more for the pleasure than the profit of his hearers. The man who is unaffected by acclamation, yet unskilled in preaching, does not truckle to the people's pleasure; but no more can he confer any real benefit upon them, because he has nothing to say. And equally, the man who is carried away with the desire for eulogies may have the ability to improve the people, but chooses instead to provide nothing but entertainment. That is the price he pays for thunders of applause.

The perfect ruler, then, must be strong in both points, to stop one being nullified by the other. When he stands up in the congregation and says things capable of stinging the careless, the good done by what he has said leaks away quickly if he then stumbles and stops and has to blush for want of words. Those who stand rebuked, being nettled by his words and unable to retaliate on him in any other way, jeer at him for his lack of skill, thinking to mask their shame by doing so. So, like a good charioteer, the preacher should have reached perfection in both these qualities, in order to be able to handle both of them as need requires. For only when he is himself beyond reproach in everyone's eyes will he be able, with all the authority he desires, to punish or pardon all who are in his charge. But until then it will not be easy to do.

But this sublimity must not only be displayed in contempt for applause; it must go further, if its benefit is not in turn to be wasted. What else, then, must he despise? Slander and envy. The right course is neither to show disproportionate fear and anxiety over ill-directed abuse (for the president will have to put up with unfounded criticism), nor simply to ignore it. We should try to extinguish criticisms at once, even if they are false and are levelled at us by quite ordinary people. For nothing will magnify a good or evil report as much as an undisciplined crowd. Being accustomed to hear and speak uncritically, they give hasty utterance to whatever occurs to them, without any regard for the truth. So we must not disregard the multitude, but rather nip their evil suspicions in the bud by convincing our accusers, however unreasonable they may be. We should leave nothing untried that might destroy an evil report. But if, when we have done all, our critics will not be convinced, then at last we must resort to contempt. For anyone who goes half-way to meet humiliation by things like this will never be able to achieve anything fine or admirable. For despondency and constant anxieties have a terrible power to numb the soul and reduce it to utter impotence.

The priest should treat those whom he rules as a father treats very young children. We are not disturbed by children's insults or blows or tears; nor do we think much of their laughter and approval. And so with these people, we should not be much elated by their praise nor much dejected by their censure, when we get these things from them out of season. This is not easy, my friend, and I think it may be impossible. I do not know whether anyone has ever succeeded in not enjoying praise. If he enjoys it, he naturally wants to receive it. And if he wants to receive it, he cannot help being pained and distraught at losing it. People who enjoy being wealthy take it hard when they fall into poverty, and those who are used to luxury cannot bear to live frugally. So, too, men who are in love with applause have their spirits starved not only when they are blamed off-hand, but even when they fail to be constantly praised. Especially is this so when they have been brought up on applause, or when they hear others being praised.

What troubles and vexations do you suppose a man endures, if he enters the lists of preaching with this ambition for applause? The sea can never be free from waves; no more can his soul be free from cares and sorrow. For though a man may have great force as a speaker (which you will rarely find), still he is not excused continual effort. For the art of speaking comes, not by nature, but by instruction, and therefore even if a man reaches the acme of perfection in it, still it may forsake him unless he cultivates its force by constant application and exercise. So the gifted have even harder work than the unskilful. For the penalty for neglect is not the same for both, but varies in proportion to their attainments. No one would blame the unskilful for turning out nothing remarkable. But gifted speakers are pursued by frequent complaints from all and sundry, unless they continually surpass the expectation which everyone has of them. Besides this, the unskilful can win great praise for small successes, but as for the others, unless their efforts are very startling and stupendous, they not only forfeit all praise, but have a host of carping critics.

For the congregation does not sit in judgement on the sermon as much as on the reputation of the preacher, so that when someone excels everyone else at speaking, then he above all needs painstaking care. He is not allowed sometimes not to succeed—the common experience of all the rest of humanity. On the contrary, unless his sermons always match the great expectations formed of him, he will leave the pulpit the victim of countless jeers and complaints. No one ever takes it into consideration that a fit of depression, pain, anxiety, or in many cases anger, may cloud the clarity of his mind and prevent his productions from coming forth unalloyed; and that in short, being a man, he cannot invariably reach the same standard or always be successful, but will naturally make many mistakes and obviously fall below the standard of his real ability. People are unwilling to allow for any of these factors, as I said, but criticize him as if they were sitting in judgement on an angel. And anyhow men are so made that they overlook their neighbour's successes, however many or great; yet if a defect comes to light, however commonplace and however long since it last occurred, it is quickly noticed, fastened on at once, and never forgotten. So a trifling and unimportant fault has often curtailed the glory of many fine achievements.

You see, my dear fellow, that the ablest speaker has all the more need for careful application, and not application only, but greater tolerance than any of those I have so far mentioned. For plenty of people keep attacking him without rhyme or reason. They hate him without having anything against him except his universal popularity. And he must put up with their acrimonious envy with composure. For since they do not cover up and hide this accursed hatred which they entertain without reason, they shower him with abuse and complaints and secret slander and open malice. And the soul which begins by feeling pain and annoyance about each of these things cannot avoid being desolated with grief. For they not only attack him by their own efforts, but they set about doing so through others as well. They often choose someone who has no speaking ability and cry him up with their praises and admire him quite beyond his deserts. Some do this through sheer ignorance and others through ignorance and envy combined, to ruin the good speaker's reputation, not to win admiration for one who does not deserve it.

And that high-minded man has to contend, not just against this kind of opponent, but often against the ignorance of a whole community. For it is impossible for a whole congregation to be made up of men of distinction; and it generally happens that the greater part of the Church consists of ignorant people. The rest are perhaps superior to these, but fall short of men of critical ability by a wider margin than the great majority fall short of them. Scarcely one or two present have acquired real discrimination. And so it is inevitable that the more capable speaker receives less applause and sometimes even goes away without any mark of approval. He must face these ups and down in a noble spirit, pardoning those whose opinion is due to ignorance, grieving over those who maintain an attitude out of envy, as miserable, pitiable creatures, and letting neither make him think the less of his powers. For if a painter of first rank who excelled all others in skill, saw the picture he had painted with great care scoffed at by men ignorant of art, he ought not to be dejected or to regard his painting as poor, because of the judgement of the ignorant; just as little should he regard a really poor work as wonderful and charming because the unlearned admired it.

Let the best craftsman be judge of his own handiwork too, and let us rate his productions as beautiful or poor when that is the verdict of the mind which contrived them. But as for the erratic and unskilled opinion of outsiders, we should not so much as consider it. So too the man who has accepted the task of teaching should pay no attention to the commendation of outsiders, any more than he should let them cause him dejection. When he has composed his sermons to please God (and let this alone be his rule and standard of good oratory in sermons, not applause or commendation), then if he should be approved by men too, let him not spurn their praise. But if his hearers do not accord it, let him neither seek it or sorrow for it. It will be sufficient encouragement for his efforts, and one much better than anything else, if his conscience tells him that he is organizing and regulating his teaching to please God. For in fact, if he has already been overtaken by the desire for unmerited praise, neither his great efforts nor his powers of speech will be any use. His soul, being unable to bear the senseless criticisms of the multitude, grows slack and loses all earnestness about preaching. So a preacher must train himself above all else to despise praise. For without this addition, knowledge of the technique of speaking is not enough to ensure powerful speech.

And even if you choose to investigate carefully the type of man who lacks this gift of eloquence, you will find he needs to despise praise just as much as the other type. For he will inevitably make many mistakes, if he lets himself be dominated by popular opinion. Being incapable of matching popular preachers in point of eloquence, he will not hesitate to plot against them, to envy them, to criticize them idly, and to do a lot of other disgraceful things. He will dare anything, if it costs him his very soul, to bring their reputation down to the level of his own insignificance. Besides this, he will give up the sweat of hard work, because a kind of numbness has stolen over his spirit. For it is enough to dispirit a man who cannot disdain praise and reduce him to a deep lethargy, when he toils hard but earns all the less approbation. When a farmer labours on poor land and is forced to farm a rocky plot, he soon gives up his toil, unless he is full of enthusiasm for his work, or is driven on by fear of starvation.

If those who can preach with great force need such constant practice to preserve their gift, what about someone who has absolutely no reserves in hand, but needs to get preaching practice by actually preaching? How much difficulty and mental turmoil and trouble must he put up with, to be able to build up his resources just a little by a lot of labour! And if any of his colleagues of inferior rank can excel him in this particular work, he really needs to be divinely inspired to avoid being seized with envy or thrown into dejection. It requires no ordinary character (and certainly not one like mine) but one of steel, for a man who holds a superior position to be excelled by his inferiors and to bear it with dignity. If the man who outstrips him in reputation is unassuming and very modest, the experience is just tolerable. But if he is impudent and boastful and vainglorious, his superior may as well pray daily to die, so unpleasant will the other man make his life by flouting him to his face and mocking him behind his back, by detracting frequently from his authority and aiming to be everything himself. And his rival will have derived great assurance in all this from the license people grant him to say what he likes, the warm interest of the majority in him, and the affection of those under his charge. Or do you not know what a passion for oratory has recently infatuated Christians? Do you not know that its exponents are respected above everyone else, not just by outsiders, but by those of the household of faith? How, then, can anyone endure the deep disgrace of having his sermon received with blank silence and feelings of boredom, and his listeners waiting for the end of the sermon as if it were a relief after fatigue; whereas they listen to someone else's sermon, however long, with eagerness, and are annoyed when he is about to finish and quite exasperated when he decides to say no more?

Perhaps this seems to you a trifling, negligible matter, because you have no experience of it. Yet it is enough to kill enthusiasm and paralyse spiritual energy, unless a man dispossesses himself of all human passions and studies to live like the disembodied spirits who are not hounded by envy or vainglory or any other disease of that sort. If there actually is anyone capable of subduing this elusive, invincible, savage monster (I mean popular esteem) and cutting off its many heads, or rather, preventing their growth altogether, he will be able to repulse all these attacks easily and enjoy a quiet haven of rest. But if he has not shaken himself free of it, he involves his soul in an intricate struggle, in unrelieved turmoil, and in the hurly-burly of desperation and every other passion. Why should I catalogue all the other troubles, which no one can describe or realize without personal experience?

St. John Chrysostom: Six Books on the Priesthood, **trans. Graham Neville (London: SPCK, 1964), pp. 127-35.**

Standing between the orthodox biblicism and the liberal optimism of the church of his day, P. T. Forsyth steered a middle course that he called "positive" theology. The greatest Congregationalist theologian of his day, he stressed the reality of the atonement, the power of grace, and the grand holiness of God. He was hailed in his time as "the preacher's theologian." His 1907 Beecher Lectures at Yale began with the words, "It is, perhaps, an overbold beginning, but I will venture to say that with its preaching Christianity stands or falls." Few commentators on the challenges of contemporary ministry have been more eloquent than Forsyth. In this selection, from his Beecher Lectures, he links the role of the preacher to the life of the congregation, the church who, as the gathered witnesses to Christ, are the true preachers of the gospel.

The Preacher and His Church
P. T. Forsyth

The one great preacher in history, I would contend, is the Church. And the first business of the individual preacher is to enable the Church to preach. Yet so that he is not its echo but its living voice, not the echo of its consciousness but the organ of its Gospel. Either he gives the Church utterance, or he gives it insight into the Gospel it utters. He is to preach to the Church from the Gospel so that with the Church he may preach the Gospel to the world. He is so to preach to the Church that he shall also preach *from* the Church. That is to say, he must be a sacrament to the Church, that with the Church he may become a missionary to the world.

You perceive what high ground I take. The preacher's place in the Church is sacramental. It is not sacerdotal, but it is sacramental. He mediates the word to the Church from faith to faith, from his faith to theirs, from one stage of their common faith to another. He does not there speak to un-faith. He is a living element in Christ's hands (broken, if need be) for the distribution and increment of Grace. He is laid on the altar of the Cross. He is not a mere reporter, nor a mere lecturer, on sacred things. He is not merely illuminative, he is augmentive. His work is not to enlighten simply, but to empower and enhance. Men as they leave him should be not only clearer but greater, not only surer but stronger, not only interested, nor only instructed, nor only affected, but fed and increased. He has not merely to show certain things but to get them home, and so home that they change life, either in direction or in scale. . . . In true preaching, as in a true sacrament, more is done than said. And much is well done which is poorly said. Let the preacher but have real doings with God and even with a stammering tongue and a loose syntax he will do much for life which has never yet been done by a finished style. The preacher may go "lame but lovely," to use Charles Lamb's fine phrase. His word may lack finish if it have hands and feet. He is a man of action. He is among the men who do things. That is why I call him a sacramental man, not merely an expository, declaratory man. In a sacrament is there not something done, not merely shown, not merely recalled? It is no mere memorial. How can you have a mere memorial of One who is always living, always present, always more potent than our act of recall is, always the mover of it? What he once put there might be a memorial, but what he is always putting there is much more than that. It is at least his organ. It is, indeed, his act. It is something practical and not spectacular. A revelation may be but something exhibited, but in a sacrament there is something effected. And the one revelation in the strict sense is the sacrament of the Cross, the Cross as an effective act of redemption. A revelation of redemption is a revelation of something done; and it is only a deed that can reveal a deed. If the preacher reveal redemption he does it by a deed, by a deed in which the Redeemer is the chief actor, by some self-reproduction by Christ, some function of the work of the Cross. He has to reproduce the word of the beginning, the word of the Cross which is really the Cross's own energy, the Cross in action. No true preaching of the Cross can be other than part of the action of the Cross. If a man preach let him preach as the Oracle of God, let him preach as Christ did, whose true pulpit was His Cross, whose Cross made disciples apostles, in whose Cross God first preached to the world, whose preaching from the Cross has done for the world what all His discourses—even His discourses—failed to do.

The preacher, in reproducing this Gospel word of God, prolongs Christ's sacramental work. The real presence of Christ crucified is what makes preaching. It is what makes of a speech a sermon, and of a sermon Gospel. This is the work of God, this continues His work in Christ, that ye should believe in Him whom He hath sent.

We do not repeat or imitate that Cross, on the one hand; and we do not merely state it, on the other. It re-enacts itself in us. God's living word reproduces itself as a living act. It is not inert truth, but quick power. All teaching about the truth as it is in Jesus culminates in the preaching of the truth which is Jesus, the self-reproduction of the word of reconciliation in the Cross. Every true sermon, therefore, is a sacramental time and act. It is God's Gospel act reasserting itself in detail. The preacher's word, when he preaches the gospel and not only delivers a sermon, is an effective deed, charged with blessing or with judgment. We eat and drink judgment to ourselves as we hear. It is not an utterance, and not a feat, and not a treat. It is a sacramental act, done together with the community in the name and power of Christ's redeeming act and our common faith. It has the real presence of the active Word whose creation it is. If Christ set up the sacrament, His Gospel set up the sermon. . . .

True preaching presupposes a Church, and not merely a public. And wherever the Church idea fades into that of a mere religious club or association you have a decay in preaching. Wherever the people are but a religious lecture society the pulpit sinks. When it is idolized it always sinks. It does not lose in interest, or in the sympathetic note, but it loses in power, which is the first thing in a Gospel. If the preacher but hold the mirror up to our finer nature the people soon forget what manner of men they are.

But you point out to me that the preaching of the Apostles was addressed to the public, that it was very largely of the gathering, of the missionary, kind. Yet, but even that began and worked from the faith it found. It began with the susceptible among the Jews. At first it was not so much converting for Gentiles as stirring for Jews. It was always with the local synagogue that Paul began when he could, with the votaries of the Old Testament Word; and while he could he worked through them or their proselytes. Jesus Himself began so. His relations beyond Israel grew out of His relations with Israel. It was His earnest dealings with Israel that provoked the Cross, which alone universalized the Gospel. So the preacher has his starting point in the stated and solemn assemblies of the Church, though he does not end there. Through these, he works also on his public who are present, though not of the Church. Then in the end he goes to the world without. But his first duty, if he is a settled pastor, and not a preaching friar, is to his Church. Nothing could be more misplaced, when a young preacher enters on a Church, than a neglect or contempt of its corporate life and creed, or a sudden inversion of these in order that he may get at the world. He has no right to stop the building that he may start else-where. He has no right to use his Church merely to provide himself with an outside pulpit. It is together that they must go to the world, he and his Church. What Christ founded was not an order of preachers, nor the institution of preaching, but a community, a Church, whose first charge His preaching should be. It is Church and preacher together that reach the world.

The preaching even to the Church, being in the presence of the public, has of course due regard to their presence. The sermon is not a mere homily to an inner circle. It is gospelling. The Church is addressed in the presence of people who are not of the Church. The preacher indeed renews for believers the reality of the Gospel; but he does it in a large way that concerns also those who have not con-fessed their faith explicitly. He dwells for the most part on the large and broad features of the Gospel rather than on individual and casuistic situations. He declares the whole counsel of God; that is, the counsel of God as a whole. If he handle individual cases, it is as illustrations of wider truth. He leaves cases of conscience to private intercourse. He is not in the pulpit a director of conscience so much as a shepherd or a seeker of souls. And he may give expression to his own private experiences only in so far as is seemly and useful for the more public aspects of his Gospel. If he is ever beside him-self, it must be privately to God; for the people's sake he is sober and sane. Preaching is not simply pastoral visitation on a large scale. Teaching from house to house meant for the apostles not vis-itation, but ministering to the Church gathered in private houses, as it had then to be.

The first *vis-à-vis* of the preacher, then, is not the world, but the Gospel community. The word is living only in a living community. Its spirit can act outwards only as it grows inwardly and animates a body duly fed and cared for. The preacher has to do this tending. He has to declare the Church's word, and to utter the Church's faith, to itself, in order that he and the Church together may declare them to the world. The Church may use, but cannot rely upon, evangelists who are evangelists and nothing else. When the preacher speaks to believers it is to build them *up as* a Christian community; when he speaks to the world it is to build them *into* a Christian community. And the Church is built up by taking sanctuary, by stopping to realize its own faith, by the repetition of its own old Gospel, by turning aside to see its great sight, by standing still to see the salvation of the Lord.

It's own old Gospel! It is not needful that the preacher should be original as a genius is, but only as a true believer is. What he brings to the Church is not something unheard of, and imported from outside, to revolutionize it. He has to offer the Church, in outer form, the word which is always within it, in order that the Church, by that presentation, may become anew what by God's grace it already is. He must be original in the sense that his truth is his own, but not in the sense that it has been no one else's. You must distinguish between novelty and freshness. The preacher is not to be original in the sense of being absolutely *new*, but in the sense of being *fresh*, of appropriating for his own personality, or his own age, what is the standing possession of the Church, and its perennial trust from Christ. He makes discovery *in* the Gospel, not *of* the Gospel. Some preachers spoil their work by an incessant strain after novelty, and a morbid dread of the commonplace. But it was one no less original than Goethe who said the great artist is not afraid of the commonplace. To be unable to freshen the commonplace is to be either dull or bizarre. Yet to be nothing but new is like a raw and treeless house shouting its plaster novelty on a beautiful old brown moor. The artist may treat revelation as discovery. He may create what he finds but as chaos. He finds but power, and he issues it in grace. But it is otherwise with the preacher. It is the converse. He finds revelation in all discovery. He finds to his hand the grace which he has to issue with power. His word is to send home a Word which was articulate from the beginning, "What we have seen and heard of the Word of life declare we to you." The artist's grace is not the preacher's. Nor is it true without modification that "all grace is the grace of God." The preacher has often been compared with the actor, and often he has succumbed to the actor's temperament, or to his arts. But there is a point of real analogy. The actor creates a part, as the phrase is; but it is only by appropriating a personality which the dramatist really created and put into his hands. And that is what the preacher has to do. He has to work less with his own personality than with the personality provided him in Christ, through Christ's work in him. He has to interpret Christ. Moreover, the actor's is a voice which is forgotten, while the poet's is a voice that remains. So also the preacher's originality is limited. By the very Spirit that moves him he speaks not of himself. He must not expect the actor's vogue. Self-assertion or jealousy are more offensive in him than in the artist. It is enough if he be a living voice; he is not a creative word. He is not the light; he but bears witness to it. . . .

There is even less room for originality of idea in the pulpit than elsewhere. What is needed is rather spontaneity of power. This is quite in keeping with the conservatism that must always play a part so much greater in the Church than in the State. The preacher not only appeals to the permanent in human nature; he is also the hierophant of a foregone revelation; he is not the organ of a new one. His foundation is laid for him once for all in Christ. His power lies not in initiation, but in appropriation. And his work is largely to assist the Church to a fresh appropriation of its own Gospel. It is not to dazzle us with brand-new aspects even of the Gospel. God forbid that I should say a word to seem to justify the dullness that infects the pulpit. Alas! If our sin crucify Christ afresh, our stupidity buries Him again. But the cure for pulpit dullness is not brilliancy, as in literature. It is reality. It is directness and spontaneity of the common life. The preacher is not there to astonish people with the unheard of; he is there to revive in them what they have long heard. He discovers a mine on the estate. The Church, by the preacher's aid, has to realize its own faith, and take home anew its own Gospel. That which was from the beginning declare we unto you—that fresh old human nature and that fresh old grace of God.

What a strength we all receive from self-expression! How we pine if it is denied! How we die if it is suppressed! It is life to a genius to get out what is in him; it is death to be stifled or neglected. If we can but express what is in us to ourselves it is often sufficient. If we can put pen to paper, paint to canvas, or the hand to clay, it may save us, even if we do not get a market or a vogue. Otherwise it is solitary confinement, or death. The flame dies for want of air. In like manner also our private prayer receives for ourselves a new value when in our solitude we utter it aloud. The aspiration gains mightily from the spoken word. The very effort to shape it in words adds to its depth, precision, confidence, and effect. It is well to sigh our prayers, but it is better to utter them. With the heart man believeth unto righteousness, but with the mouth we confess unto salvation. Righteousness is well, but it must be established and confirmed as salvation. Just so the preacher's address to the Church is really the Church preaching to the Church. It is the Church expressing itself to itself. The Church is feeling its own strength, and by the feeling it is growing in godly self-confidence, and in power to say to the world what the whole world resists.

The Christian preacher is no prophet sent to the public till he is a voice of the Church to the Church. He is but a part of the Church, yet he speaks to the whole. We tend our body with the hand, which is but an organ of the body. So the preacher tends the Church as a part of it, moved in his act, not by the part's life, but by its share in the life of the whole. He is over against the Church only as the organ is over against the organism. It is the body that turns the hand upon itself. The Church in the preacher becomes explicitly conscious of itself. Its latent faith becomes patent. It knows how much greater it is than it thought. It is amazed with itself. It realizes what a mighty matter its faith is. The flush arises to the face of its love. The gleam shines in its eye of its hope. And it *must* reach this self-expression. It is not merely the better for it. The expression is part of the reality. The form is part of the life. It is part of the joint action of the Word which is the Church's life, and of the faith that meets that Word. The sermon is an essential part of the worship.

The preacher, therefore, starts with a Church of brethren that agree with him and that believe with him; and in its power he goes to a world that does neither. What he has to do is not to exhibit himself to the Church, nor to force himself on it. He offers himself to it in the like faith, as a part of their common offering by the Eternal Spirit to God. And the stronger the Church is, so much the more it needs preaching, and the more it desires preaching, preaching not only *through* it but *to* it; just as genius demands self- expression in passionate proportion to its power. Only note that while the genius demands expression for itself the Church demands it for its

Gospel. It demands expression for its positive, objective faith and not its consciousness; its message and not merely its experience. The Eternal Word that always makes the Church has to speak to a Church whose experience is largely below the level of the faith of that Word. What makes the Church is not Christ as its founder but Christ as its tenant, as its life, as its power, the Christ living in the faith of its members in general, and of its ministers in particular. But it is a Christ that only partially comes to His own in the Church's actual experience. The faith within the Church has to speak to its half-faith, its bewildered faith, its struggling, or even its decaying faith.

What is done in preaching to the Church, therefore, is not to set out its own consciousness. At any rate, it is not the consciousness of the Church at any one stage—even the present. It is the Spirit speaking to the Churches. It is the past Church speaking to the present, the whole Church to the single Church, the ripe Church to the unripe, the faithful Church to the faltering Church, the ideal Church to the actual, the unseen to the seen. It is the great, common, universal faith addressing the faith of the local community. And, in so far as the preacher is the voice of the Church, he is the voice, not of his own Church, but of the Great Church that envelops his own. The preacher reflects the faith of the great true Church, but neither the faith nor the views of those around him. He is not giving expression to the average opinion of his congregation, or his denomination. The preacher is the mandatory of the great Church, which any congregation or sect but represents here and now. . . .

Preaching is thus the creation of the Gospel, and not our mere tribute to the Gospel; therefore, it has one great note which should appeal to the modern mind—the note of inevitability. It was the inevitable word, so prized now by the connoisseurs of style—the authentic Word. It was the triumph of the Gospel genius, the royalty of the Gospel way. It came forth with the ease, aptness and weight wielded by full and conscious power. However verbose preachers may be, preaching is not the verbosity of a Word whose truer nature would have been reticent like a ritual sacrament. The preacher may be illogical, but preaching is there by a spiritual logic, and a psychological necessity, in the Gospel itself. It was the Church's great spontaneous confession of its faith both to itself and the world. There was something almost lyric about it—as the great creeds were at first hymns. They expressed not merely belief, but triumphant irrepressible belief. Nay, it was more. It was the belief of men more than conquerors, more than triumphant. They were the harbingers and hierophants of the world's foregone but final conquest. They were more than victorious, they were redeemed. They were victorious only because redeemed. They could not be parted from Christ's love by any tribulation, anguish, peril, or sword (Rom. viii. 35-9)—not because they had overcome these things, even in His name, but because He had, already and in advance, put them under His feet for good and all, for Himself and His people. They were trophies of Christ's conquest more than victors in their own. And it was more joy to be a trophy and captive in the triumphal procession of Christ than to sit with Caesar in his car. What made them preach was a victory gained, not by them, but in them and over them. And they sang their joy in preachings that captured the world for which they were themselves also captured in Christ.

Preaching then is the Church confessing its faith.

P. T. Forsyth, *Positive Preaching and the Modern Mind* (London: Independent Press Ltd., 1907), pp. 53-68.

He was protestant liberalism's most prominent apologist. He was the preacher whose sermons helped to relate the gospel to the demands of modern life. Many would call Harry Emerson Fosdick the greatest American preacher of the twentieth century. He grew up in a dour Baptist home, but early in his studies was attracted to the developing theological liberalism of the early twentieth century. A nervous breakdown, his first year of seminary, brought him to the brink of suicide yet contributed to his ministerial character. His own emotional struggles forever marked him, giving his preaching great passion for "the real needs of real people," as he put it. His 1922 sermon "Shall the Fundamentalists Win?" was given, thanks to funds provided by John D. Rockefeller Jr., to every Protestant pastor in the country. In 1931, Fosdick mounted the pulpit of the new Riverside Church on Morningside Heights where he was to preach for decades. Every Sunday afternoon, millions of Americans listened to the National Vespers Radio Hour, *making him liberal Protestantism's most eloquent spokesperson. Fundamentalists dubbed him "Modernism's Moses." He was the great communicator and popularizer of modern Christianity, selling millions of copies of his nearly fifty books. His moving, honest, and revealing autobiography contains Fosdick's account of how he learned to preach. He once described "the essential nature of the sermon as an intimate, conversational message from soul to soul." Here is how he first entered that coversation.*

Learning to Preach
Harry Emerson Fosdick

I was tossed into my first parish over fifty years ago, like a boy thrown into deep water and told to swim when he does not know how. At the beginning I was an ignoramus about the effective preparation of a sermon. The seminary's courses in homiletics had been of slight use to me. We listened to lectures on preaching, full of good advice, I do not doubt, but lacking relevance to any actual experience of our own, and soon forgotten because not implemented in practice. You cannot teach an art simply by talking about it. Years afterward, along with Henry Sloane Coffin and others, I played a small part in helping to make the teaching of homiletics at the seminary an affair of practical drill. We brought groups of students into the chapel, heard them preach, and then fell upon them with approval where they deserved it and with rigorous criticism of their faults. That kind of training would have saved me a protracted struggle in my first pastorate, but in those old days theologues had little or nothing of such discipline. What saved me was my earlier training in public speaking so that, however little I had to say, I could somehow manage to say it.

I recall vividly the tormented weeks I spent during the first year and more in Montclair, often distraught myself and fairly driving my wife to distraction, trying to prepare sermons that would be worth preaching. Probably my memory exaggerates the occasion when improvement began. One Sunday morning, quite unexpectedly, in the midst of my sermon, the idea I was dealing with caught fire. I had a flaming few minutes when I could feel the congregation's kindling response. I am sure that they were as much surprised as I was. I had never preached like that before, and I went home sure that preaching could mean that kind of moving and effective communication of truth.

Nevertheless, it was a struggle. Preaching for me has never been easy, and at the start it was often exceedingly painful. In later years I used to envy some of my students at the seminary who from the start seemed to know instinctively how to prepare a sermon and deliver it. Ralph Sockman, for example, in his first student sermon, exhibited such mature ability and skill that I told the class he acted as though he had had twenty years of experience behind him and I doubted whether even a homiletical professor could spoil him. My road as a preacher was very rough at the beginning, but little by little I saw more clearly what I verily believed and wanted most to say and, as clairvoyance into the needs of those to whom I spoke increased, I discovered, at least occasionally, the satisfaction of preaching so that something creative happened in the listener.

Because Montclair had been religiously well taken care of already, before the Baptist congregation was organized, denominational peculiarities were stressed in the new church as a justification for its founding, and at the heart of it were some reactionary sectarians. Dr. Lorimer, hearing rumors of cantankerous elements in the congregation to which I was going, said to me in our last conversation: "Young man, never you fear the face of mortal clay!" I needed that admonition. There were, however, saving factors in the situation. The church, having already had some unpleasant experiences in its eighteen years of existence, sincerely wanted to get on with me, and were willing to put up with a good deal to do it. Moreover, on the fringes of the congregation were new people, waiting to be members if things went well. This new group was, on the whole, liberal in spirit, and the church, for every sort of reason, needed its support. So, while skating at times on thin ice, I got along. Even close communion had been the accepted custom before I arrived; no general invitation was extended to non-Baptist Christians to partake of the Lord's Supper. On that point, taking matters into my own hands, I extended an open invitation to all Christians to join in celebrating the first Lord's Supper at which I officiated. No one cared to start a fight about that with the new minister, but there was grumbling over my irregular assumption of authority.

The only crisis I had on matters of orthodoxy came after more than a year had passed. I had painfully felt my way at first, having plenty of inward troubles of my own, and my preaching, which was as much an endeavor to discover what I thought myself as it was to help anyone else, was, I suspect, not particularly disturbing. The issue between old and new theology, however, could not remain hidden, and at a meeting of the official board, when I was absent, two deacons complained about the liberal drift of my sermons. Having in hand at that time what amounted to two calls from other churches, one of them offering greater opportunity than was conceivable in Montclair, I invited those two deacons to a private conference. Not disposed to stay where I was not wanted, I told them, I put it up to them to say whether I should stay in liberty and peace or leave at once. They capitulated and, while they never agreed with me about theology, they stood by me, albeit with some pain, until the end.

The auditorium in which my pastorate began was the chapel of what was intended to be later a larger structure. As I recall the growing congregation that at last crowded us to the doors—it took less than three hundred to do it—I am reminded of the relative nature of all satisfactions. No preacher ever found more encouragement from vast assemblages of auditors than I found as I watched the growing numbers of those to whom my message was welcome in that little chapel. When the time came to venture on a building enterprise the church was ready for a fresh start altogether.

In 1911, seven years after my pastorate began, a new building on a new site was dedicated. . . .

To be sure, I found preaching two sermons on Sunday difficult. I used to burn the logwood in the morning and the chips at night, and the first sometimes made a slow blaze and the latter a thin one. Still, my congregation was merciful and sustained me with a friendliness for which I am endlessly grateful. I have seen many a young minister so maltreated by his first parish, so twisted by criticism and disheartened by meanness and coldness, that irreparable damage was done him. I was fortunate. . . .

Meanwhile, my struggle to discover how to preach went on with no little perplexity. The stereotyped routine into which old-fashioned expository preaching had fallen was impossible to me. First, elucidation of a Scriptural text, its historic occasion, its logical meaning in the context, its setting in the theology and ethic of the ancient writer; second, application to the auditors of the truth involved; third, exhortation to decide about the truth and act on it—such was the pattern in accordance with which every week multitudes of sermons were manufactured. That a vital preacher could use that model to good effect goes without saying, but there was something the matter with the model. To start with a passage from Moses, Jeremiah, Paul or John and spend the first half of the sermon or more on its historic explanation and exposition, presupposed the assumption that the congregation came to church that morning primarily concerned about the meaning of those ancient texts. That certainly was not what my congregation in Montclair was bothered about.

It was easier, however, to be impatient with the prevailing stereotype than constructively to replace it with a better method. I spent some vexatious years, impatient and floundering. "Only the preacher," I petulantly wrote, "proceeds still upon the idea that folk come to church desperately anxious to discover what happened to the Jebusites."

One difficulty was that rebels against this prevailing pattern of expository preaching commonly became topical preachers. They searched contemporary life in general and the newspapers in particular for subjects. Instead of concentrating on textual analysis, they dealt with present-day themes about which everyone was thinking. I watched those topical preachers with a dubious mind.

Week after week turning their pulpits into platforms and their sermons into lectures, they strained after new intriguing subjects, and one knew that in private they were straining even more strenuously after new intriguing ideas about them. Instead of launching out from a great text they started with their own opinions on some matter of current interest, often much farther away than a good Biblical text would be from the congregation's vital concerns and needs. Indeed, the fact that history had thought it worth while to preserve the text for centuries would cause a wise gambler to venture confidently on the text's superior vitality.

Across the years since then I have seen those topical preachers petering out and leaving the ministry. If people do not come to church anxious about what happened to the Jebusites, neither do they come yearning to hear a lecturer express his personal opinion on themes which editors, columnists and radio commentators have been dealing with throughout the week. So I floundered until personal counseling gradually led me into an approach to preaching which made it an exciting adventure.

Personal counseling does not begin full force in the experience of a young minister, fresh from the seminary. He is too callow, inexperienced, immature. Children may flock around him but adults do not naturally seek his advice. I vividly recall the first serious case of personal need presented to me—a youth from one of the church's finest families, conquered by alcohol and in utter despair. "I don't believe in God," he said to me, "but if *you* do, for God's sake pray for me, for I need him!" That was a challenge to everything I believed and preached. Few experiences in my first pastorate had so deep an effect on me as the battle in which that youth and I for long months engaged. That it ended in victory is one of the satisfying memories of my early ministry. "If you ever find anyone who does not believe in God," the youth said at last, "send him to me. I know."

In retrospect the relevance of such an experience to preaching seems obvious but only gradually did I stumble up the road until I saw it. Many other young preachers in those days were stumbling up that same road, discontented with both the prevalent expository and topical sermon patterns, but not sure how to replace them. Little by little, however, the vision grew clearer. People come to church on Sunday with every kind of personal difficulty and problem flesh is heir to. A sermon was meant to meet such needs; it should be personal counseling on a group scale. If one had clairvoyance, one would know the sins and shames, the anxieties and doubts, the griefs and disillusionments, that filled the pews, and could by God's grace bring the saving truths of the gospel to bear on them as creatively as though he were speaking to a single person. That was the place to start—with the real problems of the people. That was a sermon's specialty, which made it a sermon, not an essay or a lecture. Every sermon should have for its main business the head-on constructive meeting of some problem which was puzzling minds, burdening consciences, distracting lives, and no sermon which so met a real human difficulty, with light to throw on it and help to win a victory over it, could possibly be futile.

As I experimented with this approach I found that within a paragraph or two after a sermon started first one listener and then another would discover that the preacher was bowling down his alley, and sometimes the whole congregation would grow tense and quiet, seeing that the sermon concerned a matter of vital import to every one of them. The preacher was handling a subject they were puzzled about, or a way of living they were dangerously experimenting with, or an experience which had bewildered them, or an ideal they were striving for, or a need they had not known how to meet.

Any preacher who, with even moderate skill, is thus helping folk to solve their real problems is functioning. He never will lack an audience. He may have little learning or eloquence but he is doing the one thing which is a preacher's special business. He is delivering the goods which the community has a right to expect from the pulpit.

This did not mean that the Bible's importance in preaching diminished. Upon the contrary, I had been suckled on the Bible, knew it and loved it, and I could not deal with any crucial problem in thought and life without seeing text after text lift up its hands begging to be used. The Bible came alive to me—an amazing compendium of every kind of situation in human experience with the garnered wisdom of the ages to help in meeting them.

Nor did this "project method" shut out the best values in topical preaching. The problems that came to church on Sunday in the minds and hearts of the worshipers were not simply individual but social, economic, international. The preacher, however, did not need to deliver a lecture on them, as though he were a trained specialist in these diverse fields. He could not possibly know enough for *that*, but he could know the inner impact of those problems on his people in their defeatism and disillusionment, their agnosticism and despair, their surrender of Christian principles in the face of life's terrific realism, their reactionary clinging to old prejudices despite new light, and their class-bound loyalties to the wrong side of great issues. Let him start with the people confronting him in the pews and speak as wisely and Christianly as he could to their "business and bosoms," and he might help at least one individual that Sunday.

I have often been asked to deliver lectures on the art of preaching with a view to their subsequent publication in a book, but I have always declined. Many years ago I wrote an article for *Harper's Magazine* on "What Is the Matter with Preaching?" in which I said in gist what I am saying now, but I never expect to write a book about it. This thing that I am saying here is all I have to offer—this and a few corollaries which can be briefly noted.

I found my sermons becoming more and more co-operative enterprises between the preacher and the congregation. When a man takes hold of a real difficulty in the life and thought of his people and is trying to meet it, he finds himself not so much dogmatically thinking for them as co-operatively thinking with them. A preacher can easily play "Sir Oracle," assertive, dogmatic, flinging out his dictum as though to say "Take it or leave it," and such preaching has its appeal to credulous and emotionally impressionable minds. It has lost its influence on intelligent folk, however, and the future does not belong to it.

Later, in my classes at the seminary, I repeatedly used the story of a headmaster in his school chapel who had plunged into the first statement of his sermon theme, when a professor arose from the congregation, mounted the pulpit beside the preacher and offered a criticism of what he just had said. Excitement reigned. The headmaster answered the objection but the professor remained in the pulpit, and the sermon that day was a dialogue on a great theme of religion. The boys had never before been so entranced by a sermon. It was, of course, a prearranged affair, an experiment in having the congregation represented in the pulpit.

It certainly takes more than a preacher alone in the pulpit to make an effective sermon. If, however, the people can be there too, so that the sermon is not a dogmatic monologue but a co-operative dialogue in which the congregation's objections, questions, doubts and confirmations are fairly stated and dealt with, something worth while is likely to happen. Sometimes this can be done implicitly through the preacher's evident sympathy and understanding; sometimes it can be made explicit in paragraphs beginning "But some of you will say." Of course this style of preaching requires clairvoyance on the preacher's part into the people's thinking, but any man who lacks this has no business to preach anyway. And of course this method can be exaggerated and become a mannerism, but so can any other. We have plenty of sermons that are sheer propaganda, where preachers set out by hook or crook to put something over on the congregation. We have pugnacious sermons, where preachers wage campaigns, attack enemies, assail the citadels of those who disagree, and are in general warlike and vehement. We need more sermons that try to face people's real problems with them, meet their difficulties, answer their questions, confirm their noblest faiths and interpret their experiences in sympathetic, wise and understanding co-operation. This is the only way I could find to achieve excitement without sensationalism. Constructively to help people to meet trouble triumphantly, or to live above the mediocre moral level of a modern city, or to believe in God despite the world's evil, or to make Christ's principles standard in the face of our disordered world, is really not sensationalism. If it is well done, however, with no dodging of the difficulties, it can be vitally stimulating and can spoil all somnolent use of sermon time. An auditor, after one Sunday morning service, exclaimed: "I nearly passed out with excitement, for I did not see how you could possibly answer that objection which you raised against your own thought. I supposed you would do it somehow but I could not see how until you did it." At any rate, it was toward this style of preaching that I set my sights.

No homiletic method is without its dangers, and this one which I espoused has perils aplenty. I presented it once to a group of experienced ministers and collected a galaxy of warnings about its possible perversions. They had endeavored so precisely to deal with a real problem that Mr. Smith had vexatiously waked up to the fact that they were talking about him; or they had tried to be so fair about objections that, overstating the opposing side, they had found neither time nor ability to answer it; or they had been so practical in dealing with some definite problems that they had become trivial, failing to bring the eternal gospel to bear on the issue; or they had been so anxious to deal with felt needs in the congregation that they had forgotten still deeper needs, unfelt but real; or they had so limited the difficulties they preached about to private, psychological maladjustment that they became merely amateur pulpit psychiatrists, neglecting the public concerns of the Kingdom of God. These dangers are real, but such perversions are the fault of unskilled handling the like of which would wreck any method whatsoever.

My own major difficulty sprang from the fact that starting a sermon with a problem, however vital and urgent, suggests a discussion, a dissertation, and a treatise. A sermon, however, is more than that. The preacher's business is not merely to discuss repentance but to persuade people to repent; not merely to debate the meaning and possibility of Christian faith, but to produce Christian faith in the lives of his listeners; not merely to talk about the available power of God to bring victory over trouble and temptation, but to send people out from their worship on Sunday with victory in their possession. A preacher's task is to create in his congregation the thing he is talking about.

I learned that such direct results could be achieved through personal counseling. It was a great day when I began to feel sure that a sermon could be thus immediately creative and transforming. A good sermon is an engineering operation by which a chasm is bridged so that spiritual goods on one side—the "unsearchable riches of Christ"—are actually transported into personal lives upon the other.

Here lies the difference between a sermon and a lecture. A lecture is chiefly concerned with a *subject* to be elucidated; a sermon is chiefly concerned with an *object* to be achieved. A justifiable criticism of much modern, liberal preaching is that, though it consists of neat, analytical discourses, pertinent to real problems, and often well conceived and happily phrased, it does nothing to anyone. Such sermons are not sermons, but essays, treatises, lectures. It is lamentably easy to preach about moral courage without making anyone more courageous; to deliver a discourse on faith without creating any of that valuable article in a single life; to argue that man has power to decide and choose without causing anyone then and there to make a momentous decision.

So I went through project preaching and beyond it, and began to see how much the old preachers had to teach us. At their best they did achieve results. Their sermons were appeals to the jury and they got decisions. They knew where the great motives were and appealed to them with conclusive power. I began studying sermons of men like Phillips Brooks—not merely reading them, but analyzing sentence by sentence the steps they took toward working in their auditors the miracles they often did achieve—and I concluded that while we modern preachers talk about psychology much more than our predecessors, we commonly use it a good deal less.

After that preaching became exhilarating. It need never fail to make a transforming difference in some lives. One is not merely making a speech about religion; one is dealing with the profoundest concerns of personality, with incalculable possibilities dependent on what is said that day. My silent prayer rose each Sunday before the sermon started: "O God, some one person here needs what I am going to say. Help me to reach him!" Nothing can make preaching easy, but seen as a creative process which can transform lives, it becomes so stimulating that it reproduces in the preacher the strength it takes from him, as good agriculture replaces the soil it uses.

The supreme reward of the preacher is nothing that the public knows about. It comes in letters like this:

> More than twenty-five years ago a dirty and wretched young man crept into a church one evening and listened to your talk. . . . The drunk young man went out into the night and the words stayed with him. And things happened. He heeded the words, straightened up, went to night school for years and years until at last he graduated from _____ University, from postgraduate work at _____ University, became nationally and internationally known in his chosen field, and only recently _____ University asked him to write a new book . . . I am that man.

Harry Emerson Fosdick, *The Living of These Days: An Autobiography* (New York: Harper & Row, 1956), pp. 83-87, 92-101.

Cana Lutheran Church's little parsonage was located near the church, next to the cemetery. From there, writes Richard Lischer, his family's well was contaminated by runoff from the cemetery. "That was the joke of my first year. We couldn't drink the water because of its abnormally high Lutheran content."

Only as Lischer and his family were preparing to leave for another parish did the fathers of the church get around to repairing the church's absurd one-armed cross for an upcoming congregational anniversary. When they did so, they discovered that the cross was not made of solid copper, as had been claimed, but out of wood that had rotted from within. Young Pastor Lischer took the one-armed cross atop the peeling steeple as a kind of metaphor for a congregation that seemed sometimes to be rotting from within.

God mercifully grants most of us preachers the gift of forgetfulness of our first awkward, often painful and inept days of learning to preach in our first parish. God has graciously granted Richard Lischer the ability to vividly recall and to honestly retell of his first days as a preacher. In his memoir, Open Secrets, *Lischer captures those clumsy first days when we preachers try to find our voice, try to cobble together a word worth hearing. Yet he also indicates the gracious way that the Body of Christ reaches out to us, ministers to us in our weakness, the way that Jesus' people help us to find the words to offer the Word.*

Help Me, Jesus
Richard Lischer

I preached my first sermon in the Epiphany season on a bitterly cold morning with sleet pelting the windows of the church. The bell and the toilets had frozen up, but the church was full and warm as toast as if the old potbellied stove were still cooking.

When I was a seminarian I considered myself a good preacher, mainly because I could put words together and declaim them with Kennedyesque urgency—a legacy of mistaking myself for a liberal in prep school. I even arched my arm and stabbed the air with two fingers turned outward the way JFK did.

Like most preachers, I grossly overestimated the importance of my part in the sermon. When I thought of preaching, I did not consider it to be a congregation's reception of the word of God, but a speaker's command of the Bible's hidden meanings and applications, which were served up in a way to showcase the authority and skill of the preacher. In those days the gospel lived or died by my personal performance. My preaching was a small cloud of glory that followed me around and hung like a canopy over the pulpit whenever I occupied it. How ludicrous I must have appeared to my congregation.

In my first sermon I explained the meaning of *an* epiphany, not *the* Epiphany of God in the person of Jesus—no, that would have been too obvious—but the *category* of epiphanies in general. To this end, I drew at length on the depressing short stories of James Joyce in *Dubliners*. "Each of these stories has one thing in common," I said. "In each the central character comes to a deeper and more disturbing understanding of himself. Nothing really happens in these stories except that in the midst of the daily routine a character is unexpectedly exposed to the predicaments of estrangement in his own life. One man realizes that his wife has never loved him. Another recognizes that he is trapped in his vocation. Another finds himself to be a hopeless failure. The human condition is full of such epiphanies . . ."

Before I could talk about Jesus, I apparently found it necessary to give my farmers a crash course in the angst-ridden plight of modern man. With the help of clichés from Joyce, Heidegger, Camus, and even Walker Percy, I first converted them to existential ennui so that later in the sermon I could rescue them with carefully crafted assurances of "meaning" in a meaningless world. Along the way I defiantly refuted Marx's view of religion as an opiate that permits us to escape the hard realities of existence. It didn't concern me that the problem of *meaninglessness* had not occurred to my audience or that Marx's critique of religion rarely came up for discussion at the post office.

It's not that I minimize the importance of the major themes of modernity. No doubt my parishioners would have understood themselves better had they opened their eyes to the intellectual context of their lives. But they did not and could not. The giants of modern thought—Darwin, Marx, Nietzsche, Freud, Sartre—and the movements they unleashed, would never touch New Cana. My parishioners lived in a prison whose view was limited to the natural world and the most obvious technologies of the twentieth century. Aside from formulaic complaints about Communists, perverts, and radicals, they did not engage the modern world.

But then I did not bother to engage their world either. It did not occur to me that I needed a new education. I treated the rural life as an eccentric experience in ministry. I was a spectator once again, as I had been in college, watching a slide show of interesting scenes and odd characters. And since I was the viewer and they were the viewees, I was in control. When I preached, I always stood above my parishioners and looked down upon them.

Consequently, my sermons carried too many prerequisites to be effective. About 90 percent of my listeners had not graduated from high school; the majority of that group had not *attended* high school. There was no one with a four-year college degree in the church with the exception of a regular visitor named Darryl Sheets, our Lone Intellectual, who was principal of the high school in nearby Cherry Grove. Darryl regularly cornered me in long and fruitless conversations on the possible meanings of the Hebrew word for "young woman" in Isaiah 9:14 and how they all pointed to "Virgin." But the truth is, Darryl and his wife Marvel didn't drive all the way to Cana because of my expertise in Hebrew or the intellectual content of my sermons. Darryl was a tongue-speaking, fire-anointed charismatic who for some reason suspected that I might be one, too. It didn't take him long to figure out he was wrong, and then we saw quite a bit less of Darryl and Marvel.

My audience paid a heavy price for the gospel. The farmers had to swallow my sixties-style cocktail of existentialism and psychology before I served them anything remotely recognizable. I implicitly required them to view their world and its problems through my eyes. All I asked of them was that they pretend to be me.

The only person who appreciated my sermons was my wife, who, like me, lived from books. Tracy was completing her course work for a Ph.D. in English and, therefore, considered poetry and literary allusions to be the most natural of all forms of communication. What's a sermon without, "Perhaps Milton said it best when he wrote . . ." But among the *rest* of the congregation my preaching produced a standoff of sensibilities: If the idea for a sermon did not come from a *book*, I was not interested in pursuing it. If it did not emerge from *life*, my parishioners were not interested in hearing about it. In a few short months we had achieved homiletical gridlock.

That year some of the great Epiphany readings came from the letter to the Ephesians, which is Paul's vision of the grandeur of the church. Ephesians presents every small-town preacher with the marvelous opportunity of unveiling Jesus' presence in the midst of the common life of the congregation. "Look around you," Paul seems to say, "the church is magnificent!" It's hard to depreciate Paul's image of the "mystery hidden for ages" and its revelation in "the Body of Christ," but with the help of Joyce and Camus, I managed to whittle it down to size.

Why couldn't I see the revelation of God in our little church? In our community everyone pitched in and learned how to "pattern" a little girl with cerebral palsy. We helped one another put up hay before the rains came. We grieved when a neighbor lost his farm, and we refused to buy his tools at the auction. As a people, we walked into the fields every April and blessed the seeds before planting them. Weren't these all signs of "church" that were worthy of mention in the Sunday homily? Whatever lay closest to the soul of the congregation I unfailingly omitted from my sermons. I didn't despise these practices. I simply didn't see them.

* * *

It took me a while to improve as a preacher because no one in the congregation helped me. My first few sermons were carefully prepared, expertly given, and politely received, but my listeners maintained a studied indifference to my words, as if to say, "We *dare* you to move us. Just try it." The preacher was speaking into a dead microphone, but no one bothered to tell him.

The first time I got through to an audience was in a black church in East Alton. Before my experience at the Shiloh AME Church, I didn't know such communication was possible. One of my colleagues had organized a series of pulpit exchanges among congregations near his parish, but when it was his turn to visit Shiloh, he was ill, and I took his place.

The exchange entailed no extra work for the preachers; they simply repeated their Sunday morning sermon in the evening service.

I did the same at Shiloh—but with very different results than in my morning sermon at Cana.

My first glimpse of the sanctuary and congregation reminded me of my own small church. *We* had simple art glass windows; *they* had simple art glass windows, too, theirs depicting the same Shepherd, lambs, and angels as ours. *We* had an electronic organ and a homemade altar; *they* had the same. *We* had old people who used canes and sat in the same pews every Sunday; *they* had old people, too, with canes, fans, and hearing aids, who took their place in church with the same proprietary air.

But at the point of the sermon, our churches parted ways.

When I launched into the reprise of my Sunday morning sermon, it took the people of Shiloh about thirty seconds to recognize a preacher in trouble. An old woman in the second row said softly, *Help him, Jesus.* The entire congregation was witnessing the painful spectacle of a careful young man failing to strike fire.

Soon, others were saying, *Well? That's all right, Preach! Make it plain,* and *Come on up!* At the time, I had no idea that each of these phrases encodes a specific opinion of the sermon and a method of encouragement for the preacher. For example, when someone says rather quizzically, *Well?* in the middle of a sermon, I think it means, "That's interesting, but what are you going to do with it?"

I came from a church where *Amen* always meant "the end." When the Amens started popping like firecrackers in the *middle* of my sentences, at first I resented the interruptions, but then quickly realized that for the first time in my life I was having a conversation from the pulpit. Not only that, it was a *rhythmic* conversation! I even flexed my body in the pulpit, something our teachers warned us never to do.

The people of Shiloh helped free me from the correctness of my manuscript. At Cana I was usually so overprepared that I forgot about my hearers, but now I was actually looking at them and timing my speech with theirs. Every time one of the deacons said, *Make it plain!* I found myself smacking my next sentence like a drum. I didn't say anything out of the ordinary, but I did *smack* it. By the end of the sermon I was on the typical white preacher's high in a black-church pulpit. I was drawing energy from their responses, and loving every minute of it.

I don't want to overstate the lasting effects of my one experience at Shiloh. The black tradition of the congregation's partnership with the preacher helped me that evening, though it didn't transform me into the charismatic performer I'd always dreamed of being. But I did learn to be more interactive with the congregation. And, on occasion, I aimed my sermons at their hearts instead of their heads.

Although my own audience remained as quiet as ever, I came to realize that their silence was not the equivalent of unresponsiveness. Among Lutherans, ecstasy may take the form of a slight twitch of the eyebrow or the pursing of lips in order to suppress a smile. Sometimes a knowing glance between farmers must pass for the "Hallelujah! Preach, brother!" that is in there all right, but will never come out in this life.

Shiloh gave me something to hope for. I was waiting for my audience to become a congregation.

Richard Lischer, *Open Secrets* (New York: Doubleday, 2001), pp. 72-77.

CHAPTER SEVEN

The Pastor as Counselor

He was full of conflicts and contradictions, but these became a creative spark of genius that drove his ministry and made him a distinctive voice in the church. Born in the Netherlands in 1932, Henri Nouwen came to America as a ship's chaplain in his twenties. He eventually became hugely influential, coming to the attention of pastors while serving as a professor of psychology and pastoral care at Notre Dame, Yale, and Harvard. The last days of his life were spent among the community of L'Arche Daybreak in Richmond Hill, Ontario.

Of all his many books, received so warmly by so many contemporary Christians beyond the bounds of his Catholic faith, his most enduring will surely be The Wounded Healer. *Nouwen urged pastors to see their weaknesses, conflicts, wounds, and human frailty as resources for the healing of their people.* The Wounded Healer *embodied some of the struggles within Nouwen's own life. By his frequent admission, his own emotional life was frayed. He praised the value of solitude, yet lived in intensely public ways. He wrote about home and the love and affection of others, yet said he had difficulty finding such gifts among his own family. In his last book,* Can You Drink the Cup?, *Nouwen repeated the theme he worked so well in* The Wounded Healer: *"When each of us can hold firm to our own cup, with its many sorrows and joys, claiming it as our unique life, then we too can lift it up for others to see and encourage them to lift up their lives as well. The wounds of our individual lives, which seem intolerable when lived alone, become sources of healing when we live them as part of a fellowship of mutual care."*

While not ashamed to use the stuff of his own life as a means of thinking about ministry, Nouwen also embodied his theology in his life. He ended his career by forsaking the prestige and comfort of the academy and becoming a member of Daybreak. There he lived among people with severe developmental disabilities, people who could neither read nor care much for his writing, but who, for Henri Nouwen, embodied Christ's call to live in community where our wounds and weaknesses become a means whereby we are more closely related to the crucified Christ.

The Wounded Healer
Henri J. M. Nouwen

Introduction

In the middle of our convulsive world men and women raise their voices time and again to announce with incredible boldness that we are waiting for a Liberator. We are waiting, they announce, for a Messiah who will free us from hatred and oppression, from racism and war—a Messiah who will let peace and justice take their rightful place.

If the ministry is meant to hold the promise of this Messiah, then whatever we can learn of His coming will give us a deeper understanding of what is called for in ministry today.

How does our Liberator come? I found an old legend in the Talmud which may suggest to us the beginning of an answer:

> Rabbi Yoshua ben Levi came upon Elijah the prophet while he was standing at the entrance of Rabbi Simeron ben Yohai's cave . . . He asked Elijah, "When will the Messiah come?" Elijah replied,
> "Go and ask him yourself."
> "Where is he?"
> "Sitting at the gates of the city."
> "How shall I know him?"
> "He is sitting among the poor covered with wounds. The others unbind all their wounds at the same time and then bind them up again. But he unbinds one at a time and binds it up again, saying to himself, 'Perhaps I shall be needed: if so I must always be ready so as not to delay for a moment.' " (Taken from the tractate Sanhedrin)

The Messiah, the story tells us, is sitting among the poor, binding his wounds one at a time, waiting for the moment when he will be needed. So it is too with the minister. Since it is his task to make visible the first vestiges of liberation for others, he must bind his own wounds carefully in anticipation of the moment when he will be needed. He is called to be the wounded healer, the one who must look after his own wounds but at the same time be prepared to heal the wounds of others. . . .

I. The Wounded Minister

The Talmud story suggests that, because he binds his own wounds one at a time, the Messiah would not have to take time to prepare himself if asked to help someone else. He would be ready to help. Jesus has given this story a new fullness by making his own broken body the way to health, to liberation and new life. Thus like Jesus, he who proclaims liberation is called not only to care for his own wounds and the wounds of others, but also to make his wounds into a major source of his healing power.

But what are our wounds? They have been spoken about in many ways by many voices. Words such as "alienation," "separation," "isolation" and "loneliness" have been used as the names of our wounded condition. Maybe the word "loneliness" best expresses our immediate experience and therefore most fittingly enables us to understand our brokenness. The loneliness of the minister is especially painful; for over and above his experience as a man in modern society, he feels an added loneliness, resulting from the changing meaning of the ministerial profession itself.

1. Personal Loneliness

We live in a society in which loneliness has become one of the most painful human wounds. The growing competition and rivalry which pervade our lives from birth have created in us an acute awareness of our isolation. This awareness has in turn left many with a heightened anxiety and an intense search for the experience of unity and community. It has also led people to ask anew how love, friendship, brotherhood and sisterhood can free them from isolation and offer them a sense of intimacy and belonging. All around us we see the many ways by which the people of the western world are trying to escape this loneliness. Psychotherapy, the many institutes which offer group experiences with verbal and nonverbal communication techniques, summer courses and conferences supported by scholars, trainers and "huggers" where people can share common problems, and the many experiments which seek to create intimate liturgies where peace is not only announced but also felt—these increasingly popular phenomena are all signs of a painful attempt to break through the immobilizing wall of loneliness. . . .

. . . The Christian way of life does not take away our loneliness; it protects and cherishes it as a precious gift. Sometimes it seems as if we do everything possible to avoid the painful confrontation with our basic human loneliness, and allow ourselves to be trapped by false gods promising immediate satisfaction and quick relief. But perhaps the painful awareness of loneliness is an invitation to transcend our limitations and look beyond the boundaries of our existence. The awareness of loneliness might be a gift we must protect and guard, because our loneliness reveals to us an inner emptiness that can be destructive when misunderstood, but filled with promise for him who can tolerate its sweet pain.

When we are impatient, when we want to give up our loneliness and try to overcome the separation and incompleteness we feel, too soon, we easily relate to our human world with devastating expectations. We ignore what we already know with a deep-seated, intuitive knowledge—that no love or friendship, no intimate embrace or tender kiss, no community, commune or collective, no man or woman, will ever be able to satisfy our desire to be released from our lonely condition. This truth is so disconcerting and painful that we are more prone to play games with our fantasies than to face the truth of our existence. Thus we keep hoping that one day we will find the man who really understands our experiences, the woman who will bring peace to our restless life, the job where we can fulfill our potentials, the book which will explain everything, and the place where we can feel at home. Such false hope leads us to make exhausting demands and prepares us for bitterness and dangerous hostility when we start discovering that nobody, and nothing, can live up to our absolutistic expectations.

Many marriages are ruined because neither partner was able to fulfill the often hidden hope that the other would take his or her loneliness away. And many celibates live with the naive dream that in the intimacy of marriage their loneliness will be taken away.

When the minister lives with these false expectations and illusions he prevents himself from claiming his own loneliness as a source of human understanding, and is unable to offer any real service to the many who do not understand their own suffering.

2. Professional Loneliness

The wound of loneliness in the life of the minister hurts all the more, since he not only shares in the human condition of isolation, but also finds that his professional impact on others is diminishing. The minister is called to speak to the ultimate concerns of life: birth and death, union and separation, love and hate. He has an urgent desire to give meaning to people's lives. But he finds himself standing on the edges of events and only reluctantly admitted to the spot where the decisions are made.

In hospitals, where many utter their first cry as well as their last words, ministers are often more tolerated than required. In prisons, where men's desire for liberation and freedom is most painfully felt, a chaplain feels like a guilty bystander whose words hardly move the wardens. In the cities, where children play between buildings and old people die isolated and forgotten, the protests of priests are hardly taken seriously and their demands hang in the air like rhetorical questions. Many churches decorated with words announcing salvation and new life are often little more than parlors for those who feel quite comfortable in the old life, and who are not likely to let the minister's words change their stone hearts into furnaces where swords can be cast into plowshares, and spears into pruning hooks.

The painful irony is that the minister, who wants to touch the center of men's lives, finds himself on the periphery, often pleading in vain for admission. He never seems to be where the action is, where the plans are made and the strategies discussed. He always seems to arrive at the wrong places at the wrong times with the wrong people, outside the walls of the city when the feast is over, with a few crying women.

A few years ago, when I was chaplain of the Holland-America line, I was standing on the bridge of a huge Dutch ocean liner which was trying to find its way through a thick fog into the port of Rotterdam. The fog was so thick, in fact, that the steersman could not even see the bow of the ship. The captain, carefully listening to a radar station operator who was explaining his position between other ships, walked nervously up and down the bridge and shouted his orders to the steersman. When he suddenly stumbled over me, he blurted out: "God damn it, Father, get out of my way." But when I was ready to run away, filled with feelings of incompetence and guilt, he came back and said: "Why don't you just stay around. This might be the only time I really need you."

There was a time, not too long ago, when we felt like captains running our own ships with a great sense of power and self-confidence. Now we are standing in the way. That is our lonely position: We are powerless, on the side, liked maybe by a few crew members who swab the decks and goof off to drink a beer with us, but not taken very seriously when the weather is fine.

The wound of our loneliness is indeed deep. Maybe we had forgotten it, since there were so many distractions. But our failure to change the world with our good intentions and sincere actions and our undesired displacement to the edges of life have made us aware that the wound is still there.

So we see how loneliness is the minister's wound not only because he shares in the human condition, but also because of the unique predicament of his profession. It is this wound which he is called to bind with more care and attention than others usually do. For a deep understanding of his own pain makes it possible for him to convert his weakness into strength and to offer his own experience as a source of healing to those who are often lost in the darkness of their own misunderstood sufferings. This is a very hard call, because for a minister who is committed to forming a community of faith, loneliness is a very painful wound, which is easily subject to denial and neglect. But once the pain is accepted and understood, a denial is no longer necessary, and ministry can become a healing service.

II. The Healing Minister

How can wounds become a source of healing? This is a question which requires careful consideration. For when we want to put our wounded selves in the service of others, we must consider the relationship between our professional and personal lives.

On the one hand, no minister can keep his own experience of life hidden from those he wants to help. Nor should he want to keep it hidden. While a doctor can still be a good doctor even when his private life is severely disrupted, no minister can offer service without a constant and vital acknowledgment of his own experience. On the other hand, it would be very easy to misuse the concept of the wounded healer by defending a form of spiritual exhibitionism. A minister who talks in the pulpit about his own personal problems is of no help to his congregation, for no suffering human being is helped by someone who tells him that he has the same problems. Remarks such as, "Don't worry because I suffer from the same depression, confusion and anxiety as you do," help no one. This spiritual exhibitionism adds little faith to little faith and creates narrow-mindedness instead of new perspectives. Open wounds stink and do not heal.

Making one's own wounds a source of healing, therefore, does not call for a sharing of superficial personal pains but for a constant willingness to see one's own pain and suffering as rising from the depth of the human condition which all men share.

To some, the concept of the wounded healer might sound morbid and unhealthy. They might feel that the ideal of self-fulfillment is replaced by an ideal of self-castigation, and that pain is romanticized instead of criticized. I would like to show how the idea of the wounded healer does not contradict the concept of self-realization, or self-fulfillment, but deepens and broadens it.

How does healing take place? Many words, such as care and compassion, understanding and forgiveness, fellowship and community, have been used for the healing task of the Christian minister. I like to use the word hospitality, not only because it has such deep roots in the Judaeo-Christian tradition, but also, and primarily, because it gives us more insight into the nature of response to the human condition of loneliness. Hospitality is the virtue which allows us to break through the narrowness of our own fears and to open our houses to the stranger, with the intuition that salvation comes to us in the form of a tired traveler. Hospitality makes anxious disciples into powerful witnesses, makes suspicious owners into generous givers, and makes closed-minded sectarians into interested recipients of new ideas and insights.

But it has become very difficult for us today to fully understand the implications of hospitality. Like the Semitic nomads, we live in a desert with many lonely travelers who are looking for a moment of peace, for a fresh drink and for a sign of encouragement so that they can continue their mysterious search for freedom.

What does hospitality as a healing power require? It requires first of all that the host feel at home in his own house, and secondly that he create a free and fearless place for the unexpected visitor. Therefore, hospitality embraces two concepts: concentration and community.

1. Hospitality and Concentration

Hospitality is the ability to pay attention to the guest. This is very difficult, since we are preoccupied with our own needs, worries and tensions, which prevent us from taking distance from ourselves in order to pay attention to others.

Not long ago I met a parish priest. After describing his hectic daily schedule—religious services, classroom teaching, luncheon and dinner engagements, and organizational meetings—he said apologetically: "Yes . . . but there are so many problems . . ." When I asked, "Whose problems?" he was silent for a few minutes, and then more or less reluctantly said, "I guess—my own." Indeed, his incredible activities seemed in large part motivated by fear of what he would discover when he came to a standstill. He actually said: "I guess I am busy in order to avoid a painful self-concentration."

So we find it extremely hard to pay attention because of our intentions. As soon as our intentions take over, the question no longer is, "Who is he?" but, "What can I get from him?"—and then we no longer listen to what he is saying but to what we can do with what he is saying. Then the fulfillment of our unrecognized need for sympathy, friendship, popularity, success, understanding, money or a career becomes our concern, and instead of paying attention to the other person we impose ourselves upon him with intrusive curiosity. (See James Hillman: *Insearch*, Charles Scribner's Sons, New York, 1967, p. 18.)

Anyone who wants to pay attention without intention has to be at home in his own house—that is, he has to discover the center of his life in his own heart. Concentration, which leads to meditation and contemplation, is therefore the necessary precondition for true hospitality. When our souls are restless, when we are driven by thousands of different and often conflicting stimuli, when we are always "over there" between people, ideas and the worries of this world, how can we possibly create the room and space where someone else can enter freely without feeling himself an unlawful intruder?

Paradoxically, by withdrawing into ourselves, not out of self-pity but out of humility, we create the space for another to be himself and to come to us on his own terms. . . .

But human withdrawal is a very painful and lonely process, because it forces us to face directly our own condition in all its beauty as well as misery. When we are not afraid to enter into our own center and to concentrate on the stirrings of our own soul, we come to know that being alive means being loved. This experience tells us that we can only love because we are born out of love, that we can only give because our life is a gift, and that we can only make others free because we are set free by Him whose heart is greater than ours. When we have found the anchor places for our lives in our own center, we can be free to let others enter into the space created for them and allow them to dance their own dance, sing their own song and speak their own language without fear. Then our presence is no longer threatening and demanding but inviting and liberating.

2. Hospitality and Community

The minister who has come to terms with his own loneliness and is at home in his own house is a host who offers hospitality to his guests. He gives them a friendly space, where they may feel free to come and go, to be close and distant, to rest and to play, to talk and to be silent, to eat and to fast. The paradox indeed is that hospitality asks for the creation of an empty space where the guest can find his own soul.

Why is this a healing ministry? It is healing because it takes away the false illusion that wholeness can be given by one to another. It is healing because it does not take away the loneliness and the pain of another, but invites him to recognize his loneliness on a level where it can be shared. Many people in this life suffer because they are anxiously searching for the man or woman, the event or encounter, which will take their loneliness away. But when they enter a house with real hospitality they soon see that their own wounds must be understood not as sources of despair and bitterness, but as signs that they have to travel on in obedience to the calling sounds of their own wounds.

From this we get an idea of the kind of help a minister may offer. A minister is not a doctor whose primary task is to take away pain. Rather, he deepens the pain to a level where it can be shared. When someone comes with his loneliness to the minister, he can only expect that his loneliness will be understood and felt, so that he no longer has to run away from it but can accept it as an expression of his basic human condition. When a woman suffers the loss of her child, the minister is not called upon to comfort her by telling her that she still has two beautiful healthy children at home; he is challenged to help her realize that the death of her child reveals her own mortal condition, the same human condition which he and others share with her.

Perhaps the main task of the minister is to prevent people from suffering for the wrong reasons. Many people suffer because of the false supposition on which they have based their lives. That supposition is that there should be no fear or loneliness, no confusion or doubt. But these sufferings can only be dealt with creatively when they are understood as wounds integral to our human condition. Therefore ministry is a very confronting service. It does not allow people to live with illusions of immortality and wholeness. It keeps reminding others that they are mortal and broken, but also that with the recognition of this condition, liberation starts.

No minister can save anyone. He can only offer himself as a guide to fearful people. Yet, paradoxically, it is precisely in this guidance that the first signs of hope become visible. This is so because a shared pain is no longer paralyzing but mobilizing, when understood as a way to liberation. When we become aware that we do not have to escape our pains, but that we can mobilize them into a common search for life, those very pains are transformed from expressions of despair into signs of hope.

Through this common search, hospitality becomes community. Hospitality becomes community as it creates a unity based on the shared confession of our basic brokenness and on a shared hope. This hope in turn leads us far beyond the boundaries of human togetherness to Him who calls His people away from the land of slavery to the land of freedom. It belongs to the central insight of the Judaeo-Christian tradition, that it is the call of God which forms the people of God.

A Christian community is therefore a healing community not because wounds are cured and pains are alleviated, but because wounds and pains become openings or occasions for a new vision. Mutual confession then becomes a mutual deepening of hope, and sharing weakness becomes a reminder to one and all of the coming strength.

When loneliness is among the chief wounds of the minister, hospitality can convert that wound into a source of healing. Concentration prevents the minister from burdening others with his pain and allows him to accept his wounds as helpful teachers of his own and his neighbor's condition. Community arises where the sharing of pain takes place, not as a stifling form of self-complaint, but as recognition of God's saving promises.

Conclusion

I started this chapter with the story of Rabbi Joshua ben Levi, who asked Elijah, "When will the Messiah come?" There is an important conclusion to this story. When Elijah had explained to him how he could find the Messiah sitting among the poor at the gates of the city, Rabbi Joshua ben Levi went to the Messiah and said to him:

> "Peace unto you, my master and teacher."
> The Messiah answered, "Peace unto you,
> son of Levi." He asked, "When is the master coming?"
> "Today," he answered.
> Rabbi Yoshua returned to Elijah, who asked, "What did he tell you?"
> "He indeed has deceived me, for he said 'Today
> I am coming' and he has not come."
> Elijah said, "This is what he told you: 'Today if you
> would listen to His voice.' " (Psalm 95.7)

Even when we know that we are called to be wounded healers, it is still very difficult to acknowledge that healing has to take place today. Because we are living in days when our wounds have become all too visible. Our loneliness and isolation has become so much a part of our daily experience, that we cry out for a Liberator who will take us away from our misery and bring us justice and peace.

To announce, however, that the Liberator is sitting among the poor and that the wounds are signs of hope and that today is the day of liberation, is a step very few can take. But this is exactly the announcement of the wounded healer: "The master is coming—not tomorrow, but today, not next year, but this year, not after all our misery is passed, but in the middle of it, not in another place but right here where we are standing."

And with a challenging confrontation he says:

> O that today you would listen to his voice!
> Harden not your heart as at Meribah,
> as on that day at Massah in the desert when they tried me,
> though they saw my work. (Psalm 95.7–9)

If indeed we listen to the voice and believe that ministry is a sign of hope, because it makes visible the first rays of light of the coming Messiah, we can make ourselves and others understand that we already carry in us the source of our own search. Thus ministry can indeed be a witness to the living truth that the wound, which causes us to suffer now, will be revealed to us later as the place where God intimated his new creation.

Henri J. M. Nouwen, *The Wounded Healer: Ministry in Contemporary Society* (New York: Image Books, 1979), pp. 81-96.

The young church had been living in relative peace with the empire for a few decades when, in 250, the emperor Decius ordered renewed persecution of Christians. Only a pinch of incense at the altar of the emperor, or else a well-placed bribe, earned safety for many believers. Pastors were now required to work to strengthen the resolve of those who were considering acquiescing to the government's demands, or to find a way to absolve and to restore those who, in the face of threatened martyrdom, had forsaken the faith.

The bishop of Carthage, Cyprian, wrote a letter to the congregation at Thibaris, a town near Carthage in North Africa. Cyprian took a tough line in the face of the persecution, demanding that there be no compromise, insisting that the lapsed could not be restored to communion without correction administered by their bishops.

Roaming through Scripture, Cyprian's letter demonstrates that martyrdom is not a momentary intrusion into the life of the church, but rather the permanent state of life for the faithful in the Old and New Testaments. In martyrdom, Christians are given the opportunity to come especially close to their crucified Lord. He ends his pastoral epistle by predicting the apocalyptic dissolution of the empires of this world and God's just wrath upon those who now brought the emperor's wrath upon the church. Sure enough, Decius suddenly died within the year.

Yet, eight years later, in another imperial persecution of the church, Cyprian embodied his own exhortation when he too joined the noble army of martyrs.

(On) Facing Martyrdom
Cyprian

Cyprian to the people abiding at Thibaris, greeting. I had indeed thought, beloved brethren, and prayerfully desired—if the state of things and the condition of the times permitted, in conformity with what you frequently desired—myself to come to you; and being present with you, then to strengthen the brotherhood with such moderate powers of exhortation as I possess. But since I am detained by such urgent affairs, that I have not the power to travel far from this place, and to be long absent from the people over whom by divine mercy I am placed, I have written in the meantime this letter, to be to you in my stead. For as, by the condescension of the Lord instructing me, I am very often instigated and warned, I ought to bring unto your conscience also the anxiety of my warning. For you ought to know and to believe, and hold it for certain, that the day of affliction has begun to hang over our heads, and the end of the world and the time of Antichrist to draw near, so that we must all stand prepared for the battle; nor consider anything but the glory of life eternal, and the crown of the confession of the Lord; and not regard those things which are coming as being such as were those which have passed away. A severer and a fiercer fight is now threatening, for which the soldiers of Christ ought to prepare themselves with uncorrupted faith and robust courage, considering that they drink the cup of Christ's blood daily, for the reason that they themselves also may be able to shed their blood for Christ. For this is to wish to be found with Christ, to imitate that which Christ both taught and did, according to the Apostle John, who said, "He that saith he abideth in Christ, ought himself also so to walk even as He walked." Moreover, the blessed Apostle Paul exhorts and teaches, saying, "We are God's children; but if children, then heirs of God, and joint-heirs with Christ; if so be that we suffer with Him, that we may also be glorified together."

Which things must all now be considered by us, that no one may desire anything from the world that is now dying, but may follow Christ, who both lives for ever, and quickens His servants, who are established in the faith of His mane. For there comes the time, beloved brethren, which our Lord long ago foretold and taught us was approaching, saying, "The time cometh, that whosoever killeth you will think that he doeth God service. And these things they will do unto you, because they have not known the Father nor me. But these things have I told you, that when the time shall come, ye may remember that I told you of them." Nor let any one wonder that we are harassed with constant persecutions, and continually tried with increasing afflictions, when the Lord before predicted that these things would happen in the last times, and has instructed us for the warfare by the teaching and exhortation of His words. Peter also, His apostle, has taught that persecutions occur for the sake of our being proved, and that we also should by the example of righteous men who have gone before us, be joined to the love of God by death and sufferings. For he wrote in his epistle, and said, "Beloved, think it not strange concerning the fiery trial which is to try you, nor do ye fall away, as if some new thing happened unto you; but as often as ye partake in Christ's sufferings, rejoice in all things, that when His glory shall be revealed, ye may be glad also with exceeding joy. If ye be reproached in the name of Christ, happy are ye; for the name of the majesty and power of the Lord resteth on you, which indeed on their part is blasphemed, but on your part is glorified." Now the apostles taught us those things which they themselves also learnt from the Lord's precepts and the heavenly commands, the Lord Himself thus strengthening us, and saying, "There is no man that hath left house, or land, or parents, or brethren, or sisters, or wife, or children, for the kingdom of God's sake, who shall not receive sevenfold more in this present time, and in the world to come life everlasting." And again, He says, "Blessed are ye when men shall hate you, and shall separate you from their company, and shall cast you out, and shall reproach your name as evil for the Son of Man's sake. Rejoice ye in that day, and leap for joy; for, behold your reward is great in heaven."

The Lord desired that we should rejoice and leap for joy in persecutions, because, when persecutions occur, then are given the crowns of faith, then the soldiers of God are proved, then the heavens are opened to martyrs. For we have not in such a way given our name to warfare that we ought only to think about peace, and draw back from and refuse war, when in this very warfare the Lord walked first—the Teacher of humility, and endurance, and suffering—so that what He taught to be done, He first of all did, and what He exhorts to suffer, He Himself first suffered for us. Let it be before your eyes, beloved brethren, that He who alone received all judgment from the Father, and who will come to judge, has already declared the decree of His judgment and of His future recognition, foretelling and testifying that He will confess those before His Father who confess Him, and will deny those who deny Him. If we could escape death, we might reasonably fear to die. But since, on the other hand, it is necessary that a mortal man should die, we should embrace the occasion that comes by divine promise and condescension, and accomplish the ending provided by death with the reward of immortality; nor fear to be slain, since we are sure when we are slain to be crowned.

Nor let any one, beloved brethren, when he behold our people drive away and scattered by the fear of persecution, be disturbed at not seeing the brotherhood gathered together, nor hearing the bishops discoursing. All are not able to be there together, who may not kill, but who must be killed. Wherever, in those days, each one of the brethren shall be separated from the flock for a time, by the necessity of the season, in body, not in spirit, let him not be moved at the terror of that flight; nor, if he withdraw and be concealed, let him be alarmed at the solitude of the desert place. He is not alone, whose companion in flight Christ is; he is not alone who, keeping God's temple wheresoever he is, is not without God. And if a robber should fall upon you, a fugitive in the solitude or in the mountains; if a wild beast should attack you; if hunger, or thirst, or cold should distress you, or the tempest and the storm should overwhelm you hastening in a rapid voyage over the seas, Christ everywhere looks upon His soldier fighting; and for the sake of persecution, for the honour of His name, gives a reward to him when he dies, as He has promised that He will give in the resurrection. Nor is the glory of martyrdom less that he has not perished publicly and before many, since the cause of perishing is to perish for Christ. That Witness who proves martyrs, and crowns them, suffices for a testimony of his martyrdom.

Let us, beloved brethren, imitate righteous Abel, who initiated Martyrdoms, he first being slain for righteousness' sake. Let us imitate Abraham, the friend of God, who did not delay to offer his son as a victim with his own hands, obeying God with a faith of devotion. Let us imitate the three children Ananias, Azarias, and Misael, who, neither frightened by their youthful age nor broken down by captivity, Judea being conquered and Jerusalem taken, overcame the king by the power of faith in his own kingdom; who, when bidden to worship the image which Nebuchadnezzar the king had made, stood forth stronger both than the king's threats and the flames, calling out and attesting their faith by these words: "O king Nebuchadnezzar, we are not careful to answer thee in this matter. For the God whom we serve is able to deliver us from the burning fiery furnace; and He will deliver us out of thine hands, O king. But if not, be it known unto thee, that we do not serve thy gods, nor worship the golden image which thou hast set up." They believed that they might escape according to their faith, but they added, "and if not," that the king might know that they could also die for the God they worshipped. For this is the strength of courage and of faith, to believe and to know that God can deliver from present death, and yet not to fear death nor to give way, that faith may be the more mightily proved. The uncorrupted and unconquered might of the Holy Spirit broke forth by their mouth, so that the words which the Lord in His Gospel spoke are seen to be true: "But when they shall seize you, take no thought what ye shall speak; for it shall be given you in that hour what ye shall speak. For it is not ye that speak, but the Spirit of your Father which speaketh in you." He said that what we are able to speak and to answer is given to us in that hour from heaven, and supplied; and that it is not then we who speak, but the Spirit of God our Father, who, as He does not depart nor is separated from those who confess Him, Himself both speaks and is crowned in us. So Daniel, too, when he was required to worship the idol Bel, which the people and the king then worshipped, in asserting the honour of his God, broke forth with full faith and freedom, saying, "I worship nothing but the Lord my God, who created the heaven and the earth."

What shall we say of the cruel tortures of the blessed martyrs in the Maccabees, and the multiform sufferings of the seven brethren, and the mother comforting her children in their agonies, and herself dying also with her children? Do not they witness the proofs of great courage and faith, and exhort us by their sufferings to the triumphs of martyrdom? What of the prophets whom the Holy Spirit quickened to the foreknowledge of future events? What of the apostles whom the Lord chose? Since these righteous men were slain for righteousness' sake, have they not taught us also to die? The nativity of Christ witnessed at once the martyrdom of infants, so that they who were two years old and under were slain for his name's sake. An age not yet fitted for the battle appeared fit for the crown. That it might be manifest that they who are slain for Christ's sake are innocent, innocent infancy was put to death for His name's sake. It is shown that none is free from the peril of persecution, when even these accomplished martyrdoms. But how grave is the case of a Christian man, if he, a servant, is unwilling to suffer, when his masters first suffered; and that we should be unwilling to suffer for our own sins, when he had no sin of his own suffered for us! The Son of God suffered that He might make us sons of God, and the son of man will not suffer that he may continue to be a son of God! If we suffer from the world's hatred, Christ first endured the world's hatred. If we suffer reproaches in this world, if exile, if tortures, the Maker and Lord of the world experienced harder things than these, and He also warns us, saying, "If the world hated you, remember that it hated me before you. If ye were of the world, the world would love its own: but because ye are not of the world, but I have chosen you out of the world, therefore the world hated you. Remember the word that I said unto you, The servant is not greater than his lord. If they have persecuted me, they will also persecute you." Whatever our Lord and God taught, He also did, that the disciple might not be excused if he learns and does not.

Nor let any one of you, beloved brethren, be so terrified by the fear of future persecution, or the coming of the threatening Antichrist, as not to be found armed for all things by the evangelical exhortations and precepts, and by the heavenly warnings. Antichrist is coming, but above him comes Christ also. The enemy goeth about and rageth, but immediately the Lord follows to avenge our sufferings and our wounds. The adversary is enraged and threatens, but there is One who can deliver us from his hands. He is to be feared whose anger no one can escape, as He himself forewarns, and says: "Fear not them which kill the body, but are not able to kill the soul; but rather fear Him which is able to destroy both body and soul in hell." And again: "He that loveth his life, shall lose it; and he that hateth his life in this world, shall keep it unto life eternal." And in the Apocalypse He instructs and forewarns, saying, "If any man worship the beast and his image, and receive his mark in his forehead or in his hand, the same also shall drink of the wine of the wrath of God, mixed in the cup of His indignation, and he shall be tormented with fire and brimstone in the presence of the holy angels, and in the presence of the Lamb; and the smoke of their torments shall ascend up for ever and ever; and they shall have no rest day nor night, who worship the beast and his image."

For the secular contest men are trained and prepared, and reckon it a great glory of their honor if it should happen to them to be crowned in the sight of the people, and in the presence of the emperor. Behold a lofty and great contest, glorious also with the reward of a heavenly crown, inasmuch as God looks upon us as we struggle, and extending His view over those whom He had condescended to make His sons, He enjoys the spectacle of our contest. God looks upon us in the warfare, and fighting in the encounter of faith; His angels look on us, and Christ looks on us. How great is the dignity, and how great the happiness of the glory, to engage in the presence of God, and to be crowned, with Christ for a judge! Let us be armed, beloved brethren, with our whole strength, and let us be prepared for the struggle with an uncorrupted mind, with a sound faith, with a devoted courage. Let the camp of God go forth to the battle-field which is appointed to us. Let the sound ones be armed, lest he that is sound should lose the advantage of having lately stood; let the lapsed also be armed, that even the lapsed may regain what he has lost: let honour provoke the whole; let sorrow provoke the lapsed to the battle. The Apostle Paul teaches us to be armed and prepared, saying, "We wrestle not against flesh and blood, but against powers, and the princes of this world and of this darkness, against spirits of wickedness in high places. Therefore put on the whole armour, that ye may be able to withstand in the most evil day, that when ye have done all ye may stand; having your loins girted about with truth, and having put on the breastplate of righteousness; and your feet shod with the preparation of the Gospel of peace; taking the shield of faith, wherewith ye shall be able to quench all the fiery darts of the wicked one; and the helmet of salvation, and the sword of the Spirit, which is the word of God."

Let us take these arms, let us fortify ourselves with these spiritual and heavenly safeguards, that in the most evil day we may be able to withstand, and to resist the threats of the devil: let us put on the breastplate of righteousness, that our breast may be fortified and safe against the darts of the enemy: Let our feet be shod with evangelical teaching, and armed, so that when the serpent shall begin to be trodden and crushed by us, he may not be able to bite and trip us up: let us bravely bear the shield of faith, by the protection of which, whatever the enemy darts at us may be extinguished: let us take also for protection of our head the helmet of salvation, that our ears may be guarded from hearing the deadly edicts; that our eyes may be fortified, that they may not see the odious images; that our brow may be fortified, so as to keep safe the sign of God; that our mouth may be fortified, that the conquering tongue may confess Christ its Lord: Let us also arm the right hand with the sword of the Spirit, that it may bravely reject the deadly sacrifices; that, mindful of the Eucharist, the hand which has received the Lord's body may embrace the Lord Himself, hereafter to receive from the Lord the reward of heavenly crowns.

Oh, what and how great will that day be at its coming, beloved brethren, when the Lord shall begin to count up His people, and to recognise the deservings of each one by the inspection of His divine knowledge, to send the guilty to Gehenna, and to set on fire our persecutors with the perpetual burning of a penal fire, but to pray to us the reward of our faith and devotion! What will be the glory and how great the joy to be admitted to see God, to be honoured to receive with Christ, thy Lord God, the joy of eternal salvation and light—to greet Abraham, and Isaac, and Jacob, and all the patriarchs, and prophets, and apostles, and martyrs—to rejoice with the righteous and the friends of God in the kingdom of heaven, with the pleasure of immortality given to us—to receive there what neither eye hath seen, nor ear heard, neither hath entered into the heart of man! For the apostle announces that we shall receive greater things than anything that we here either do or suffer, saying, "The sufferings of this present time are not worthy to be compared with the glory to come thereafter which shall be revealed in us." When that revelation shall come, when that glory of God shall shine upon us, we shall be as happy and joyful, honoured with the condescension of God, as they will remain guilty and wretched, who, either as deserters from God or rebels against Him, have done the will of the devil, so that it is necessary for them to be tormented with the devil himself in unquenchable fire.

Let these things, beloved brethren, take hold of our hearts; let this be the preparation of our arms, this our daily and nightly meditation, to have before our eyes and ever to revolve in our thoughts and feelings the punishments of the wicked and the rewards and the deservings of the righteous: what the Lord threatens by way of punishment against those that deny Him; what, on the other hand, he promises by way of glory to those that confess Him. If, while we think and meditate on these things, there should come to us a day of persecution, the soldier of Christ instructed in His precepts and warnings is not fearful for the battle, but is prepared for the crown. I bid you dearest brethren, ever heartily farewell.

Cyprian, Epistle LV, To the People of Thibaris, Exhorting to Martyrdom, trans. Ernest Wallis, *The Ante-Nicene Fathers*, ed. Alexander Roberts and James Donaldson (Buffalo: Christian Literature Company, 1886), vol. V, pp. 347-50.

Toward the end of his worldwide, incredibly effective ministry, I had the privilege of teaching with Samuel D. Proctor at Duke. By this time his days as seminary president, head of the Peace Corps, and pastor of New York's Abyssinian Baptist Church had made him into one of America's premier senior preachers. Although he was active in politics, the struggle for civil rights for African Americans, and various national and international causes, he was at heart a pastor, as this selection shows. Although he was a member of a free church, a lifelong Baptist, this passage, written late in life, shows his exceedingly high view of ministry as part of the high priesthood of Christ. Here he focuses upon the high pastoral task of intercession, of priestly ministry in bringing the faithful before the throne of God in prayer and in other pastoral work.

The Pastor as Intercessor
Samuel D. Proctor

For we are not, like so many, peddlers of God's word;
but as [persons] of sincerity, as commissioned by God, in the
sight of God we speak in Christ.
                    —2 Corinthians 2:17 (RSV)

We have this treasure in earthen vessels, to show that the tran-
scendent power belongs to God and not to us.
                    —2 Corinthians 4:7 (RSV)

The most frightening moment in a pastor's life occurs with the realization that there are people counting on him or her to light the pathway to an understanding of God and a transforming relationship with Jesus Christ. It is one thing to teach someone to swim, to use a computer, to roast a turkey, or to play chess; but it is something of another magnitude entirely to say, "Watch me, and I will lead you to a knowledge of God. Listen to me and copy my life, and I will lead you to a life-changing experience with Jesus Christ."

. . . Scarcely anyone could feel really capable of making any such assertion unless it was qualified by acknowledging that no one stands in such a place by his or her own authority or merits, but only as one who is saved, forgiven, and serving by the grace of God. . . .

177

The Pastor's Intercessory Role

Some communions ascribe to priests and pastors a sacerdotal function—a formal, efficacious, vicarious presentation of one's appeal for forgiveness and the official pardon, the *mea culpa* and the *Nunc Dimittis*. Other fellowships grant congregational autonomy, recognize neither hierarchical nor sacerdotal function for pastors, believe in the priesthood of all believers, and allow no intermediary between God and the penitent soul.

In the one case the priest has a more precise role as an intercessor. In the other case the pastor's intercessory role is implicit, not explicit. The pastor is an intercessor not by title or ordinance but by function and efficacy. In both cases, however, the same end is sought, trying to effect a right relationship, a reconciled relationship, an atoning and redemptive relationship between God and the believer.

It is more difficult to describe this function when it works well than when it fails. When it works well, it culminates in a loud "Hallelujah!" and a glorious "Amen!" When it is a bungling failure, the end is pitiable. When a seeker turns to a pastor and finds in him or her a stranger to God who has lost his or her own soul to idolatry and hollow pretense, the consequences are a disgrace. There is little wonder why a person like Moses, who had high ability, strong convictions, and indefatigable endurance, felt unworthy when he heard the call of God. "Moses said to God, 'Who am I that I should go to Pharaoh, and bring the sons of Israel out of Egypt?' " (Exodus 3:11 RSV). And listen to Isaiah's response to God's call, "Woe is me! For I am lost; for I am a man of unclean lips, and I dwell in the midst of a people of unclean lips; for my eyes have seen the King, the Lord of hosts" (Isaiah 6:5 RSV).

Those who have served effectively as intercessors, who have gained great respect and appreciation as pastors, whose names are passed around as examples and models of excellence in ministry are likely to disclaim any merit in this area, and are likely to ask for an intercessor on their own behalf. They know enough about God to know how great the gulf really is, and enough about sin to know how great is the burden of our guilt. But thank God! They also know how boundless God's mercy is, and they have been emboldened to come to the throne of grace on their own behalf, and on behalf of those who lean on them. They hear the words of the writer of Hebrews resonating in their hearts:

> "We have not a high priest who is unable to sympathize with our weaknesses, but one who in every respect has been tempted as we are, yet without sin. Let us then with confidence draw near to the throne of grace, that we may receive mercy and find grace to help in time of need." (Hebrews 4:15-16 RSV)

This remains one of the pastor's most vital ministries, and it intersects with every other aspect of the office. Not only in the pulpit or at the altar, but in every relationship there is the possibility of helping someone to begin a closer walk with God. Thus pastors need to devote time to considering ways in which their ministry can be impeded—the pain and agony of continued estrangement from God; the initiative that God has taken to evoke our response and surrender; the intercessor as an instrument of God's grace.

The Importance of a Disciplined Life

In my early youth we played in the streets because our community had no playgrounds or community centers. We were familiar with all of the cars that regularly traveled through our streets, interrupting our games. We knew who lived where and which cars were parked where and for how long. When one car parked in the same place frequently, for long periods, our curiosity was pricked. When we found that it was the car of the pastor of a large church, we indulged in all sorts of jokes, gossip, and unkind speculation. This distinguished gentleman never had the faintest clue that his error and indiscretion seriously diminished our esteem for the clergy, at an early stage in life. The role of intercessor demands rigorous discipline.

Recently, and most pathetically, two famous television evangelists fell suddenly into ill-repute while commanding audiences of millions of viewers. Many of their listeners were persons of modest means and limited educational opportunity who had given them their trust, believing that these evangelists were sent especially to meet their needs. Their sudden disgrace was bewildering to many. That cost in spiritual terms remains incalculable.

Such dramatic disappointments notwithstanding, there is a more troublesome enemy of trust that undermines the intercessor, the one who leads others to God. It is the direction in which the intercessor's own life has been moving. There is no set standard of income or comfort for a pastor, priest, or rabbi. This is a subject that remains open for discussion. But excessive consumption suggests that the pastor's interest is in something other than leading persons to God. For a pastor, a lifestyle that is marked by material indulgence and luxury is clearly incompatible with the cultivation of those spiritual qualities that would help one lead others to find God. Those who live close to God find that a simple, uncluttered life and a lean profile are more conducive to service, to discipleship, and to a prayerful, worshipful spirit. They find self-aggrandizement, materialistic display, and personal comfort a distraction. It is a different focus altogether.

This is a matter of integrity. When someone makes a commitment to follow Christ, the question arises, What kind of life did Christ lead? The one who loves Christ experiences this as a matter of fidelity and commitment. Many find that serious tension arises in regard to their obedience to Christ and their life in the world. This issue can get complicated, especially when one has a family and when one serves an affluent parish. For the pastor, the bottom line is that affection for the things of this world impacts his or her effectiveness in leading people to God. The role of intercessor gets blurred and confused when one's priorities are unclear.

Contemporary American culture can be fairly characterized as sensate, hedonistic, secular, and godless. Sadly, the church and church leadership have made peace with this materialistic emphasis. We have mimicked the corporate culture and the consumer ethos with a blind servitude, and we have behaved in ways alien to the spirit of our Lord Christ. We look more like disciples of Charles Darwin than of Jesus of Nazareth. The price we have paid for this error as ministers is that when we invite others to join us in search of God, too often they have trouble taking us seriously because they have not recognized in us a hunger and a thirst for God. They see us, rather, succumbing to an easy conformity—emulating a greedy, narcissistic, hedonistic culture and its idolatrous lifestyle.

The role of intercessor awaits candidates who understand its urgency and who are willing to make the necessary commitment.

Because true intercessors are so rare, every one of us can name on one hand those few persons in a lifetime who have helped us to find the path to God. Most of them lived in relative obscurity but were well known to those whose lives they touched. Many of us would gladly trade the perfunctory and superficial plaudits that we have proudly collected in exchange for a few names of those who would testify that they found their way to God through our ministry.

This impediment to real intercession runs even deeper. America's economic and military powers are a source of serious spiritual crisis for all of us. Our high standard of living and our national chauvinism amount to a kind of idolatry that inhibits our quest for a closer relationship to God. Even if we had a new reformation in the churches, the spirit and ethos of our nation are tilted toward secularism. All of this makes the task of the intercessor one of even more serious discipline and intentionality. These impediments and hindrances notwithstanding, it is the work of God, and in it we are not alone.

This brings us to the heart of the matter: God calls us pastors to guard our ministries with zealous care and to be certain that we surrender ourselves to Christ with a devotion that will cause others to copy us as we copy Christ, thus finding their way into the presence of God. In this surrender we offset those impediments that are so subtle and pervasive.

Proclaiming a New Life

Our preaching, our counseling, and our teaching present opportunities to proclaim that the anguish, the alienation, and the deep frustrations that follow us daily are due largely to our detachment from God. Cut off from the source, we wither like cut flowers. Perhaps the most creative aspect of the work of the pastor is to convince those afar off that what they want most out of life can be found, only and sufficiently, in their surrender to God in Christ. Jesus came to fill life with meaning and purpose, joy and satisfaction. Somehow the idea prevails that following Christ amounts to nothing but painful denial. Following Christ does include denial of self and sin, but it also includes the fulfillment found in a new life of creative service and rich fellowship.

I learned a significant lesson during my brief tour as associate director of the Peace Corps. We set high standards for volunteers, but to our surprise we could have filled all of our available positions with volunteers from Los Angeles and New York alone. The finest college graduates in the country wanted a chance to engage in hard work on another continent in a developing country without modern conveniences among persons of another culture, sharing the local fare with mostly poor and illiterate people, for a salary of fifty dollars a month! They found the challenge so fulfilling that when their two-year tour ended, they had to be forced to return home. In this experience I saw many of Christ's teachings fulfilled. When we give freely, we receive freely. When we seek to save our own lives, we lose them; but when we lose our lives for Christ's sake, we truly find them.

Interceding and seeking to lead persons into a right relationship with God admits no secondary agenda, such as swelling the church roster, recruiting another tither, saving a marriage, finding a new youth leader, or proving our skills in evangelism. The only appropriate motivation is being obedient to our calling and helping any and every person near us to know the love of God and the blessing of living in God's favor and fellowship. This is all the reward we seek. The persons we lead to God in Christ need to know that the enrichment of one's spiritual life—a closer walk with God—has all sorts of corollary benefits.

Living estranged from God, cut off from the strength and direction that the life of faith provides, we risk all kinds of misdirection and shallow resources. We become directed by the culture, making it on our nerves and our glands, making it on the customs and the habits we inherit from others. But God designed us. God created us. God cares about our destiny, and when we try to live without God, we deny ourselves the strength and support available from God. This is what the intercessor yearns to communicate.

Lacking the support and nurture that faith in God provides, no one's life functions at its best. Many are struggling with careers that do not match their interests or abilities. Since one's occupation is such an important aspect of life, choosing a suitable career is vital. A career chosen solely on the basis of money or location or prevailing market conditions, in the absence of any larger personal commitment, can lead to years of unhappiness and can spoil every aspect of life. But when one chooses to invest time, talent, and commitment in response to a need, where one senses a stewardship, where one can connect his or her daily chores to the larger purposes of God in the world, every day at work is a gift of God. Someone who has to work at a job for the income can still defer his or her real vocation to evening hours and weekends. Even then the fulfillment that comes from doing what one feels called to do, if only part-time, becomes a blessing.

Marriage is an important part of life, and when the intercessor succeeds in bringing engaged couples to God before they marry, they are able to prepare for the kind of understanding, forgiveness, patience, caring, and selfless support that makes marriage more than a forced contract or a tired friendship. It becomes a dynamic relationship that grows richer and more fulfilling with each passing year.

A new life with God reflects itself in our careers and in the close relationships of family life in dramatic ways. The intercessor does use such blessings as an enticement. Knowing God is an end in itself, but there are benefits, the most observable of which is the strength to endure life's vicissitudes and vagaries without falling apart.

Without God in our lives we do all sorts of strange things to seek ballast and stability. Some simply drop their identity entirely, becoming a mere reflection of what is going on, chasing every lifestyle, fashion, or indulgence that bids for a following. Another loses his or her personhood and becomes a montage of the many samples of wasteful living on display. Any intercessor who saves a life from such confusion by bringing it to God is an honor to God. What results from such wasteful living is often a loss of self-esteem, an abandonment of pride, indulgence in promiscuous, recreational sex, abuse of narcotics, and sometimes criminal activities. But a life with God, mercifully, moves in another direction. One who knows God avoids such spiritual suicide and "rises up with wings as eagles, runs without growing weary, and walks without fainting."

Proclaiming God's Initiative

Looking further into the pastor's service as intercessor, we find the very special privilege of proclaiming constantly, in an unbroken and joyful refrain, what God has already done in Christ to make clear how the initiative has already been taken and the invitation is extended perpetually. This is the crux of our faith, that the same God—who gave us the big brain; who put speed in the legs of the cheetah and music in the throat of the lark; who made a world out of nothing and set the movement of the moon and the stars in their courses; who equipped us to reason, to rhyme, and to reproduce; who fixed the laws of physics, music, medicine, and morality in immutable regularity; who tuned our hearts for love and praise and celebration—in the fullness of time, took on a robe of flesh and entered time in the little town of Bethlehem, shared our human limitations, grew up in a carpenter's house, was baptized in the Jordan, was tempted forty days in the desert, and for three years went about doing good—healing the sick, cleansing lepers, and calling sinners to repentance. For our sake he shed the love of God abroad by submitting to a cruel death on a Roman cross. And God has given him a name above all names, and it is in that name that we are invited to come out of our sin and separation and be received into the presence of God. And then sing with William Cowper:

> The dearest idol I have known,
> Whate'er that idol be,
> Help me to tear it from Thy throne,
> And worship only Thee.
> Return, O holy Dove, return,
> Sweet messenger of rest;
> I hate the sins that made Thee mourn,
> And drove Thee from my breast.
> O for a closer walk with God,
> Calm and heavenly frame,
> A light to shine upon the road
> That leads me to the Lamb.

All of this is the work of the intercessor, who finds us tangled in all of the thickets of confusion, mired in the muck of sin and guilt, and hiding in the shadows of shame. He goes before us and leads us into newness of life. Have mercy!

Much of our preaching has to do with concerns of the moment, with people trying to cope with the daily grind of life, with responding to a local crisis and putting some kind of a face on the evening news. We are compelled to be current, just as Isaiah, Amos, and Micah dealt with the news of their day. Jeremiah went to jail for being relevant. It is the pastor's job. We are called upon also to keep up with the seasonal festivals and celebrations that call us all away from life's tedium.

Before life is over, however, we have to stand before the big picture and point out the details to those who come to us only in spaced intervals, mostly at funerals. We are the ones who interrupt vacation planning, shopping for new cars, preparing for weddings, campaigning for a friend's election, visiting children at college, rushing to the mall, the market, the dentist, or the beautician. And somehow in all of this the echo of the voice of pastor resounds in a solemn refrain:

> LORD, thou hast been our dwelling place in all generations.
> Before the mountains were brought forth, or ever thou hadst formed the earth and the world, even from everlasting to everlasting, thou art God. (Psalm 90:1-2 KJV)

This may seem like an interruption, but it is a part of the ongoing agenda of life from beginning to end. The reality of God, as well as the reality of our standing in God's sight, is the most profound issue of life. We are physical beings, but we are equipped for a spiritual transformation whereby this old Adam becomes a new creation, and we are given a rebirth. Our transformed spiritual nature becomes our new definition. We are all candidates for this second birth, and this is the main work of the pastor. While we may succeed at interpreting the details of the horizontal dimension of life, we have not finished until we have dealt with that vertical dimension, our personal relationship to God, and have worked as an intercessor, bringing persons into an awareness of their true destiny.

There is a temptation for pastors to compete with other professionals. "Merely" being a pastor does not bring great social prestige, for it too often implies intellectual dullness. This is partly due to the fact that pastors are paid so little. Licensure for the pastorate is not subjected to the same degree of scrutiny imposed on other professionals. The state examines and licenses plumbers, dentists, beauticians, embalmers, pharmacists, nurses, opticians, architects, and manicurists, but pastors are sent forth on their own word and the approval of their church, locally or through its hierarchy. This exemption that the state grants to the clergy causes some pastors to feel denigrated, diminished, and degraded.

It remains, therefore, for the pastor to recognize the significance of the task left to the intercessor. Beyond commenting on the news, feeding the hungry, giving shelter to the homeless, fighting racism and bigotry, raising money for scholarships, building new housing with public grants, helping to get students into college and innocent people out of jail, praying for the sick and burying the dead, marrying young lovers and baptizing their offspring—the task left to the intercessor is to find the stone that the builders rejected, the cornerstone, God's love for us all so that a way has been provided for us to transcend the travail of life and to discover the balm of Gilead, the saving power of Christ, and eternal fellowship with God.

Matters of the Spirit

. . . The intercessor believes that Christ will always lead us to eternal fellowship with God, and the intercessor pursues his or her faith in God's unseen hand in human affairs with the same confidence of the astronaut, the scientist, and the sea captain charting a way over the vast expanse of the deep.

The pastor stands alone, different from the politician, the social worker, the entrepreneur, the engineer, the physician, and the jurist. All of these deal with a segment—a significant segment—of the human enterprise, but the pastor—alone—steps back from it all, examines it from God's perspective, and tries to give it all meaning, purpose, and direction. And he accomplishes this without physical power or civil authority. The pastor has only the power of example, the power of trust, the power of respect, and the power of the love of God shed abroad in Jesus Christ.

It is amazing, therefore, that for all of these generations, in spite of the failure, the apostasy, the impediments, and the inertia, faithful pastors have been effective intercessors. Without public recognition or awareness, they shine as the stars in the night. They have brought many to righteousness.

Samuel D. Proctor and Gardner C. Taylor, with Gary V. Simpson, *We Have This Ministry: The Heart of the Pastor's Vocation* **(Valley Forge, Pa.: Judson Press, 1966), pp. 31-50.**

CHAPTER EIGHT

The Pastor as Teacher

In the pressurized, heated environment that was twentieth-century Mississippi, some good souls were crushed, others were made into tough, courageous witnesses. Martyrs and saints. Will Campbell grew up poor in Mississippi, poor and Baptist. In these selections from his classic Brother to a Dragonfly, *Campbell first tells of his "plunge into the preaching world" at age sixteen, holding in his hand the large Bible that had been given to East Fork Baptist Church by the Ku Klux Klan and bearing the Klan's insignia. While stationed with the army on an island in the Pacific, he read Howard Fast's* Freedom Road, *and Campbell's eyes were opened not only to the evil of Southern racism but also to the connection between Southern racism and the oppression of poor whites in the South. He went on to graduate from Yale Divinity School and returned to his native state as a chaplain at Old Miss, a self-described "missioner to the Confederacy, bridge between white and black."*

Of his many wonderful histories, novels, and political writings, his greatest is Brother to a Dragonfly. *Campbell tells his own history as a prophet of God's justice in the context of the tragic life of his brother Joe. Joe was a pharmacist and drug addict and, by the grace of God, Campbell's most severe and loving critic, critic of the church as well. In the second passage, Campbell describes how, the day he heard of the murder of Jonathan Daniel, brother Joe and friend P. D. East ganged up on him and "made a Christian out of me." During that fateful conversation, on that sad day, Campbell was slapped in the face with the radical significance of Christ's death on the cross, comprehended the dramatic, comprehensive, world-changing quality of Jesus' redemption of the world. Or, as Campbell puts it in his famous one-line definition of Christianity, "We are all bastards and God loves us anyway."*

Brother to a Dragonfly
Will D. Campbell

My plunge into the preaching world came suddenly and without much warning. The word had made the rounds that Dave was going to be a preacher. But there had never been anything formal about it. I had mastered the art of public praying and for the past two summers had impressed some of the more pious ones at revival meetings—Hebron, Glading, Thompson, and, of course, East Fork—with long and well-worded prayers which, they had said to one another and to relatives, sounded for the world like a preacher praying. "That boy can pray as sweet a prayer as you ever heard!" Our East Fork pastor, J. Price Brock, had taken an interest in me and would sometimes take me on his preaching circuit. The hour of preaching at each church was arranged to fit the convenience of the preacher. One at nine, another at eleven. Across the county line, thirty miles of dirt road away, still another church would meet at two in the afternoon. Then back to the last by seven that night. He introduced me to his congregations and began to insist that I read certain books. The first was a little handbook on personal timidity. He had noticed that I never talked to anyone on his church fields unless asked a question, would not go to the dinner table until specifically asked, did not shake hands unless the other's hand was offered first. He did not outright say that I had to overcome my shyness if I were going to be a successful preacher but I got the message. Such practical and social habits as that seemed more important than what I might believe about one theological point or another. Interesting that I should find the same thing true throughout years of theological training. The training was for success, not faithfulness to Christian orthodoxy. . . .

. . . Gladys Anderson I think, suggested that we should ask Brother Brock to let us have a youth day service at church. Based on that performance, everyone thought it would be a good idea. So in five minutes it was all planned. I would be pastor, Evie Lee would play the piano, Delton as song leader, and so on through the list of church functions including collecting the offering, a job reserved for the deacons.

The youth day was set for late June and until the day came I spent more time practicing my sermon than doing anything else. I continued to work in the field, but if plowing, the sermon outline was tacked on the rung between the two plow handles where I could preach to the rear end of the horse. And I did it with varying enthusiasm. At times I wished that I had never appeared behind that pulpit. But most of the time I felt that I could not wait until the day arrived. Daddy asked on more than one occasion if I would be ready, stating that he had rather I not plow another day than to fail in my first preaching endeavor. He also pointed out one night when we were having our daily Bible readings that my voice was not very strong. I told him of a preacher secret I had heard from Norma Jane, Brother Brock's wife. She had told me that when they were first married she had him drink a glass of pineapple juice before he went into the pulpit on Sunday morning. I had already planned to have a can of pineapple juice on hand that Sunday morning as part of my last minute preparations.

Joe would, of course, come home from the CCC Camp for the occasion. Grandpa Will Parker would be there for sure, Aunt Dolly and other kin from "across the river."

The sermon was called "In the Beginning." The Scripture reading was, appropriately, the first chapter of Genesis, or at least major portions of it. The sermon told of how this was a beginning for us, of how our class could be compared to the creation story. The majority of it dealt with the fact that the Biblical account said, "In the beginning God created the heavens and the earth . . ." and that the rest of the Bible had to do with earth and what happened there and not with heaven. I was a sixteen-year-old fundamentalist, but for some reason which I have never understood I had never taken much to preachments about other worlds—above or below. It was, in many ways, heretical and modernistic for East Fork. But on that occasion I could have denounced Christianity as a capitalistic myth cunningly designed to keep the masses under control, and our youth choir could have sung Ukrainian folk songs, and our Sunday School superintendent could have lectured on "The Origin of Species," and all the people would have said "Amen." Never had they been so proud of us. I chided the oldsters and chastised them lightly for being irregular at Sunday night services and this was the most appreciated part of all. It meant that Dave was not to be a preacher who would tolerate sin, and would denounce it no matter how unpopular it made him. (Somehow the pride of some of those in attendance that day went sour when the little preacher years later turned to denouncing social sins.)

Everyone in the graduating class had some part in the service. And we were all roundly hugged and congratulated and commended for having done so splendidly. Uncle Hilary, or "Uncle Fork" as we called him, Grandpa Campbell's half-brother, father of my buddy Thaxton, or "Snooky," and the one who was considered a drunk though he was in fact a moderate drinker, allowed to all standing around after the service that they should remember that day for they would be hearing much from the little preacher. Ray Turner, a great teacher in any age, simply whispered, "Plow deep," the R.F.D. version of "Right on." Aunt Ida, not really Aunt but sister to Aunt Donnie, wife of Uncle Fork, who lived with them and was considered rich because she lived on some kind of mysterious disability insurance policy, kissed me and cried. Joe made no comment but gave me the kind of look that told me he had been extremely proud of what I had done. For I had stood up, laid my dollar Ingram watch on the pulpit—an act which had nothing to do with when I began or stopped for it was all written down, a fact which brought the only criticism from one aunt, which Mamma dismissed as jealousy because one of her boys was not making a preacher—and said my piece. . . .

I was a full-fledged preacher, entitled to buy Coca-Colas at clergy discount.

* * *

Joe came to the door and called us in. "Brother, you know a Jonathan Daniel?" "Yea. Sure. I know Jon Daniel Why?" "Well, he's dead." Joe had heard a news bulletin but had no details. It was not hard to believe for I had been with Jonathan at a conference a few weeks earlier and knew what he was about

He was a student from the Episcopal Theological Seminary in Cambridge, Massachusetts who was involved in registering black citizens to vote in Lowndes County, Alabama. A few days earlier I had learned that Jon was in jail in that county along with a number of others. We waited to hear the national news which carried a detailed account.

Jonathan and Richard Morrisroe, a Roman Catholic priest from Chicago, had just been released from the Lowndes County jail in

Hayneville. Because of some confusion in a telephone conversation there was no one there to meet them when they, and twenty-five others, had been released. Jonathan, Richard, and two black students stopped at a small grocery store on the edge of the little town. Despite the fact that the majority of the woman's trade was black people, she became alarmed at their presence and called a special deputy named Thomas Coleman who arrived on the scene before the four could finish their cold drinks and leave. Armed with his own shotgun he fired as the four were leaving the premises, killing Jonathan instantly with the first shot, turning immediately upon Father Morrisroe, the pellets from the second shot leaving him mortally wounded on the gravel outside the little one-room, unpainted shack which was the store. The two young black women fled in terror and were unharmed. Coleman went to the telephone and called Colonel Al Lingo, Commissioner of Public Safety in Alabama and told him, "I've just shot two preachers. You better get on down here."

That was the news. That was all we knew. My young friend Jonathan Daniel was dead and his friend lay mortally wounded, listed in critical condition. I sat in stunned silence. Joe snapped the television off and came over and kissed me on the head. "I'm sorry, Brother." P. D. said nothing.

I made some phone calls to get more details and to see if there was something we should be doing. Joe and P. D. sat in a silent room, mourning with me over the death of a friend, saying little, forgetting to turn the lights on when darkness came. When I re-entered the room they were speaking in whispers, like people do in a funeral parlor when there is a casket in the room. I could see them outlined against the street light which cast a beam through a crack in the venetian blind, reflecting itself in a huge mirror and returning across the room to bring form to these two big men sitting facing each other as if playing chess. P. D. spoke first. "Well, Brother, what you reckon your friend Mr. Jesus thinks of all this?" I allowed that I guessed he was pretty sad about it. He stood up and turned an overhead light on, went to the kitchen and came back with some beer and cheese. He spoke again as his hulking frame sank into a bigger chair. "Brother, what about that definition of Christianity you gave me that time? Let's see if it can pass the test."

Years before, when P. D. had his paper going, he liked to argue about religion. Most of it was satire, but I would often take it upon myself to set him straight on one theological point or another. He had long since deserted and disavowed the Methodist Church of his foster parents, had tried being a Unitarian and had taken instruction from the local rabbi and was considering declaring himself a Jew. He referred to the Church as "the Easter chicken." Each time I saw him he would ask, "And what's the state of the Easter chicken, Preacher Will?" I knew he was trying to goad me into some kind of an argument and decided to wait him out. One day he explained.

"You know, Preacher Will, that Church of yours and Mr. Jesus is like an Easter chicken my little Karen got one time. Man, it was a pretty thing. Dyed a deep purple. Bought it at the grocery store."

I interrupted that *white* was the liturgical color for Easter but he ignored me. "And it served a real useful purpose. Karen loved it. It made her happy. And that made me and her Mamma happy. Okay?"

I said, "Okay."

"But pretty soon that baby chicken started feathering out. You know, sprouting little pin feathers. Wings and tail and all that. And you know what? Them new feathers weren't purple. No sirree bob, that damn chicken wasn't really purple at all. That damn chicken was a Rhode Island Red. And when all them little red feathers started growing out from under that purple it was one hell of a sight. All of a sudden Karen couldn't stand that chicken any more."

"I think I see what you're driving at, P. D."

"No, hell no, Preacher Will. You don't understand any such thing for I haven't got to my point yet."

"Okay. I'm sorry. Rave on."

"Well, we took that half-purple and half-red thing out to her Grandma's house and threw it in the chicken yard with all the other chickens. It was still different, you understand. That little chicken. And the other chickens knew it was different. And they resisted it like hell. Pecked it, chased it all over the yard. Wouldn't have anything to do with it. Wouldn't even let it get on the roost with them. And that little chicken knew it was different too. It didn't bother any of the others. Wouldn't fight back or anything. Just stayed by itself. Really suffered too. But little by little, day by day, that chicken came around. Pretty soon, even before all the purple grew off it, while it was still just a little bit different, that damn thing was behaving just about like the rest of them chickens. Man, it would fight back, peck the hell out of the ones littler than it was, knock them down to catch a bug if it got to it in time. Yes sirree bob, the chicken world turned that Easter chicken around. And now you can't tell one chicken from another. They're all just alike. The Easter chicken is just one more chicken. There ain't a damn thing different about it."

I knew he wanted to argue and I didn't want to disappoint him.

"Well, P. D., the Easter chicken is still useful. It lays eggs, doesn't it?"

It was what he wanted me to say. "Yea, Preacher Will. It lays eggs. But they all lay eggs. Who needs an Easter chicken for that? And the Rotary Club serves coffee. And the 4-H Club says prayers. The Red Cross takes up offerings for hurricane victims. Mental Health does counseling, and the Boy Scouts have youth programs."

I told him I agreed and that it had been a long time since I would not have agreed but that that didn't have anything to do with the Christian Faith. He looked a little hurt and that was when he asked me to define the Christian Faith. But he had a way of pushing one for simple answers. "Just tell me what this Jesus cat is all about. I'm not too bright but maybe I can get the hang of it." The nearest I ever came to giving him a satisfactory answer was once when I blasted him for some childish "can God make a rock so big He couldn't pick it up" criticism of the Faith. He blasted right back. "Okay. If you would tell me what the hell the Christian Faith is all about maybe I wouldn't make an ass of myself when I'm talking about it. Keep it simple. In ten words or less, what's the Christian message?" We were going someplace, or coming back from someplace when he said, "Let me have it. Ten words." I said, "We're all bastards but God loves us anyway." He swung his car off on the shoulder and stopped, asking me to say it again. I repeated: "We're all bastards but God loves us anyway." He didn't comment on what he thought about the summary except to say, after he had counted the number of words on his fingers, "I gave you a ten word limit. If you want to try again you have two words left." I didn't try again but he often reminded me of what I had said that day.

Now, sitting in the presence of two of the most troubled men I have ever known, I was about to receive the most enlightening theological lesson I had ever had in my life. Not Louisiana College, Tulane, Wake Forest, or Yale Divinity School. But sitting here in a heavily mortgaged house in Fairhope, Alabama. P. D. East and Joseph Lee Campbell, as teachers. And I as pupil.

"Yea, Brother. Let's see if your definition of the Faith can stand the test." My calls had been to the Department of Justice, to the American Civil Liberties Union, and to a lawyer friend in Nashville. I had talked of the death of my friend as being a travesty of justice, as a complete breakdown of law and order, as a violation of Federal and State law. I had used words like redneck, backwoods, woolhat, cracker, Kluxer, ignoramus and many others. I had studied sociology, psychology, and social ethics and was speaking and thinking in those concepts. I had also studied New Testament theology.

P. D. stalked me like a tiger. "Come on, Brother. Let's talk about your definition." At one point Joe turned on him, "Lay off, P. D. Can't you see when somebody is upset?" But P. D. waved him off, loving me too much to leave me alone.

"Was Jonathan a bastard?"

I said I was sure that everyone is a sinner in one way or another but that he was one of the sweetest and most gentle guys I had ever known.

"But was he a bastard?" His tone was almost a scream. "Now that's your word. Not mine. You told me one time that everybody is a bastard. That's a pretty tough word. I know. Cause I *am* a bastard. A born bastard. A real bastard. My Mamma wasn't married to my Daddy. Now, by god, you tell me, right now, yes or no and not maybe, was Jonathan Daniel a bastard?"

I knew that if I said no he would leave me alone and if I said yes he wouldn't. And I knew my definition would be blown if I said no.

So I said, "Yes."

"All right. Is Thomas Coleman a bastard?"

That one was a lot easier. "Yes. Thomas Coleman is a bastard."

"Okay. Let me get this straight now. I don't want to misquote you. Jonathan Daniels *was* a bastard. Thomas Coleman *is* a bastard. Right?" Joe the Protector was on his feet.

"Goddammit, P. D. that's a sacrilege. Knock it off! Get off the kid's back."

P. D. ignored him, pulling his chair closer to mine, placing his huge, bony hand on my knee. "Which one of these two bastards do you think God loves the most?" His voice now was almost a whisper as he leaned forward, staring me directly in the eyes.

I made some feeble attempt to talk about God loving the sinner and not the sin, about judgment, justice, and brotherhood of all humanity. But P. D. shook his hands in a manner of cancellation. He didn't want to hear about that.

"You're trying to complicate it. Now you're the one always told me about how simple it was. Just answer the question." His direct examination would have done credit to Clarence Darrow.

He leaned his face closer to mine, patting first his own knee and then mine, holding the other hand aloft in oath-taking fashion.

"Which one of these two bastards does God love the most? Does he love that little dead bastard Jonathan the most? Or does He love that living bastard Thomas the most?"

Suddenly everything became clear. Everything. It was a revelation. The glow of the malt which we were well into by then seemed to illuminate and intensify it. I walked across the room and opened the blind, staring directly into the glare of the street light. And I began to whimper. But the crying was interspersed with laughter. It was a strange experience. I remember trying to sort out the sadness and the joy. Just what was I crying for and what was I laughing for? Then this too became clear.

I was laughing at myself, at twenty years of a ministry which had become, without my realizing it, a ministry of liberal sophistication. An attempted negation of Jesus, of human engineering, of riding the coattails of Caesar, of playing on his ballpark, by his rules and with his ball, of looking to government to make and verify and authenticate our morality, of worshiping at the shrine of enlightenment and academia, of making an idol of the Supreme Court, a theology of law and order and of denying not only the Faith I professed to hold but my history and my people—the Thomas Colemans. Loved. And if loved, forgiven. And if forgiven, reconciled. Yet sitting then in his own jail cell, the blood of two of his and my brothers on his hands. The thought gave me a shaking chill in a non-air-conditioned room in August. I had never considered myself a liberal. I didn't think in those terms. But that was the camp in which I had pitched my tent. Now I was not so sure.

Joe and P. D. came and stood beside me, Joe pulling me to him in sympathetic embrace, P.D. handing me his half-emptied beer. I closed the blind and sat down, taking a sip of the beer and passing it back to P. D. who in turn sipped and passed it on to Joe. And we passed it round and round until it was gone.

The lesson was over. Class dismissed. But I had one thing I must say to the teacher.

"P. D.?"

"Yea, Brother?"

"I've got to amend the definition."

"Okay, Brother. Go ahead. You know you always had them two words left."

"We're all bastards but you've got to be the biggest bastard of us all."

"How's that, Brother?"

"Because, damned if you ain't made a Christian out of me. And I'm not sure I can stand it."

P. D. thought that was just about the funniest thing he had ever heard.

Our three-man wake for Jonathan and mourning for Thomas (funny that these should be their names—Jonathan, lover of David; Thomas, dubious of resurrection) continued, and between trips to refrigerator and bathroom my learning continued as we talked of history, civil rights and Gospel.

At one point Joe asked what we thought the court would do with Thomas Coleman since he had already pleaded guilty, had admitted that he had killed Jonathan and mortally wounded Richard. We all agreed that he would be released, that the climate of fear was such in Alabama at the time that no white jury would convict a man for killing a Yankee agitator.

Now P. D. wanted to argue with the conversion he had led me to. I tried to point out the parallel between the Alabama Court and God. Joe was only listening, and P. D. wasn't buying.

"Look, you stupid idiot. We agree that they're *gonna* turn him loose. But that ain't the same as saying they *ought* to turn him loose.

They ought to fry the son of a bitch. You know that! He *killed* a man. A good man."

I agreed that the notion that a man could go to a store where a group of unarmed human beings are drinking soda pop and eating moon pies, fire a shotgun blast at one of them, tearing his lungs and heart and bowels from his body, turn on another and send lead pellets ripping through his flesh and bones, and that God would set him free is almost more than I could stand. But unless that is precisely the case then there is no Gospel, there is no Good News. Unless that is the truth we have only bad news, we are back with law alone.

P. D. saw that as sheer lunacy. And said so with considerable embellishment. Then, turning to Joe, he sighed, "Brother Will wants to play church! Come on, gang. Let's play church!" He motioned Joe to a chair, pulling another up beside him, folding his hands to a position of prayer. "Brother Will is the preacher. Me and you is the congregation."

I decided to play church and began to preach. "Here's all I'm trying to say, Brothers. I'm trying to say what you brought me suddenly to see with two questions. When Thomas killed Jonathan he committed a crime against the State. When Thomas killed Jonathan he committed a crime against God. The strange, the near maddening thing about this case, is that both these offended parties have rendered the same verdict—not for the same reasons, not in the same way, but the verdict is the same—acquittal."

"Shit, Will, you're saying George Wallace is God Almighty. And George Wallace wouldn't even make a good Devil." Joe kicked his foot, missing, then kicking again. "You don't interrupt the preacher, fool. And you don't say 'shit' in church!"

"No. George Wallace frees him to go and kill again. The other liberates him to obedience to Christ. Acquittal by law is the act of Caesar. Render unto him what is his. The State, by its very nature and definition, can do anything it wills to do—Hitler must have proved at least that much. Acquittal by resurrection takes us back to our little definition of the Faith. And takes us into a freedom where it would never occur to us to kill somebody."

The teacher wasn't having the lesson now. "Brother, you're just as crazy as hell! There are a bunch of lunatics out there, absolute madmen! Killers! Hell, maybe you'll be next. Or even worse, maybe *I'll* be next. Mad men have to be restrained! I say, fry the son of a bitch."

"Okay. You say they have to be restrained. Let's talk about that. The truth is, law is not restraining them. If law is for the purpose of preventing crime every wail of a siren calls out its failure. Every civil rights demonstration attests to the courts' inability to provide racial justice. Every police chief who asks for a larger appropriation because of the rising crime rate is admitting his own failure. Every time a law has to be *enforced* it is a failure.

"Sure. The Thomas Colemans must be restrained. Exactly. Then where is the fruit? When *will* he be restrained? Certainly not by legislation and court decisions. Of those we have plenty. And in the legislative and court decisions he watches a truce being signed between his two traditional enemies, black leaders and the Federal government. And that, no doubt, is necessary. But meanwhile, the rejections continue, the killings go on, the hostilities mount and intensify to be set loose wholesale yet again on another day.

"If you want to argue, P. D., on what will work and what won't work then let's put it there. I'll go to the mat with you on that."

Joe sat tight on the chair P. D. had assigned him, clutching the rungs of the seat, staring straight at the designated preacher. P. D. did not move.

We were moving into territory familiar to both of them. Joe stood up and yawned. "I've seen this movie, Brothers. I know about law. I've been divorced." P. D. leaned backward in his chair, burped as discreetly as he could and whispered, "Brothers, we're getting a little bit tight."

Conversion is at once a joyous and painful experience. If it was not the beginning of my ministry it was certainly a turning point. And it was certainly the most significant training I had received since we sat at our father's fireside and listened to him read the Bible every night.

And it was a personal lesson as well. For being pushed by P. D. East, in the presence of Joe, to see Thomas Coleman, murderer of my friend, in the light of the Gospel turned me back to where I had once been, years before, a path from which I had strayed. It was the beginning of a process—the process of coming to terms with one's own history, whatever that history might be.

I, like many another Southern liberal, had tried to deny that history, to flee from it, to so insulate myself from it in learning and action and sophistication that it would appear never to have existed. I had become a doctrinaire social activist, without consciously choosing to be. And I would continue to be some kind of a social activist. But there was a decided difference. Because from that point on I came to understand the nature of tragedy. And one who understands the nature of tragedy can never take sides. And I had taken sides. Many of us who were interested in racial justice had taken sides and there were good reasons in history for doing what we did. We who left home, or were pushed from home when Mamma or Daddy couldn't understand, were just a little bit prideful of our alienation from them, and a little bit arrogant in our newfound liberation and assumed sophistication. We justified it in terms of the suffering, the injustices, the blatant hostilities and economic deprivations black people had had heaped upon them. There was drama and romance in the Civil Rights Movement and we who had no home at home sought that home in the black cause. Because we did not understand the nature of tragedy we learned the latest woolhat jokes, learned to cuss Mississippi and Alabama sheriffs, learned to say "redneck" with the same venomous tones we had heard others, or ourselves, say "nigger." We did not understand that those we so vulgarly called "redneck" were a part of the tragedy. They had been victimized one step beyond the black. They had had their head taken away by cunning, skillful and well-educated gentlemen and ladies of the gentry. And so we, my people and Joe's and P. D.'s, picked the wrong enemy. We were right in aligning ourselves with the black sufferer. But we were wrong in not directing some of our patience and energy and action to a group which also had a history. A history of slavery. The redneck's slavery, called indentured servanthood, was somewhat, but only somewhat unlike that of black slaves. He was told that if he would serve the master for five years, or seven years, he would then be free in a new and prosperous and promising land in a new world. But freedom to what, and in what? Freedom to flounder, to drift, to wander west in search of what had been promised but never delivered. Freedom to compete in the wilderness with wealthy landholders, with black labor, to fight a war to defend that system as well as his own peonage, to come back home and watch the aristocrat as he tried to meet the basic needs of those he had formerly owned and the handouts of the Freemen's Bureau to those declared free but still valuable as working property, while he had no assistance at all. No wonder that he had to find a Jonah. And no wonder, as he strived to match the cultural and economic status of the aristocrat he became a living denial of his own servanthood, teaching his grandchildren that his fathers landed at Plymouth Rock. And no wonder that such deception resulted in the paranoia, the hostilities, bigotries and prejudices which he had harbored over the years. It was all in the libretto and scenario.

I thought of those things as I thought of Thomas Coleman, and as I reviewed my ministry and considered my conversion.

My ministry had become one of law, not of grace. While I had tried to keep in mind all along that the central theme of the triumph of grace over law was clear in the New Testament, I had come to act as if I didn't believe it. I knew that while St. Paul stopped short of a rigid antinomian position, a complete disregard for law, he did make it clear that to abide *in* grace was more radical than to abide *by* law. And such law as he did emphasize was not law in the sense of entreaties of the State to make us behave, but an ethos, a condition of being, *In Christ*. I had not quite accepted that freedom before, marching instead under the banner and umbrella of social science and legislation, Caesar and politics, a litigious gospel which is no gospel at all.

I moved to sit facing P. D. as Joe had sat earlier. The beams of light shining between the slats of the Venetian blinds seemed somehow brighter than before.

"Where's Brother?"

It could have been either of us who asked. Then we heard the sounds, sounds meant to be whispers, through the plastered walls. Joe was confessing his misdeeds to Josephine and asking if he could come home. We knew they would soon be back together.

Five years after our theological evening, on New Year's Day, P. D. died of an acute liver ailment. His fourth bride, whom he had married as a nineteen-year-old Wellesley sophomore and whom he said he loved more than any woman he had ever known, called to tell me. "But as you know," she added, "P. D. was not much on religion and funerals and all that, so there will be no service."

But there was. On the final page of his autobiography, *The Magnolia Jungle,* he had suggested some words he hoped Easton King, Clarence Jordan, or I would see fit to say:

> These are the remains of P. D. East. He had a heart and he had a hatchet. They were both the same size. One could hardly determine the difference between the two. He lived and died confused and frustrated. He did not know where he came from, nor did he know why. And for years he worried about it. Finally, one day he stopped worrying about it. He realized that where he came from and who he was mattered little. He realized that what he was and where he was going did matter. And that was all he knew. It was about all he cared to know. His beloved Magnolia Jungle needed a path. It needed a clearing so that all of us could look up and see the light of the sky—the face of God. Let it be said of P. D. East: with his heart and his hachet he hacked like hell!

Easton was dead. So was Clarence Jordan. So John Howard Griffin and I, along with a mutual friend at Koinonia Farm, did the funeral on a telephone conference call. It was a fitting memorial for a man who took delight in being a pagan, befriended my brother when no one else would, and led me to the Lord.

Will D. Campbell, *Brother to a Dragonfly* (New York: Continuum International Publishing Group, Inc., 2000), pp. 75-78, 217-28.

He had a voice, a distinctive voice, and for more than half a century it thundered forth, first from his city pastorate in Detroit at Bethel Evangelical Church from 1915 to 1928, then as Professor of Applied Christianity at Union Theological Seminary in New York until his retirement in 1960. His aim was to expound a "vital prophetic Christianity," which he defended and practiced as a critique of American social and political institutions from the standpoint of "Christian realism."

But before becoming perhaps American Protestant Christianity's most influential social ethicist, Reinhold Niebuhr was a pastor of a German-American congregation in the shadow of Henry Ford's smokestacks in Detroit. His candid, typically visceral and earnest thoughts on his first days in the pastorate were later published as Leaves From the Notebook of a Tamed Cynic. *Although not as intellectually renowned as his 1939 Gifford Lectures,* The Nature and Destiny of Man, *this pastoral diary may prove to be Niebuhr's most enduring contribution to the church. Today, much of his social ethics sounds dated, peculiarly lacking in theological content, mostly mid-twentieth-century anthropology with only a thin Christian veneer. But nearly a century later,* Leaves From the Notebook of a Tamed Cynic *still resonates with the trials and tribulations of the idealistic young pastor, still delights with its honest reflections upon what it is like to be a pastor enmeshed in the lives of God's people who are called to be an outpost of the kingdom of God in the middle of a conflicted and fallen, though still beloved and being redeemed creation.*

Niebuhr tells us that in 1920, he laid aside some of the intellectual, that is, theological, problems that had troubled him in seminary and instead found delight in consideration of the practical "ethical problems" that he encountered in his parish. This focus upon the ethical, the political, and the practical rather than the theological typified Niebuhr's special contribution to North American Christianity and, for good or ill, tended to set the tone for generations of Niebuhr's pastoral heirs.

Leaves From the Notebook of a Tamed Cynic
Reinhold Niebuhr

1920

I am really beginning to like the ministry. I think since I have stopped worrying so much about the intellectual problems of religion and have begun to explore some of its ethical problems there is more of a thrill in preaching. The real meaning of the gospel is in conflict with most of the customs and attitudes of our day at so many places that there is adventure in the Christian message, even if you only play around with its ideas in a conventional world. I can't say that I have done anything in my life to dramatize the conflict between the gospel and the world. But I find it increasingly interesting to set the two in juxtaposition at least in my mind and in the minds of others. And of course ideas may finally lead to action.

A young woman came to me the other day in—and told me that my talk on forgiveness in the C_____ Church of that town several months ago has brought about a reconciliation between her mother and sister after the two had been in a feud for five years. I accepted the news with more outward than inward composure. There is redemptive power in the message! I could go on the new courage that came out of that little victory for many a month.

I think I am beginning to like the ministry also because it gives you a splendid opportunity to have all kinds of contacts with people in relationships in which they are at their best. You do get tired of human pettiness at times. But there is nevertheless something quite glorious about folks. That is particularly true when you find them bearing sorrow with real patience. Think of Mrs. ____ putting up with that drunkard of a husband for the sake of her children— and having such nice children. One can learn more from her quiet courage than from many a book. . . .

1922

Just received a pitiful letter from a young pastor who is losing his church because he has been "too liberal." I suppose there are churches which will crucify a leader who tries to lead them into the modern world of thought and life. Yet here I have been all these years in a conservative communion and have never had a squabble about theology. I suppose that is partly due to the fact that there were so few people here when I came that no one had to listen to me if he didn't like my approach. Those who have come have associated themselves with us because they were in general agreement with "our gospel." They have come, however, from conservative communions and churches. But of course they have been mostly young people.

If preachers get into trouble in pursuance of their task of reinterpreting religious affirmations in the light of modern knowledge I think it must be partly because they beat their drums too loudly when they make their retreats from untenable positions of ancient orthodoxy. The correct strategy is to advance at the center with beating drums and let your retreats at the wings follow as a matter of course and in the interest of the central strategy. You must be honest, of course, but you might just as well straighten and shorten your lines without mock heroics and a fanfare of trumpets.

The beauty of this strategy is that there is enough power at the center for a real advance and enough opposition for a real conflict. If you set the message of a gospel of love against a society enmeshed in hatreds and bigotries and engulfed in greed, you have a real but not necessarily a futile conflict on your hands. There is enough natural grace in the human heart to respond to the challenge of the real message in the gospel—and enough original sin in human nature to create opposition to it. The sorriest preachers are those who preach a conventional morality while they try to be intellectually and theologically radical.

Men will not make great intellectual readjustments for a gospel which does not greatly matter. If there is real adventure at the center of the line the reserves are drawn from the wings almost unconsciously. . . .

1924

I am not surprised that most prophets are itinerants. Critics of the church think we preachers are afraid to tell the truth because we are economically dependent upon the people of our church. There is something in that, but it does not quite get to the root of the matter. I certainly could easily enough get more money than I am securing now, and yet I catch myself weighing my words and gauging their possible effect upon this and that person. I think the real clue to the tameness of a preacher is the difficulty one finds in telling unpleasant truths to people whom one has learned to love.

To speak the truth in love is a difficult, and sometimes an almost impossible, achievement. If you speak the truth unqualifiedly, that is usually because your ire has been aroused or because you have no personal attachment to the object of your strictures. Once personal contact is established you are very prone to temper your wind to the shorn sheep. It is certainly difficult to be human and honest at the same time. I'm not surprised that most budding prophets are tamed in time to become harmless parish priests.

At that, I do not know what business I have carping at the good people who are doing the world's work and who are inevitably enmeshed to a greater or less degree in the iniquities of society. Conscience, Goethe has observed, belongs to the observer rather than the doer, and it would be well for every preacher to realize that he is morally sensitive partly because he is observing and not acting. What is satisfying about the ministry is to note how far you can go in unfolding the full meaning of the Christian gospel provided you don't present it with the implication that you have attained and are now laying it as an obligation upon others.

If the Christian adventure is made a mutual search for truth in which the preacher is merely a leader among many searchers and is conscious of the same difficulties in his own experience which he notes in others, I do not see why he cannot be a prophet being forced into itinerancy. . . .

1924

Arrived in ____ today and spoke this noon to a group of liberal people. The meeting was arranged by the secretary of the Y.W.C.A. I poked fun at them a little for enjoying their theological liberalism so much in this part of the country, while they were afraid of even the mildest economic and political heresy. Of course that didn't quite apply to the people at the table, but it does apply to this whole section. There is no one quite so ridiculous as a preacher who prides himself upon his theological radicalism in a city where the theological battle was won a generation ago, while he meanwhile speaks his convictions on matters of economics only in anxious whispers.

I was asked to visit ____ (leading preacher) and see whether I could not interest him in our organization. He was an interesting study. He told me of his important connections in the city, of his tremendous church program, of the way he had increased the budget of his church, of his building plans, of the necessity "of fighting on one front at a time," of his theological battles; and he ended by declining to join the liberal group which sought his aid.

He thought it would not be advisable, considering his heavy responsibilities, to imperil the many great "causes" to which he was devoting his life by identifying himself with a radical movement. I didn't mind his cowardice so much, though he tried to hide it, as his vanity, which he took no pains to hide. I could just see him cavorting weekly before his crowd of doting admirers.

Obviously one of his chief difficulties is that he is good looking. A minister has enough temptations to vanity without bearing the moral hazard of a handsome face. If this young fellow had only been half as homely as old Dr. Gordon he might have a chance of acquiring a portion of his grace. But I don't want to drive that generalization too far. I know one or two saintly preachers who could pose for a collar ad.

1924

Had a letter today informing me that the First ____ church in ____ has called a new pastor. After trying futilely to find the right man, who was to have as much scholarship as his predecessor and more "punch," they decided to raise his salary to $15,000. I don't know whether that was the factor which finally solved their problem, but at any rate they have the man they want. I suppose it is not easy to get a combination of Aristotle and Demosthenes, and on the current market, that ought to be worth $15,000. Nevertheless there must be some limit to this matter of oversized salaries.

There ought to be some questioning, too, about the growing tendency of churches to build their congregations around pulpit eloquence. What kind of fundamental ethical question can a man be eloquent about when he draws that much cash, particularly since a Croesus or two usually has to supply an undue portion of it? I don't know anything about the prophet of the Lord who accepted this call, but I venture to prophesy that no sinner in that pagan city will quake in his boots in anticipation of his coming.

The idea of a professional good man is difficult enough for all of us who are professionally engaged as teachers of the moral ideal. Of course, "a man must live," and it is promised that if we seek first the kingdom and its righteousness "all these things shall be added unto us." But I doubt whether Jesus had a $15,000 salary in mind. If the things that are added become too numerous they distract your attention terribly. To try to keep your eye on the main purpose may only result in making you squint-eyed. I hope the new prophet won't begin his pastorate with a sermon on the text, "I count all things but loss."

1924

I was a little ashamed of what I wrote recently about ministers' salaries, but today I was strangely justified in my criticism. Walking into a store to buy a hat I met an old friend who told me about his new preacher. His church had tried for a long while to secure the right man, and then by dint of a special campaign they raised the salary from $6,000 to $10,000. That is obviously more than most of the people in the congregation make. He said to me with considerable pride, "You ought to hear our new preacher. My, but he is a great talker!" Then he came close and whispered to me out of hearing of the other customers: "He ought to be. We are paying him ten thousand dollars." The cynicism was quite unconscious.

Reinhold Niebuhr, *Leaves From the Notebook of a Tamed Cynic* (Louisville, Ky.: Westminster/John Knox Press, 1990), pp. 27-56.

George Herbert's seventeenth-century England was a place of change and intellectual turmoil. Herbert himself turned his back upon a promising academic career when he entered the Anglican pastorate. Perhaps this helps account for the sense of unrest and struggle that permeates his poems. He is more interesting as a poet than as a dispenser of advice to parsons. His complex, strange poem, "The Temple," is a wonder of insight, image, and startling juxtapositions. Herbert proved himself to be a master of the poetic art (he was greatly admired by our T. S. Eliot) as he walks us through a church building, step-by-step. His "Aaron," included here, named for the father of priests (see Exod. 28), reveals Herbert's own sense of both his unworthiness for the high vocation of pastor and yet the gracious manner in which Christ gives us "another heart and breast." Christ clothes us poor parsons in virtues not our own, in order that, in our ministry before the congregation, we are "well drest."

Though to our ears, Herbert's The Country Parson *(1652) sounds more than a little pedantic and tiresome, it has exercised great influence upon pastors for centuries as a trusted guide, a handbook for parish ministry. Herbert's stress upon the humility of the parson, the need for independent dignity in the parson's conduct among the congregation, for spiritual disciplines, and for unfailing loyalty to Christ alone, all set the tone for thinking about the virtues of a Protestant pastor. His was a high sense of pastoral privilege and responsibility. The church is the source of Christ's salvation of the world, and the parson is the chief embodiment of that means of grace.*

As a student of classical rhetoric at Trinity College, Cambridge, Herbert elevated preaching as the chief pastoral task. The pastor is mainly a teacher and, in preaching, the pastor teaches by example, through close examination of and care for the congregation, and by compassionately, skillfully adapting his pulpit speech to the particular needs of the congregation.

Herbert's high view of the ordained ministry is also somewhat fatiguing. In his chapter on "The Parson's Church," he advises his fellow clergy to ensure that the church has "walls plastered, windows glazed, floor paved, seats whole, firm, and uniform," "the church swept, and kept clean, without dust or cobwebs, and at great festivals strawed, and stuck with boughs, and perfumed with incense." Truly for Herbert, parish ministry, even out in the country, is a demanding vocation.

The Country Parson
George Herbert

Of a Pastor

A Pastor is the Deputy of Christ for the reducing[4] of Man to the Obedience of God. This definition is evident, and contains the direct steps of Pastoral Duty and Authority. For first, Man fell from God by disobedience. Secondly, Christ is the glorious instrument of God for the revoking[5] of Man. Thirdly, Christ being not to continue on earth, but after he had fulfilled the work of Reconciliation, to be received up into heaven, he constituted Deputies in his place, and these are Priests. And therefore Saint *Paul* in the beginning of his Epistles, proffesseth this: and in the first to the *Colossians*[6] plainly avoucheth, that he *fills up that which is behind of the afflictions of Christ in his flesh, for his Body's sake, which is the Church.* Wherein is contained the complete definition of a Minister. Out of this Charter of the Priesthood may be plainly gathered both the Dignity thereof, and the Duty: The Dignity, in that a Priest may do that which Christ did, and by his authority, and as his Vicegerent. The Duty, in that a Priest is to do that which Christ did, and after his manner, both for Doctrine and Life. . . .

The Parson's Life

The Country Parson is exceeding exact in his Life, being holy, just, prudent, temperate, bold, grave in all his ways. And because the two highest points of Life, wherein a Christian is most seen, are Patience, and Mortification; Patience in regard of afflictions, Mortification in regard of lusts and affections, and the stupifying and deading of all the clamorous powers of the soul, therefore he hath thoroughly studied these, that he may be an absolute Master and commander of himself, for all the purposes which God hath ordained him. Yet in these points he labors most in those things which are most apt to scandalize his Parish. And first, because

---

4. *reducing.* Bringing back from error.
5. *revoking.* Restoring or recalling to correct way of life.
6. *first to the Colossians.* Col. 1:24-25.

Country people live hardly,[7] and therefore as feeling their own sweat, and consequently knowing the price of money, are offended much with any, who by hard usage increase their travail, the Country Parson is very circumspect in avoiding all covetousness, neither being greedy to get, nor niggardly to keep, nor troubled to lose any worldly wealth; but in all his words and actions slighting, and disesteeming it, even to a wond'ring, that the world should so much value wealth, which in the day of wrath hath not one dram of comfort for us. Secondly, because Luxury is a very visible sin, the Parson is very careful to avoid all the kinds thereof, but especially that of drinking, because it is the most popular vice; into which if he come, *he prostitutes himself* both to shame, and sin, and by having *fellowship, with the unfruitful works of darkness*,[8] he disableth himself of authority *to reprove them:* For sins make all equal, whom they find together; and then they are worst, who ought to be best. Neither is it for the servant of Christ to haunt Inns, or Taverns, or Ale-houses, *to the dishonor of his person and office.* The Parson doth not so, but orders his Life in such a fashion, that when death takes him, as the Jews and *Judas* did Christ, he may say as He did, *I sat daily with you teaching in the Temple.*[9] Thirdly, because Country people (as indeed all honest men) do much esteem their word, it being the Life of buying, and selling, and dealing in the world; therefore the Parson is very strict in keeping his word, though it be to his own hindrance, as knowing, that if he be not so, he will quickly be discovered, and disregarded: neither will they believe him in the pulpit, whom they cannot trust in his Conversation. As for oaths, and apparel, the disorders thereof are also very manifest. The Parson's yea is yea, and nay nay: and his apparel plain, but reverend, and clean, without spots, or dust, or smell; the purity of his mind breaking out, and dilating itself even to his body, clothes, and habitation. . . .

---

7. *hardly.* Hard and difficult lives.
8. Eph. 5:11.
9. Luke 22:53.

Aaron[494]

Holiness on the head,
Light and perfections on the breast,
Harmonious bells below, raising the dead
To lead them unto life and rest.
Thus are true Aarons drest.

Profaneness in my head,
Defects and darkness in my breast,
A noise[495] of passions ringing me for dead
Unto a place where is no rest.
Poor priest thus am I drest.

Only another head
I have, another heart and breast,
Another music, making live not dead,
Without whom I could have no rest:
In him I am well drest.

Christ is my only head,
My alone only heart and breast,
My only music, striking me ev'n dead;
That to the old man I may rest,
And be in him new drest.[496]

So holy in my head,
Perfect and light in my dear breast,
My doctrine tun'd by Christ, (who is not dead,
But lives in me while I do rest)
Come people; Aaron's drest.

---

494. Title. See Exod. 28.
495. *noise*. A band of musicians.
496. See Col. 3:9-10 and Gal 2:20.

George Herbert, *The Country Parson, The Temple* (Ramsey, N.J.: Paulist Press, 1981), pp. 55-57, 300.

CHAPTER NINE

The Pastor as Evangelist

Lesslie Newbigin was one of the great missionaries and great theologians of mission in the twentieth century. His Foolishness to the Greeks *interpreted the current state of the church in the industrialized West from the standpoint of Newbigin's experiences as a missionary and bishop of the Church of South India. His insights transformed the way much of the church in North America reconceived its task. Many pastors after Newbigin no longer saw themselves as custodians of Christendom but rather as missionaries to a society that was no longer, if it ever was, Christian. In the late 1960s, Newbigin composed a series of lectures for his pastors in Madras, short talks on the duties of their ministry in the Church of South India. Here Newbigin, great theorist of Christian evangelization, speaks simply and practically to his pastors in their role as evangelist.*

The Pastor as Evangelist
Lesslie Newbigin

The scripture says, "No one who believes in him will be put to shame." For there is no distinction between Jew and Greek; the same Lord is Lord of all and bestows his riches upon all who call upon him. For, "every one who calls upon the name of the Lord will be saved."

But how are men to call upon him in whom they have not believed? And how are they to believe in him of whom they have never heard? And how are they to hear without a preacher? And how can men preach unless they are sent? As it is written, "How beautiful are the feet of those who preach good news!"

Romans 10:11-15

It is characteristic of the Christian message that it speaks of hearing good news, rather than of receiving spiritual enlightenment. The word Gospel just means "good news," and from a very early time it became practically a technical term for the Christian message. Evangelism—telling the good news—has been central to the Christian way of life from the beginning. The passage which we have read from Romans 10 gives the logic of it. You cannot get to know about Jesus unless someone goes and tells you. There has to be a journey, a going, a mission. That simple piece of logic underlies the whole splendid ministry of St. Paul as we see it described in the Acts and interpreted in the Letters. It underlies some of the most moving chapters in Christian history—the mission of the Irish to Germany, of the early Jesuits to South India, of the Protestant missions of the 18th and 19th centuries, of Azariah to the jungle of Dornakal and of Kagawa to the slums of Tokyo. The haunting phrase of Isaiah—How beautiful are the feet of those who bring good news—has been remembered in generation after generation, because they truly expressed what men felt.

How is it, then, that the words "Evangelism" and "Evangelist," have become so unpopular? How has it come that we use the name "Evangelist" for the lowest category of church worker—half-trained, half-paid and half-starved? How does it come that respectable Christians feel uncomfortable with the very idea of evangelism? An American missionary friend of mine told me recently of a congregation which had offered him a large sum of money, provided he would promise that it would not be used for evangelism. In response to the questionnaire sent out to pastorates at the time of the last Diocesan Council, one pastorate answered to the question: Are you doing any evangelism? with the words: I hope not. How has this state of affairs come about? I think there are several reasons.

1. There is the fact that we have often confused evangelism with proselytisation. I mean that we have not been people simply full of good news which we had to share with all our friends: we have been agents of an organisation trying to strengthen itself in the world by getting more members and more influence. I know that it is not easy to draw a sharp line between these two in practice. But the difference in spirit and motive is there, and ordinary people quickly recognise it. I do not need to dwell on this. We can all

recognise the proselytising spirit in other people, even if we do not recognise it so easily in ourselves.

2. There is the fact that we have corrupted our evangelism by trying to exploit the weaknesses of others. We have almost come to take it for granted that organised evangelism is directed towards those who are in a weaker position than ourselves. We send evangelists to backward villages, to slums, to people who are sick in hospital, to those in jail, to the hill tribes. We do not send evangelists to the lawyers, the businessmen, the legislators. Above all, the whole picture of evangelism in our world is coloured by the fact that it has been dominated by the massive power of the white races directed towards the coloured peoples who were under their political and economic power. Even where there has not been this exploitation of a political or economic or cultural weakness, we have tended in our evangelism to try to get at the weak spots of others, their secret sins and failures, as a means of getting leverage for the Gospel. This, as Bonhoeffer pointed out in one of his letters, is something very remote from the spirit of the man who is simply eager to share good news.

3. There is the fact that, in our evangelism, we have departed from Christ's own way—the way of the incarnation. Jesus became man—completely one among those for whom he came. We do not. We remain at a distance. I am thinking of the typical evangelistic effort which our pastorates put on from time to time. We go to a village, stand in the street, sing a few lyrics, perhaps shout a few texts through a loudspeaker, deliver a message and go home to supper. We do not become really involved with the people. We do not sit down beside them and listen to their thoughts, their problems, their hopes. Certainly we are not "tempted in all points as they are." Our model is not the incarnation of the Word of God, but the methods of a modern commercial or political advertiser.

4. I think there is also another fact which we are less willing to face. I think that behind the disrepute of the word evangelism there is a real break-down of faith in the Gospel. At least I think we must humbly face this possibility. I have never forgotten the first public meeting that I attended a few days after coming to India as a young missionary. It was arranged by the public of Chingleput to congratulate the Church of Scotland Mission on the completion of 100 years of work in that town. The speech of the Municipal Chairman

was a model of courtesy. He said something like this: "When the first missionaries came here from Scotland, we were very suspicious of them. We thought that they had come to convert us to Christianity. Now as we watch them we can see that our suspicions were quite unjustified. These people are perfect gentlemen, with no such improper motives. We can welcome them without any reservations."

What has happened to us? Have we become wiser than our fathers—or less faithful?

Among the duties of presbyters as enjoined in the CSI Constitution is the responsibility "to use every opportunity to preach the Gospel to non-Christians and to bring men to the obedience of the faith."

These words make it very clear that we are not ordained to this ministry just to look after Christians. Many of our Church members think that we are simply paid to look after them, and get seriously annoyed if we devote too much time to those outside the fellowship. It has happened more than once that a pastor has been rebuked by the elders of the congregation for spending too much time with Hindus, and told bluntly that he is paid to look after the Christians and not to spend his time with others. But this is a total misunderstanding of our ordination. The people for whom we are responsible before God as the result of our ordination vows are not just the members of the church, but all the people of our parish or diocese, whether they are Christians or not. It is an essential part of our ministry that we are appointed to lead God's people in evangelism.

But we must go deeper than this. The truth is that we do not truly understand the Gospel if we spend all our time preaching it to Christians. A French layman, Michel Philibert, has written an excellent little book called *Christ's Preaching and Ours,* in which he shows that we simply cannot transfer the language of the Gospels about the announcement of the good news to those who had not heard it and apply it directly to our weekly preaching to people who have heard the Gospel innumerable times. If we know only the latter situation, we do not know what the Gospel is. The Gospel is communication of news to those who do not know it, and we only really understand it as we are involved in so communicating it. I would testify from my own limited experience that I have never felt the reality of the Gospel more fully than when I was regularly involved in a ministry to the condemned prisoners in the Madurai Jail. It is in a situation where the Gospel is really being received as NEWS that you understand what it is.

What can we say constructively about our role in leading God's people in evangelism? Let me begin with a phrase which has been used by many who are not happy with traditional ways of evangelism—the phrase *Christian presence*. This phrase has both a negative and positive reference. Negatively it draws attention to the fact, which I referred to earlier, that in much of our traditional evangelism we have not really been fully present to those to whom we spoke. We have addressed them, perhaps shouted at them, but we have not been *with* them. We have not "sat where they sat." We have not become part of their situation as Jesus has become part of our human situation. "Christian presence" points to the true way of the incarnation. Positively the phrase may be developed along the following lines. When we read the Gospels we see that the presence of Jesus was itself the presence of the Kingdom of God. Jesus was, in a sense, himself the good news which he announced. If, then, the Church is truly faithful, then the Church's presence in any situation will be itself good news. The real presence of the people of God in a village, in a slum, in a situation of conflict or of despair, will be itself good news, and a source of hope.

Having said this, however, I must say that I do not think the idea of "Christian presence" can replace evangelism in the life of the Church. Jesus was not only himself the good news, but he was also himself the evangelist. His deeds were interpreted by words. He *proclaimed* good news. It was not that every deed of love had to be interpreted by a sermon, or that every teaching had to be illustrated by an act. Certainly not. But nevertheless the same Jesus who did the works of love also interpreted these works of love by his announcement of the coming of God's reign. Both deeds and words were essential to his ministry. Neither was a substitute for the other. The words interpreted the deeds and the deeds authenticated the words.

So it has to be in the life of the Church. I have criticised the kind of evangelism which "is words without real presence." But presence alone is not enough. None of us is so like Jesus that our presence can be a substitute for the naming of his name. We must

217

faithfully follow him by taking up the Cross and being, as Luther said, a sort of Christ for our neighbours. But we still have to point them to that one Cross on Calvary by which the world is redeemed, and there is no substitute for that. The exclusive use of the concept of presence could mean a betrayal.

We have to keep hold of both parts of the truth. Our evangelism will be futile if it is mere words not authenticated by deeds. But our deeds will be futile if they do not eventually find their full meaning in the message of the Gospel which has to be proclaimed by words. At this moment in the life of our Church I think that the most important thing to say is this: it is as we are truly present with our neighbours, bearing with them the sin and sorrow of the world, that we shall be in a position to point them to Jesus in such a way that they will recognise him as Saviour.

The Good News of the Kingdom

Now after John was arrested, Jesus came to Galilee, preaching the gospel of God, and saying, "The time is fulfilled, and the kingdom of God is at hand; repent, and believe in the gospel."
Mark 1:14-15

There are not many passages in the New Testament dealing explicitly with evangelism. Evangelism does not seem to have been seen by the first Christians as a problem, or as a duty. One gets the impression that the new life in Christ is something which glows with its own light. Witness is not something commanded but something promised. "When the Holy Spirit comes upon you, you will be my witnesses." However, it is of course also true that Jesus preached, and that he commanded his disciples to go into all the world and preach. What, exactly, was the Gospel which he preached, and which he commanded his disciples to preach?

The first passage to be looked at is Mark's account of the beginning of the ministry of Jesus. "Jesus came into Galilee, preaching the Gospel of God, and saying: 'The time is fulfilled, and the kingdom of God is at hand; repent and believe in the gospel' " (Mark 1:14-15). Here we have the beginning of the preaching of the Gospel. The good news is that the kingdom of God is at hand. God's time for this has come. World history is not a meaningless jumble of events. It is not a game. God is doing something, and this work of God has its times and seasons. He has been preparing for this over many ages, and now the time has come for something new and decisive.

This new thing is that the rule or reign of God has drawn near. This is the heart of the good news. In a world full of injustice and evil, a world which seems to be ruled not by God but by the devil, God's rule has come near. In a world where God is not known, he has made himself known. The day for which the suffering servants of God have waited has dawned. The reign of God is at hand.

But what, exactly, does this "at hand" mean? Has it come, or is it still to come? Is our Gospel about something which has happened, or about something which is going to happen? Where does the accent fall? As I ask this question, I think of two occasions on which I was engaged in street preaching. One was in Kancheepuram, where a catechist, after telling a good story, took a big breath and began: "Two thousand years ago, in a country called Palestine, there was a man called Jesus." The crowd began to melt away. Why should we bother about something 2,000 years ago? The other occasion was in a small country town. The preacher was a well-known evangelist. His message was simple: "Jesus is coming; are you ready to meet him?" The crowd gathered round. Something which is just going to happen excites more interest than something which happened 2,000 years ago. But how are we to preach the Gospel? If the good news is: "Jesus is coming soon"—what does "soon" mean after 2,000 years? If the good news is: "The reign of God has come," why is there still so much evil in the world?

We cannot begin to answer these questions until we look at the last part of Jesus' announcement. "Repent, and believe the good news." To repent means to turn round and face in a different direction. People were waiting for the reign of God—waiting eagerly. But it was coming from the direction opposite to the way they were looking. They would not see it unless they turned right round and faced the other way.

Not only is repentance (turning round) required, but also faith. Even when you turn round you do not *see* the reign of God. The Jews wanted to see it, and asked for some proof that it was there. Jesus answered with parables, stories of ordinary life which challenged his hearers to see what they had been blind to, to recognise the signs of the reign of God, and to believe in its reality. If the reign of God were obvious to everybody, there would be no need of faith. If it were completely hidden, there would be no possibility of faith. What is given in the coming of Jesus is the reign of God as a revealed mystery. Those who have eyes to see will see; others will not. His announcement is therefore a challenge to faith.

The centre of the revealed mystery of the reign of God is the Cross. There the power of God is revealed—but it is revealed as weakness. The glory of God is revealed—but it is revealed as humiliation. The victory of God is revealed—but it is revealed as defeat. To the ordinary eyes of what the Bible calls "flesh" that is to say, to the eyes of men facing in the direction that men usually face, trusting in the things that men usually trust, the Cross is weakness, humiliation, defeat. To those who turn round, face the other way, and *believe*, it is power, glory, victory.

For this reason the preaching of the Gospel acts like a sword—dividing men from one another. Some will believe; some—a majority—will not. That is the situation to which the parable of the sower is addressed. One can imagine how surprising and perplexing that parable must have been to those who expected the reign of God to come with the kind of power and glory that men recognise. Nothing could be farther from that picture than this one of the seed—much of which proves unable to survive the pressures of the environment, only a small part of which bears fruit.

In the light of all this, how shall we interpret the announcement that the reign of God has come near? In some places, as we know, it is interpreted as a past event. "If it is by the Spirit of God that I cast out demons, then the Kingdom of God has come upon you" (Matt. 12:28). In other places it is something yet to come. "When you pray, say: 'Thy kingdom come' " (Matt. 6:10). What is the relation between these two?

God's reign has come into the world in the coming of Jesus. That is the good news. But the reign of God is present in Jesus to faith. It is a reality which is hidden from those who have not undergone a radical repentance, a complete turning round so as to face in the opposite direction. The reign of God shows its presence in Jesus' deeds of love and compassion, and in the deeds done in his name and through his power. It is present supremely in his Cross and resurrection. There is the place where faith finds the supreme proof of the presence of the reign of God in the midst of the life of the world.

But this presence will not always be a hidden presence. The resurrection of Jesus, and the words that he spoke to his disciples after he was risen, are the sure promises that the power of the Kingdom will in the end manifestly rule over all men and all creation. Those who have turned round and believed the hidden presence of the kingdom, long ardently for that day when what is now hidden will be manifest to all men.

Meanwhile, God respects our freedom. He does not force men to accept his rule. There is freedom to believe or to disbelieve. A forced allegiance would be a false allegiance. God wants nothing less than the willing commitment of our whole being—which means radical repentance of faith.

What does this mean for our evangelism? It means, first, that the *context* of our evangelism will be (as it was in the ministry of Jesus) those works of love and power in which men may—by faith—be able to recognise the signs of the presence of the Kingdom. Where the Church is really continuing the ministry of Jesus—healing the sick, liberating the captives, seeking the lost, reconciling enemies, challenging injustice—then there is a possibility that men may be able to recognise and believe in the real presence of the reign of God.

But it also means, second, that we have to point beyond these things to the reality of which they are only signs. Our "good works" are highly ambiguous. They do not themselves manifest the holiness and love of God. At best they can be signs which can lead men to ask whether—after all—the reign of God is a reality. If that question is followed up, it will lead to suffering, to the Cross. We have to point men explicitly beyond these signs to Jesus and his Cross. Our good works cannot save men from their real enemy. But they can point men to the one who can.

It means, thirdly, that we have to call men insistently to repentance and faith. "Have you come to convert us?" was the question put by a local resident to one of our workers in the Slum Sanitation Project. The only possible answer is "Yes." If we are not clear about that, then our social service has no future. It only achieves its real purpose if it leads men to change their attitudes, to turn round and face the other way, to believe in the reality of God's rule and to become committed to his service, to be not mere recipients of charity but agents of change.

I do not mean by this to say that every piece of social service we do has to be accompanied by a sermon and a specific call to discipleship. It was not so in Jesus' ministry. There are times when it is good to speak directly about the Kingdom of God, and other times when it is better to be silent. What I mean is this: that the ministry of the Church as a whole should be manifestly and explicitly both a ministry of love and service and compassion, and also a ministry of proclamation and enlistment—the proclamation of the coming of the reign of God in Jesus, and the enlistment of men for the service of that reign. Within that total ministry there is room for a variety of special callings, but the world should be in no doubt that the Church stands for both these things and that they belong together.

If I am not mistaken, our current evangelism hardly ever uses the category of the Kingdom of God. And yet the original preaching of the Gospel on the lips of Jesus was—precisely—the announcement of the coming of that Kingdom. I believe that we may recover a true evangelism for our day if we return to that original language (translated into the idiom of our own time and place) as the basic category for our proclamation of the Gospel.

Lesslie Newbigin, *The Good Shepherd: Meditations on Christian Ministry in Today's World* (Grand Rapids, Mich.: Wm. B. Eerdmans, 1977), pp. 58-67.

The Gospels present Jesus and his disciples as those on a journey. Christian discipleship is a matter of leaving somewhere and journeying with Jesus to a place that one might not have gone had not one been invited, pushed, pulled, prodded there by the risen Christ. Christian life does not come naturally but is rather the result of the risen Christ's ability to transform, convert, beckon, and allure. That most of us who are Christian expect, even long for such radical transformation is due, in no small part, to the testimonial of a bishop in North Africa, Augustine of Hippo. Throughout his youthful years Augustine struggled with faith in God, a struggle that culminated in a dramatic conversion in a garden, under a tree, while reading from Paul's Letter to the Romans. Over a decade after this event, about the year 400, Augustine took time from his busy dealings as a bishop of the church to write about his conversion to Christ. It was his attempt to better understand that journey and to display his journey in such a way that the journeys of others might be enlightened by it. The result was not only one of the great masterpieces of Western writing but also the paradigmatic account of the power of Christ to reach in, to intrude, to speak, to seize a life and commandeer it for his kingdom. The selection here is from Book Six of Confessions, *in which Augustine recounts how he "wrangled with myself," wrestling with deep conflicts. Discussions with good friends who were Christian both attracted and repulsed him. He read the* Life of Anthony *and was much impressed but still could not make the step toward baptism and Christian commitment. He found much that was noble about the Christian way of life, but the desires of his body prevented him from taking up that way. Eventually, he was to find that this struggle deep within himself, which he describes so eloquently, was also a struggle with God. His journey deeper within himself was, in reality, an alluring of his life toward God. In all his twisting and turning, his conflict and consternation, his life was gradually being prepared for that day under the tree when he at last found the source of his lifelong yearning, and Augustine's restless heart found rest in God.*

Confessions
St. Augustine (trans. by R. S. Pine-Coffin)

6

O Lord, my Helper and my Redeemer, I shall now tell and confess to the glory of your name how you released me from the fetters of lust which held me so tightly shackled and from my slavery to the things of this world. I continued to lead my usual life, but I was growing more and more unsettled and day after day I poured out my heart to you. I went to your church whenever I had time from my work, which was a painful load upon my shoulders. Alypius was with me, now taking respite from his legal work after a third term of office as assessor. He was looking for clients who would pay him for his advice, just as my pupils paid me for skill in words, if it is possible to teach such an art. As a gesture of friendship to Alypius and me, Nebridius had consented to act as assistant to a great friend of ours named Verecundus, a Milanese, who was a teacher of grammar. . . .

One day when for some reason that I cannot recall Nebridius was not with us, Alypius and I were visited at our house by a fellow-countryman of ours from Africa, a man named Ponticianus, who held a high position in the Emperor's household. He had some request to make of us and we sat down to talk. He happened to notice a book lying on a table used for games, which was near where we were sitting. He picked it up and opened it and was greatly surprised to find that it contained Paul's epistles, for he had supposed that it was one of the books which used to tax all my strength as a teacher. Then he smiled and looked at me and said how glad he was, and how surprised, to find this book, and no others, there before my eyes. He of course was a Christian and a faithful servant to you, our God. Time and again he knelt before you in church repeating his prayers and lingering over them. When I told him that I studied Paul's writings with the greatest attention, he began to tell us the story of Antony, the Egyptian monk, whose name was held in high honour by your servants, although Alypius and I had never heard it until then. When Ponticianus realized this, he went into greater detail, wishing to instill some knowledge of this great man into our ignorant minds, for he was very surprised that we had not heard of him. For our part, we too were astonished to hear of the wonders you had worked so recently, almost in our own times, and witnessed by so many, in the true faith and in the Catholic Church. . . .

After this he went on to tell us of the groups of monks in the monasteries, of their way of life that savours of your sweetness, and of the fruitful wastes of the desert. All of this was new to us.

There was a monastery at Milan also, outside the walls, full of good brethren under the care of Ambrose, but we knew nothing of this either. Ponticianus continued to talk and we listened in silence. Eventually he told us of the time when he and three of his companions were at Trêves. One afternoon, while the Emperor was watching the games in the circus, they went out to stroll in the gardens near the city walls. They became separated into two groups, Ponticianus and one of the others remaining together while the other two went off by themselves. As they wandered on, the second pair came to a house which was the home of some servants of yours, men poor in spirit, to whom the kingdom of heaven belongs.[1] In the house they found a book containing the life of Antony. One of them began to read it and was so fascinated and thrilled by the story that even before he had finished reading he conceived the idea of taking upon himself the same kind of life and abandoning his career in the world—both he and his friend were officials in the service of the State—in order to become your servant. All at once he was filled with the love of holiness. Angry with himself and full of remorse, he looked at his friend and said, "What do we hope to gain by all the efforts we make? What are we looking for? What is our purpose in serving the State? Can we hope for anything better at Court than to be the Emperor's friends? Even so, surely our position would be precarious and exposed to much danger? We shall meet it at every turn, only to reach another danger which is greater still. And how long is it to be before we reach it? But if I wish, I can become the friend of God at this very moment."

After saying this he turned back to the book, labouring under the pain of the new life that was taking birth in him. He read on and in his heart, where you alone could see, a change was taking place. His mind was being divested of the world, as could presently be seen. For while he was reading, his heart leaping and turning in his breast, a cry broke from him as he saw the better course and determined to take it. Your servant now, he said to his friend, "I have torn myself free from all your ambitions and have decided to serve God. From this very moment, here and now, I shall start to serve him. If you will not follow my lead, do not stand in my way." The other answered that he would stand by his comrade, for such

---

1. See Matt. 5:3.

service was glorious and the reward was great. So these two, now your servants, built their tower at the cost which had to be paid, that is, at the cost of giving up all they possessed and following you.[1]

At this moment Ponticianus and the man who had been walking with him in another part of the garden arrived at the house, looking for their friends. Now that they had found them they said that it was time to go home, as the daylight was beginning to fade. But the other two told them of the decision they had made and what they proposed to do. They explained what had made them decide to take this course and how they had agreed upon it, and they asked their friends, if they would not join them, at least not to put obstacles in their way. Ponticianus said that he and the other man did not change their old ways, but they were moved to tears for their own state of life. In all reverence they congratulated the others and commended themselves to their prayers. Then they went back to the palace, burdened with hearts that were bound to this earth; but the others remained in the house and their hearts were fixed upon heaven. Both these men were under a promise of marriage, but once the two women heard what had happened, they too dedicated their virginity to you.

7

This was what Ponticianus told us. But while he was speaking, O Lord, you were turning me around to look at myself. For I had placed myself behind my own back, refusing to see myself. You were setting me before my own eyes so that I could see how sordid I was, how deformed and squalid, how tainted with uclers and sores. I saw it all and stood aghast, but there was no place where I could escape from myself. If I tried to turn my eyes away they fell on Ponticianus, still telling his tale, and in this way you brought me face to face with myself once more, forcing me upon my own sight so that I should see my wickedness and loathe it. I had known it all along, but I had always pretended that it was something different. I had turned a blind eye and forgotten it.

---

1. See Luke 14:28-34.

But now, the more my heart warmed to those two men as I heard how they had made the choice that was to save them by giving themselves up entirely to your care, the more bitterly I hated myself in comparison with them. Many years of my life had passed—twelve, unless I am wrong—since I had read Cicero's *Hortensius* at the age of nineteen and it had inspired me to study philosophy. But I still postponed my renunciation of this world's joys, which would have left me free to look for that other happiness, the very search for which, let alone its discovery, I ought to have prized above the discovery of all human treasures and kingdoms or the ability to enjoy all the pleasures of the body at a mere nod of the head. As a youth I had been woefully at fault, particularly in early adolescence. I had prayed to you for chastity and said "Give me chastity and continence, but not yet." For I was afraid that you would answer my prayer at once and cure me too soon of the disease of lust, which I wanted satisfied, not quelled. I had wandered on along the road of vice in the sacrilegious superstition of the Manichees, not because I thought that it was right, but because I preferred it to the Christian belief, which I did not explore as I ought but opposed out of malice.

I had pretended to myself that the reason why, day after day, I staved off the decision to renounce worldly ambition and follow you alone was that I could see no certain goal towards which I might steer my course. But the time had now come when I stood naked before my own eyes, while my conscience upbraided me. "Am I to be silent? Did you not always say that you would not discard your load of vanity for the sake of a truth that was not proved? Now you know that the truth is proved, but the load is still on your shoulders. Yet here are others who have exchanged their load for wings, although they did not wear themselves out in the search for truth or spend ten years or more in making up their minds."

All the time that Ponticianus was speaking my conscience gnawed away at me like this. I was overcome by burning shame, and when he had finished this tale and completed the business for which he had come, he went away and I was left to my own thoughts. I made all sorts of accusations against myself. I cudgelled my soul and belaboured it with reasons why it should follow me now that I was trying so hard to follow you. But it fought back. It would not obey and yet could offer no excuse. All its old arguments were exhausted and had been shown to be false. It remained silent and afraid, for as much as the loss of life itself it feared the stanching of the flow of habit, by which it was wasting away to death.

8

My inner self was a house divided against itself. In the heart of the fierce conflict which I had stirred up against my soul in our common abode, my heart, I turned upon Alypius. My looks betrayed the commotion in my mind as I exclaimed, "What is the matter with us? What is the meaning of this story? These men have not had our schooling, yet they stand up and storm the gates of heaven while we, for all our learning, lie here grovelling in this world of flesh and blood! Is it because they have led the way that we are ashamed to follow? Is it not worse to hold back?"

I cannot remember the words I used. I said something to this effect and then my feelings proved too strong for me. I broke off and turned away, leaving him to gaze at me speechless and astonished. For my voice sounded strange and the expression of my face and eyes, my flushed cheeks, and the pitch of my voice told him more of the state of my mind than the actual words that I spoke.

There was a small garden attached to the house where we lodged. We were free to make use of it as well as the rest of the house because our host, the owner of the house, did not live there. I now found myself driven by the tumult in my breast to take refuge in this garden, where no one could interrupt that fierce struggle, in which I was my own contestant, until it came to its conclusion. What the conclusion was to be you knew, O Lord, but I did not. Meanwhile I was beside myself with madness that would bring me sanity. I was dying a death that would bring me life. I knew the evil that was in me, but the good that was soon to be born in me I did not know. So I went out into the garden and Alypius followed at my heels. His presence was no intrusion on my solitude, and how could he leave me in that state? We sat down as far as possible from the house. I was frantic, overcome by violent anger with myself for not accepting your will and entering into your covenant. Yet in my bones I knew that this was what I ought to do. In my heart of hearts I praised it to the skies. And to reach this goal I needed no chariot or ship. I need not even walk as far as I had come from the house to the place where we sat, for to make the journey, and to arrive safely, no more was required than an act of will. But it must be a resolute and whole-hearted act of the will, not some lame wish which I kept turning over and over in my mind, so that it had to wrestle with itself, part of it trying to rise, part falling to the ground.

During this agony of indecision I performed many bodily actions, things which a man cannot always do, even if he wills to do them. If he has lost his limbs, or is bound hand and foot, or if his body is weakened by illness or under some other handicap, there are things which he cannot do. I tore my hair and hammered my forehead with my fists; I locked my fingers and hugged my knees; and I did all this because I made an act of will to do it. But I might have had the will to do it and yet not have done it, if my limbs had been unable to move in compliance with my will. I performed all these actions, in which the will and the power to act are not the same. Yet I did not do that one thing which I should have been far, far better pleased to do than all the rest and could have done at once, as soon as I had the will to do it, because as soon as I had the will to do so, I should have willed it wholeheartedly. For in this case the power to act was the same as the will. To will it was to do it. Yet I did not do it. My body responded to the slightest wish of my mind by moving its limbs at the least hint from me, and it did so more readily than my mind obeyed itself by assenting to its own great desire, which could be accomplished simply by an act of will.

9

Why does this strange phenomenon occur? What causes it? O Lord in your mercy give me light to see, for it may be that the answer to my question lies in the secret punishment of man and in the penitence which casts a deep shadow on the sons of Adam. Why does this strange phenomenon occur? What causes it? The mind gives an order to the body and is at once obeyed, but when it gives an order to itself, it is resisted. The mind commands the hand to move and is so readily obeyed that the order can scarcely be distinguished from its execution. Yet the mind is mind and the hand is part of the body. But when the mind commands the mind to make an act of will, these two are one and the same and yet the order is not obeyed. Why does this happen? What is the cause of it? The mind orders itself to make an act of will, and it would not give this order unless it willed to do so; yet it does not carry out its own command. But it does not fully will to do this thing and therefore its orders are not fully given. It gives the order only in so far as it wills, and in so far as it does not will the order is not carried out. For the will commands that an act of will should be made, and it gives this command to itself, not to some other will. The reason, then, why the command is not obeyed is that it is not given with the full will. For if the will were full, it would not command itself to be full, since it would be so already. It is therefore no strange phenomenon partly to will to do something and partly to will not to do it. It is a disease of the mind, which does not wholly rise to the heights where it is lifted by the truth, because it is weighed down by habit. So there are two wills in us, because neither by itself is the whole will, and each possesses what the other lacks.

10

There are many abroad who talk of their own fantasies and lead men's minds astray.[1] They assert that because they have observed that there are two wills at odds with each other. . . . we must therefore have two minds of different natures, one good, the other evil. *Let them vanish at God's presence as the smoke vanishes.*[1] As long as they hold these evil beliefs they are evil themselves, but even they will be good if they see the truth and accept it, so that your apostle may say to them *Once you were all darkness; now, in the Lord you are all daylight.*[2] These people want to be light, not in the Lord, but in themselves, because they think that the nature of the soul is the same as God. In this way their darkness becomes denser still, because in their abominable arrogance they have separated themselves still further from you, who are *the true Light which enlightens every soul born into the world.*[3] I say to them "Take care what you say, and blush for shame. Enter God's presence, and find there enlightenment; *here is no room for downcast looks.*"[4]

1. Titus 1:10.
1. Ps. 67:3 (68:2).
2. Eph. 5:8.
3. John 1:9.
4. Ps. 33:6 (34:5).

When I was trying to reach a decision about serving the Lord my God, as I had long intended to do, it was I who willed to take this course and again it was I who willed not to take it. It was I and I alone. But I neither willed to do it nor refused to do it with my full will. So I was at odds with myself. I was throwing myself into confusion. All this happened to me although I did not want it, but it did not prove that there was some second mind in me besides my own. It only meant that my mind was being punished. *My action did not come from me, but from the sinful principle that dwells in me.*[5] It was part of the punishment of a sin freely committed by Adam, my first father.

If there were as many different natures in us as there are conflicting wills, we should have a great many more natures than merely two. Suppose that someone is trying to decide whether to go to the theatre or to the Manichees' meeting-house. The Manichees will say, "Clearly he has two natures, the good one bringing him here to us and the bad one leading him away. Otherwise, how can you explain this dilemma of two opposing wills?" I say that the will to attend their meetings is just as bad as the will to go off to the theatre, but in their opinion it can only be a good will that leads a man to come to them. Suppose then that one of us is wavering between two conflicting wills and cannot make up his mind whether to go to the theatre or to our church. Will not the Manichees be embarrassed to know what to say? Either they must admit—which they will not do—that it is a good will which brings a man to our church, just as in their opinion it is a good will which brings their own communicants and adherents to their church; or they must presume that there are two evil natures and two evil minds in conflict in one man. If they think this, they will disprove their own theory that there is one good and one evil will in man. The only alternative is for them to be converted to the truth and to cease to deny that when a man tries to make a decision, he has one soul which is torn between conflicting wills.

So let us hear no more of their assertion, when they observe two wills in conflict in one man, that there are two opposing minds in him, one good and the other bad, and that they are in conflict because they spring from two opposing substances and two opposing

---

5. Rom. 7:17.

principles. For you, O God of truth, prove that they are utterly wrong. You demolish their arguments and confound them completely. It may be that both the wills are bad. For instance, a man may be trying to decide whether to commit murder by poison or by stabbing; whether he should swindle another man out of one part of his property or another, that is, if he cannot obtain both; whether he should spend his money extravagantly on pleasure or hoard it like a miser; or whether he should go to the games in the circus or to the theatre, when there is a performance at both places on the same day. In this last case there may be a third possibility, that he should go and rob another person's house, if he has the chance. There may even be a fourth choice open to him, because he may wonder whether to go and commit adultery, if the occasion arises at the same time. These possibilities may all occur at the same moment and all may seem equally desirable. The man cannot do all these things at once, and his mind is torn between four wills which cannot be reconciled—perhaps more than four, because there are a great many things that he might wish to do. But the Manichees do not claim that there are as many different substances in us as this.

It is just the same when the wills are good. If I question the Manichees whether it is good to find pleasure in reading Paul's Epistles or in the tranquil enjoyment of a Psalm or in a discussion of the Gospel, they will reply in each case that it is good. Supposing, then, that a man finds all these things equally attractive and the chance to do all of them occurs at the same time, is it not true that as long as he cannot make up his mind which of them he most wants to do his heart is torn between several different desires? All these different desires are good, yet they are in conflict with each other until he chooses a single course to which the will may apply itself as a single whole, so that it is no longer split into several different wills.

The same is true when the higher part of our nature aspires after eternal bliss while our lower self is held back by the love of temporal pleasure. It is the same soul that wills both, but it wills neither of them with the full force of the will. So it is wrenched in two and suffers great trials, because while truth teaches it to prefer one course, habit prevents it from relinquishing the other.

11

This was the nature of my sickness. I was in torment, reproaching myself more bitterly than ever as I twisted and turned in my chain. I hoped that my chain might be broken once and for all, because it was only a small thing that held me now. All the same it held me. And you, O Lord, never ceased to watch over my secret heart. In your stern mercy you lashed me with the twin scourge of fear and shame in case I should give way once more and the worn and slender remnant of my chain should not be broken but gain new strength and bind me all the faster. In my heart I kept saying "Let it be now, let it be now!" and merely by saying this I was on the point of making the resolution. I was on the point of making it, but I did not succeed. Yet I did not fall back into my old state. I stood on the brink of resolution, waiting to take fresh breath. I tried again and came a little nearer to my goal, and then a little nearer still, so that I could almost reach out and grasp it. But I did not reach it. I could not reach out to it or grasp it, because I held back from the step by which I should die to death and become alive to life. My lower instincts, which had taken firm hold of me, were stronger than the higher, which were untried. And the closer I came to the moment which was to mark the great change in me, the more I shrank from it in horror. But it did not drive me back or turn me from my purpose: it merely left me hanging in suspense.

I was held back by mere trifles, the most paltry inanities, all my old attachments. They plucked at my garment of flesh and whispered, "Are you going to dismiss us? From this moment we shall never be with you again, for ever and ever. From this moment you will never again be allowed to do this thing or that, for evermore." What was it, my God, that they meant when they whispered "this thing or that"? Things so sordid and so shameful that I beg you in your mercy to keep the soul of your servant free from them! These voices, as I heard them, seemed less than half as loud as they had been before. They no longer barred my way, blatantly contradictory, but their mutterings seemed to reach me from behind, as though they were stealthily plucking at my back, trying to make me turn my head when I wanted to go forward. Yet, in my state of indecision, they kept me from tearing myself away, from shaking myself free of them and leaping across the barrier to the other side, where you were calling me. Habit was too strong for me when it asked "Do you think you can live without these things?"

But by now the voice of habit was very faint. I had turned my eyes elsewhere, and while I stood trembling at the barrier, on the other side I could see the chaste beauty of Continence in all her serene, unsullied joy, as she modestly beckoned me to cross over and to hesitate no more. She stretched out loving hands to welcome and embrace me, holding up a host of good examples to my sight. With her were countless boys and girls, great numbers of the young and people of all ages, staid widows and women still virgins in old age. And in their midst was Continence herself, not barren but a fruitful mother of children, of joys born of you, O Lord, her Spouse. She smiled at me to give me courage, as though she were saying, "Can you not do what these men and these women do? Do you think they find the strength to do it in themselves and not in the Lord their God? It was the Lord their God who gave me to them. Why do you try to stand in your own strength and fail? Cast yourself upon God and have no fear. He will not shrink away and let you fall. Cast yourself upon him without fear, for he will welcome you and cure you of your ills." I was overcome with shame, because I was still listening to the futile mutterings of my lower self and I was still hanging in suspense. And again Continence seemed to say, "Close your ears to the unclean whispers of your body, so that it may be mortified. It tells you of things that delight you, but not such things as the law of the Lord your God has to tell."[1]

In this way I wrangled with myself, in my own heart, about my own self. And all the while Alypius stayed at my side, silently awaiting the outcome of this agitation that was new in me.

12

I probed the hidden depths of my soul and wrung its pitiful secrets from it, and when I mustered them all before the eyes of my heart, a great storm broke within me, bringing with it a great deluge of tears. I stood up and left Alypius so that I might weep and cry to my heart's content, for it occurred to me that tears were best shed in solitude. I moved away far enough to avoid being embarrassed even by his presence. He must have realized what my

---

1. See Ps. 118:85 (119:85).

feelings were, for I suppose I had said something and he had known from the sound of my voice that I was ready to burst into tears. So I stood up and left him where we had been sitting, utterly bewildered. Somehow I flung myself down beneath a fig tree and gave way to the tears which now streamed from my eyes, the sacrifice that is acceptable to you.[1] I had much to say to you, my God, not in these very words but in this strain: *Lord, will you never be content?*[2] *Must we always taste your vengeance? Forget the long record of our sins.*[3] For I felt that I was still the captive of my sins, and in my misery I kept crying "How long shall I go on saying 'tomorrow, tomorrow'? Why not now? Why not make an end of my ugly sins at this moment?"

I was asking myself these questions, weeping all the while with the most bitter sorrow in my heart, when all at once I heard the singsong voice of a child in a nearby house. Whether it was the voice of a boy or a girl I cannot say, but again and again it repeated the refrain "Take it and read, take it and read." At this I looked up, thinking hard whether there was any kind of game in which children used to chant words like these, but I could not remember ever hearing them before. I stemmed my flood of tears and stood up, telling myself that this could only be a divine command to open my book of Scripture and read the first passage on which my eyes should fall. For I had heard the story of Antony, and I remembered how he had happened to go into a church while the Gospel was being read and had taken it as a counsel addressed to himself when he heard the words *Go home and sell all that belongs to you. Give it to the poor, and so the treasure you have shall be in heaven; then come back and follow me.*[1] By this divine pronouncement he had at once been converted to you.

So I hurried back to the place where Alypius was sitting, for when I stood up to move away I had put down the book containing Paul's Epistles. I seized it and opened it, and in silence I read the first passage on which my eyes fell: *Not in revelling and drunkenness, not in lust and wantonness, not in quarrels and rivalries. Rather, arm yourselves with the Lord Jesus Christ; spend no more thought on*

1. See Ps. 50:19 (51:17).
2. Ps. 6:4 (6:3).
3. Ps. 78:5, 8 (79:5, 8).
1. Matt. 19:21.

nature and nature's appetites.[2] I had no wish to read more and no need to do so. For in an instant, as I came to the end of the sentence, it was as though the light of confidence flooded into my heart and all the darkness of doubt was dispelled.

I marked the place with my finger or by some other sign and closed the book. My looks now were quite calm as I told Alypius what had happened to me. He too told me what he had been feeling, which of course I did not know. He asked to see what I had read. I showed it to him and he read on beyond the text which I had read. I did not know what followed, but it was this: *Find room among you for a man* of *over-delicate conscience.*[3] Alypius applied this to himself and told me so. This admonition was enough to give him strength, and without suffering the distress of hesitation he made his resolution and took this good purpose to himself. And it very well suited his moral character, which had long been far, far better than my own.

Then we went in and told my mother, who was overjoyed. And when we went on to describe how it had all happened, she was jubilant with triumph and glorified you, *who are powerful enough, and more than powerful enough, to carry out your purpose beyond all our hopes and dreams.*[4] For she saw that you had granted her far more than she used to ask in her tearful prayers and plaintive lamentations. You converted me to yourself, so that I no longer desired a wife or placed any hope in this world but stood firmly upon the rule of faith, where you had shown me to her in a dream so many years before. And you *turned her sadness into rejoicing,*[1] into joy far fuller than her dearest wish, far sweeter and more chaste than any she had hoped to find in children begotten of my flesh.

---

2. Rom. 13:13, 14. Saint Augustine does not quote the whole passage, which begins *"Let us pass our time honourably, as by the light of day, not in revelling and drunkenness,"* etc.

3. Rom. 14:1.

4. Eph. 3:20.

1. Ps. 29:12 (30:11).

Saint Augustine, *Confessions,* trans. R. S. Pine-Coffin (London: Penguin, 1961), pp. 166-79.

CHAPTER TEN

The Pastor as Prophet

Stanley Hauerwas, the irrepressible one, and I, the polite one, arrived at Duke Divinity School to assume our places on the Duke faculty during the same week in the summer of 1984. Hauerwas is one of this country's most learned and thoughtful theological ethicists. I am just a simple, Bible-believing Methodist preacher. Whether the convergence of our two paths has been a good or a bad thing for theological education has been a matter of some debate over the years. Resident Aliens *was about the most popular book either of us wrote. Its strident polemic struck a chord with thousands of pastors and laity. Yet others, mostly in the theological academy, condemned the book's "arrogant simplicity." This passage on truthfulness in ministry occurs toward the end of the book and helps to explain why many within the theological establishment did not take kindly to our book. Here, two theological professors who have given our professional lives to making clergy, confess and critique the ways that seminary education can be a means of unfaithfully constricting the very prophets the church needs to hear.*

Resident Aliens *caused such a stir, so disrupted our lives, so impacted the discussion of ministry in the North American church that we wrote a sequel, describing what we had learned from the book and the ensuing debate. The very last sentence in the sequel,* Where Resident Aliens Live, *advises pastors, "If you call on God, God will be there, and it will frighten the hell out of you."*

Empowerment for Ministry
Stanley Hauerwas and William H. Willimon

We want to empower people for ministry in today's church. The writer to the Ephesians prayed for empowerment to speak the truth boldly. He wrote in chains. The "chains" that bind us today and render today's pastors impotent may not be so recognizable as those which held the writer to the Ephesians, but they are no less threatening.

Contemporary pastors are chained because so much current thinking about the church and its ministry is meant to disempower rather than to empower people. What happens when people come to seminary? We teach them courses that disempower them rather than give them the skills to claim their ministries with joy and excitement. For example, what happens when a seminarian takes a course in Old or New Testament? The student is introduced to critical apparatus and historical-critical issues that are determined by and limited to historical-critical skills. The first week is spent analyzing the documentary hypothesis for the composition of the first chapters of the book of Genesis as if the most important questions to be put to scripture are historical, literary, and scientific. Yet what does that have to do with ministry? We have argued that questions related to ministry tend primarily to be social, political, and ecclesial rather than arising out of the modern penchant to reduce all knowledge to the scientific and the historical and all research method to the individual and the private. The tools and the skills tend to be inappropriate to the way the church ought to go about its business of discerning the Word of its Lord.

Worse, the unfortunate seminarian is gradually convinced that he or she will never obtain all of the critical tools and linguistic skills required to extend the interpretive issues posed by the academicians, who live by the historical-critical method of biblical interpretation. Knowledge of the original biblical languages is most helpful to pastors—as a constant warning that many biblical notions cannot easily be translated into modern thought forms. Unfortunately, biblical languages are often taught in order to advance the debates of the academy rather than to address the needs of the church. A pastor despairs of ever knowing enough to do the sort of historical and linguistic investigation which is commended in seminary as the only way to uncover or recover "what the text meant." What "the text means for us" is, of course, said to be the theologian and pastor's task.

The result is that, when the seminarian is out and in his or her first parish, the young pastor throws up the hands, throws in the towel, and decides to preach his or her personal opinions. If I can't preach biblically, I might as well preach subjectively. Such subjectivity might not be a bad way to preach if, by subjective, we meant conversation with the saints of the church such as Luther, Augustine, and Calvin and what they had to say about biblical passages. Unfortunately, most of the time that is not what we mean by subjectivity. What we usually mean is that we have learned to preach by the seat of our pants.

As pastors, we need to be *clear* about our source of authority. One way to do that is to preach from scripture, specifically, to preach from the ecumenical lectionary. A pastor wishes to preach, say, on abortion. But the pastor is troubled because she knows that the congregation is deeply divided on this issue. To preach on abortion sounds as if the preacher is simply airing her own opinions. Clerical authority thus becomes expressed as, "We indulge our preacher by giving her the right to speak for fifteen or twenty minutes on her own opinion of what's right." The very act of reading and preaching from scripture is a deeply moral act in our age, a reminder of the source of pastoral authority. When the preacher uses the lectionary, the preacher makes clear that he or she preaches what he or she has been *told* to preach. That is important because it makes clear that the *story* forms us. This is the church's way of reminding itself of how it subverts the world.

Tragically, many of us are trying to preach without scripture and to interpret scripture without the church. Fundamentalist biblical interpretation and higher criticism of the Bible are often two sides of the same coin. The fundamentalist interpreter has roots in the Scottish Common Sense school of philosophy (fundamentalism is such a modernist heresy), which asserted that propositions are accessible to any thinking, rational person. Any rational person ought to be able to see the common sense of the assertion that God created the heavens and the earth. A Christian preacher merely has to assert these propositions, which, because they are true, are understandable to anybody with common sense.

The historical-critical method denies the fundamentalist claim. Scripture, higher criticism asserts, is the result of a long historical process. One must therefore apply sophisticated rules and tools of historical analysis to a given biblical text, because one cannot understand the text without understanding its true context. Presumably, anybody who applies the correct historical tools will be able to understand the text.

Both the fundamentalist and the higher critic assume that it is possible to understand the biblical text without training, without moral transformation, without the confession and forgiveness that come about within the church. Unconsciously, both means of interpretation try to make everyone religious (that is, able to understand and appropriate scripture) without everyone's being a member of the community for which the Bible is Scripture. Perhaps the recent enthusiasm for so-called inductive preaching—preaching that attempts to communicate the gospel indirectly, inductively through stories rather than through logical, deductive reasoning—is an attempt to understand scripture without being in the church. Inductive preaching presents the gospel in a way that enables everyone to "make up his or her own mind." But we suspect that scripture wonders if we have a mind worth making up! Minds worth making up are those with critical intelligence, minds trained to judge the true from the false on the basis of something more substantial than their own, personal subjectivism.

So, to a rather embarrassing degree, preaching depends on the recovery of the integrity of the Christian community. Here is a community breaking out of the suffocating tyranny of American individualism in which each of us is made into his or her own tyrant. Here is an alternative people who exist, not because each of us made up his or her own mind but because we were *called*, called to submit our lives to the authority of the saints.

Not that we are much better off in our seminary courses in theology and ethics. There we are introduced to assorted theories of moral rationality and justification. We debate whether or not a deontological or a teleological ethic is to be preferred; or what is the correct understanding of love and justice. Christian ethics and theology are reduced to intellectual dilemmas, schemes of typology rather than an account of how the church practically discusses what it ought to be. The situation is aggravated as contemporary theologians and ethicists write for other theologians and ethicists rather than for those in ministry. Which helps explain why those in ministry read fewer and fewer books on theology and ethics. It also explains why we have the new discipline of "practical theology," which is supposed to translate academic theology into something usable. Theology, to be Christian, is by definition practical. Either it serves the formation of the church or it is trivial and inconsequential. Preachers are the acid test of theology that would be Christian. Alas, too much theology today seems to have as its goal the convincing of preachers that they are too dumb to understand real theology. Before preachers buy into that assumption, we would like preachers to ask themselves if the problem lies with theologies which have become inconsequential.

Behind the disempowerment of the ministry through the seminary is the hidden agenda of convincing those in the ministry that they are not smart enough to teach in seminary. That is why those of us who take the trouble to get Ph.D.'s are paid to continue to teach in seminaries, where we then disempower new generations of ministers by bringing them to seminary in order to convince them that their vocation is not to be a professor!

Of course, we are drawing an exaggerated picture. Unfortunately, there is also truth in what we say. It is good to set aside some people to read and to write books in order to teach those who are called into the pastoral ministry. These people are reminders that seminary is not just a place where pastors are trained but also a place where we provide time for some to dedicate their lives to the intellectual love of God. Seminary professors like us rightfully spend much of their lives reading books so that the Christian tradition may not be lost but be a continuing conversation between us and the dead. The dead are not dead insofar as we are bound together in the communion of saints, living and dead, and therefore our conversation cannot be limited to those who now live. As we said earlier, pastors are significant only because of what needs to happen in the church. Now we add that seminary professors like us are significant only because of who pastors need to be.

Which helps explain why we very much hope that what we have written has been a beginning for the kind of *empowerment* that we believe is possible for today's church. Pastors fail if they have not evoked an exciting sense of adventure among their parishioners. Seminary professors have failed if we have not helped to empower pastors to evoke the sense of adventure in the laity. As we have said often, the fundamental challenge before us is ecclesial. Clever new theologies may keep seminary professors from being bored, but they will also distract them from their central mission as seminary professors and they will certainly not renew the church. The roller coaster of clever new theologies has subjected clergy to one fad after another and has misled pastors into thinking that their problem was intellectual rather than ecclesial.

Renewal comes, not through isolated, heroic thinkers, but rather in the church through the everyday activity of people such as those in the examples we have drawn on. We believe that renewal comes through an appreciation of the continuing empowerment, by word and sacrament, which, in each age, creates a church worthy to hear the Word and to receive the body and blood of Christ.

> Therefore remember that at one time you Gentiles in the flesh, . . . were at that time separated from Christ, alienated from the commonwealth of Israel, and strangers to the covenants of promise, having no hope and without God in the world. But now in Christ Jesus you who once were far off have been brought near in the blood of Christ. For he is our peace, who has made us both one, and has broken down the dividing wall of hostility, . . . and might reconcile us both to God in one body through the cross, thereby bringing the hostility to an end. . . . So then you are no longer strangers and sojourners, but you are fellow citizens with the saints and members of the household of God, built upon the foundation of the apostles and prophets, Christ Jesus himself being the cornerstone, in whom the whole structure is joined together and grows into a holy temple in the Lord; in whom you also are built into it for a dwelling place of God in the Spirit. (Eph. 2:11-22)

By the Working of God's Power

. . . The church is dying a slow death at the hands of pastors who are nice, pastors who are themselves miserable because they are attempting to "help people" with no basis for that help, and no safeguard for themselves, other than their desire to be nice and help people. Indeed, one of us is tempted to think that there is not much wrong with the church that could not be cured by God calling about a hundred really insensitive, uncaring, and offensive people into the ministry!

A better way is for us to be so confident that the gospel is true that we dare not say less to the people we are called to serve.

Power arises from truthfulness. The power of Christian clergy lies, not in their cultural significance, but in their service to the living truth who is Jesus Christ. Although Christianity is not about "liberation" as the world defines it, we are about *power,* and there is no need for a false humility among Christians about our lack of power. Servanthood is power insofar as it is obedience to the One who is the way, the truth, and the life. Clergy must not assume that their disempowerment by the culture means that they have no power. A Christian pastor is a powerful person because only the pastor has been given the authority to serve the eucharist and to preach the Word for the church—to point to the very presence of God among us. That is power.

So the real challenge for clergy is not how to live as powerless persons in a world that recognizes only the power of politics. The challenge is how to be a person who is morally capable of exercising the awesome power of Word and sacrament as bestowed by God and God's church. Clergy become dangerous when they act as if they are so powerless that they could not hurt people. Imagine a medical student coming to medical school saying, "I want to be a doctor, but I do not want to take any courses in anatomy because I do not enjoy anatomy." The medical school would say, in effect, "To heck with your personal preferences. We do not want you cutting on people if you do not know anatomy!"

Yet many seminaries allow future pastors to avoid mastery of church history or theology—perhaps because the seminary assumes that, after all, the clergy cannot kill anybody through their ignorance. To the church is given the awesome power to bind and to loose, to convict and to forgive. Look what Peter did to poor Ananias and Sapphira. We must therefore be people who respect the power God has given us and who learn to exercise that power faithfully.

Jonathan Edwards, who never hesitated to speak the truth as it was delivered to him, asked fellow pastors:

> Why should we be afraid to let persons that are in an infinitely miserable condition know the truth, or to bring them into the light for fear it should terrify them? It is light that must convert them, if ever they are converted. The more we bring sinners into the light while they are miserable and the light is terrible to them, the more likely it is that by and by the light will be joyful to them. The ease, peace and comfort that natural men enjoy, have their foundation in darkness and blindness; therefore as that darkness

vanishes and they are terrified: but that is no good argument why we should endeavor to bring back their darkness that we may promote their present comfort. (*Thoughts on the Revival of Religion in New England, 1740 to which is prefixed A Narrative of the Surprising Work of God in Northampton, Mass., 1735* [New York: American Tract Society, n.d.], *pp. 244-45*)

We believe that the pastoral ministry today is being robbed of its vitality and authority by participating in a charade of protecting people from the truth that is the gospel, which is our true empowerment.

For pastors to speak the truth boldly, they must be freed from fear of their congregations. While others may seek to embolden pastors by psychological appeals for the strengthening of clerical ego, we have sought to empower pastors through an appeal to the theological basis of their ministry. We therefore agree with Walter Brueggemann when he says "Pastoral vitality is related to a concrete sense of what God is doing in the world, If one has not made a bold decision about that, then one must keep juggling and vacillating" (*Hopeful Imagination* [Philadelphia: Fortress Press, 1986], p. 16). In chains, the writer to First Church Ephesus could still claim the power to speak and to minister to his congregation on the basis of God's vocation:

> Of this gospel I was made a minister according to the gift of God's grace which was given me by the working of his power. To me, though I am the very least of all the saints, this grace was given, to preach to the Gentiles the unsearchable riches of Christ, and to make all men see what is the plan of the mystery hidden for ages in God who created all things; that through the church the manifold wisdom of God might now be made known to the principalities and powers in the heavenly places. This was according to the eternal purpose which he has realized in Christ Jesus our Lord, in whom we have boldness and confidence. (Eph. 3:7-12)

A pastor finds the guts to speak the truth because he or she has found this biblical basis for pastoral care: Jesus Christ, "in whom we have boldness and confidence." Lacking such confidence, pastors become fearful creatures. After all, pastors have a front row seat to observe the lies by which people live, the shallowness, the quiet desperation, or raging anger by which people react to a life without significance. Self-protection makes cowards of us all.

We believe that pastoral fear can be overcome because the people Jesus calls to be the church, for all their infidelity, are still capable of hearing the truth. A ministry built on fear of the people can never be a happy one. Undoubtedly, people come to church for a host of wrong reasons. But the pastor is able to help them find the words to acknowledge, sometimes to their own surprise, that they are here because God has willed them to be here, despite all their wrong reasons. People may come to church to get their marriages fixed, or for help in raising chaste, obedient children, or simply to be with a few relatively nice people rather than to be alone. The pastor is essential for helping us cut through our wrong reasons for being at church and helping us to see that God is a relentless, utterly unscrupulous, infinitely resourceful god who is determined to have us, good reasons or bad. And that is why we rejoice; that is why we call our meal "eucharist."

For everyone who has demanded to know if we are liberal or conservative, someone else has wondered if there is anything "new" in what we say here. We have no stake in saying something new. That is a favorite game of academia and is of little use to a church more interested in saying something true than something new. However, if there is a new emphasis in what we write, it has to be a renewed confidence in the integrity of Christian convictions as embodied in the life and work of the church. Early on we asserted that the challenge facing today's Christians is not the necessity to translate Christian convictions into a modern idiom, but rather to form a community, a colony of resident aliens which is so shaped by our convictions that no one even has to ask what we mean by confessing belief in God as Father, Son, and Holy Spirit.

The biggest problem facing Christian theology is not translation but enactment. No doubt, one of the major reasons for the great modern theologians who strove to translate our language for modernity was that the church had become so inept at enactment. Yet no clever theological moves can be substituted for the necessity of the church being a community of people who embody our language about God, where talk about God is used without apology because our life together does not mock our words. The church is the visible, political enactment of our language of God by a people who can name their sin and accept God's forgiveness and are thereby enabled to speak the truth in love. Our Sunday worship has a way of reminding us, in the most explicit and ecclesial of ways, of the source of our power, the peculiar nature of our solutions to what ails the world.

God has graciously refused to leave us to our own devices but has come out to meet us in Jesus of Nazareth and his church. So one of the best ways to know God is to take a good look at the lives of those whom God has claimed—the saints.

Of course, that is just the reason many people say they do not believe in God. They look at this collection of "saints" called the church and say that they cannot see anybody who looks much different from somebody who does not believe. Part of the problem may be that these onlookers have a too limited, or even too paganly extravagant idea of God, which prevents their seeing God when God meets them in the life of Gladys or Paul. More than likely, we Christians have failed to become like the One we adore.

We have confidence in the boldness of pastors and the potential truthfulness of their congregations because we do not believe God has abandoned the world. A great deal is wrong with us as the church today, and who should know that any better than the church's pastors. Yet, thank God, we are not so unfaithful as to be utterly unable to locate the saints.

Stanley Hauerwas and William H. Willimon, *Resident Aliens: Life in the Christian Colony* **(Nashville: Abingdon, 1989), pp. 160-72.**

CHAPTER ELEVEN

The Pastor as Leader

In January of 1963, eight prominent "liberal" clergymen in Birmingham, Alabama, published an open letter asking Martin Luther King Jr. to withdraw from their city in order that there be time for gradual racial integration to occur through the working of the court system. In April, King wrote a letter to them while in jail. That letter has become one of King's most beloved and widely published pieces. Evoking the prophets of old, King spoke as a pastor to fellow pastors, chiding them for their lack of compassion, their failure of nerve; above all, their inability to be the bold leaders the church deserved.

Letter from Birmingham Jail
Martin Luther King Jr.

Author's Note: This response to a published statement by eight fellow clergymen from Alabama (Bishop C. C. J. Carpenter, Bishop Joseph A. Durick, Rabbi Hilton L. Grafman, Bishop Paul Hardin, Bishop Holan B. Harmon, the Reverend George M. Murray, the Reverend Edward V. Ramage and the Reverend Earl Stallings) was composed under somewhat constricting circumstances. Begun on the margins of the newspaper in which the statement appeared while I was in jail, the letter was continued on scraps of writing paper supplied by a friendly Negro trusty, and concluded on a pad my attorneys were eventually permitted to leave me. Although the text remains in substance unaltered, I have indulged in the author's prerogative of polishing it for publication.

April 16, 1963

My Dear Fellow Clergymen,

While confined here in the Birmingham city jail, I came across your recent statement calling my present activities "unwise and untimely." Seldom do I pause to answer criticism of my work and ideas. If I sought to answer all the criticisms that cross my desk, my secretaries would have little time for anything other than such correspondence in the course of the day, and I would have no time for constructive work. But since I feel that you are men of genuine good will and that your criticisms are sincerely set forth, I want to try to answer your statement in what I hope will be patient and reasonable terms.

I think I should indicate why I am here in Birmingham, since you have been influenced by the view which argues against "outsiders coming in." I have the honor of serving as president of the Southern Christian Leadership Conference, an organization operating in every southern state, with headquarters in Atlanta, Georgia. We have some eighty-five affiliated organizations across the South, and one of them is the Alabama Christian Movement for Human Rights. Frequently we share staff, educational and financial resources with our affiliates. Several months ago the affiliate here in Birmingham asked us to be on call to engage in a nonviolent direct-action program if such were deemed necessary. We readily consented, and when the hour came we lived up to our promise. So I, along with several members of my staff, am here because I was invited here. I am here because I have organizational ties here.

But more basically, I am in Birmingham because injustice is here. Just as the prophets of the eighth century B.C. left their villages and carried their "thus saith the Lord" far beyond the boundaries of their home towns, and just as the Apostle Paul left his village of Tarsus and carried the gospel of Jesus Christ to the far corners of the Greco-Roman world, so am I compelled to carry the gospel of freedom beyond my own home town. Like Paul, I must constantly respond to the Macedonian call for aid.

Moreover, I am cognizant of the interrelatedness of all communities and states. I cannot sit idly by in Atlanta and not be concerned about what happens in Birmingham. Injustice anywhere is a threat to justice everywhere. We are caught in an inescapable net-work of mutuality, tied in a single garment of destiny. Whatever affects one directly, affects all indirectly. Never again can we afford to live with the narrow, provincial "outside agitator" idea. Anyone who lives inside the United States can never be considered an out-sider anywhere within its bounds.

You deplore the demonstrations taking place in Birmingham. But your statement, I am sorry to say, fails to express a similar con-cern for the conditions that brought the demonstrations. I am sure that none of you would want to rest content with the superficial kind of social analysis that deals merely with effects and does not grapple with underlying causes. It is unfortunate that demonstra-tions are taking place in Birmingham, but it is even more unfortu-nate that the city's white power structure left the Negro community with no alternative.

In any nonviolent campaign there are four basic steps: collection of the facts to determine whether injustices exist; negotiation; self-purification; and direct action. We have gone through all these steps in Birmingham. There can be no gainsaying the fact that racial injustice engulfs this community. Birmingham is probably the most thoroughly segregated city in the United States. Its ugly record of brutality is widely known. Negroes have experienced grossly unjust treatment in the courts. There have been more unsolved bombings of Negro homes and churches in Birmingham than in any other city in this nation. These are the hard, brutal facts of the case. On the basis of these conditions, Negro leaders sought to negotiate with the city fathers. But the latter consistently refused to engage in good-faith negotiation.

Then, last September, came the opportunity to talk with leaders of Birmingham's economic community. In the course of the negoti-ations, certain promises were made by the merchants—for exam-ple, to remove the stores' humiliating racial signs. On the basis of these promises, the Reverend Fred Shuttlesworth and the leaders of the Alabama Christian Movement for Human Rights agreed to a moratorium on all demonstrations. As the weeks and months went by, we realized that we were the victims of a broken promise. A few signs, briefly removed, returned; the others remained.

As in so many past experiences, our hopes had been blasted, and the shadow of deep disappointment settled upon us. We had no alternative except to prepare for direct action, whereby we would present our very bodies as a means of laying our case before the conscience of the local and national community. Mindful of the difficulties involved, we decided to undertake a process of self-purification. We began a series of workshops on nonviolence, and we repeatedly asked ourselves: "Are you able to accept blows without retaliating?" "Are you able to endure the ordeal of jail?" We decided to schedule our direct-action program for the Easter season, realizing that except for Christmas, this is the main shopping period of the year. Knowing that a strong economic-withdrawal program would be the by-product of direct action, we felt that this would be the best time to bring pressure to bear on the merchants for the needed change.

Then it occurred to us that Birmingham's mayorality election was coming up in March, and we speedily decided to postpone action until after election day. When we discovered that the Commissioner of Public Safety, Eugene "Bull" Connor, had piled up enough votes to be in the run-off, we decided again to postpone action until the day after the run-off so that the demonstrations could not be used to cloud the issues. Like many others, we waited to see Mr. Connor defeated, and to this end we endured postponement after postponement. Having aided in this community need, we felt that our direct-action program could be delayed no longer.

You may well ask: "Why direct action? Why sit-ins, marches and so forth? Isn't negotiation a better path?" You are quite right in calling for negotiation. Indeed, this is the very purpose of direct action. Nonviolent direct action seeks to create such a crisis and foster such a tension that a community which has constantly refused to negotiate is forced to confront the issue. It seeks so to dramatize the issue that it can no longer be ignored. My citing the creation of tension as part of the work of the non-violent resister may sound rather shocking. But I must confess that I am not afraid of the word "tension." I have earnestly opposed violent tension, but there is a type of constructive, nonviolent tension which is necessary for growth. Just as Socrates felt that it was necessary to create a tension in the mind so that individuals could rise from the bondage of myths and half-truths to the unfettered realm of creative analysis and objective appraisal, so must we see the need for nonviolent gadflies to create the kind of tension in society that will help men rise from the dark depths of prejudice and racism to the majestic heights of understanding and brotherhood.

The purpose of our direct-action program is to create a situation so crisis-packed that it will inevitably open the door to negotiation. I therefore concur with you in your call for negotiation. Too long has our beloved Southland been bogged down in a tragic effort to live in monologue rather than dialogue. . . .

. . . My friends, I must say to you that we have not made a single gain in civil rights without determined legal and nonviolent pressure. Lamentably, it is an historical fact that privileged groups seldom give up their privileges voluntarily. Individuals may see the moral light and voluntarily give up their unjust posture; but, as Reinhold Niebuhr has reminded us, groups tend to be more immoral than individuals.

We know through painful experience that freedom is never voluntarily given by the oppressor; it must be demanded by the oppressed. Frankly, I have yet to engage in a direct-action campaign that was "well timed" in the view of those who have not suffered unduly from the disease of segregation. For years now I have heard the word "Wait!" It rings in the ear of every Negro with a piercing familiarity. This "Wait" has almost always meant "Never." We must come to see, with one of our distinguished jurists, that "justice too long delayed is justice denied."

We have waited for more than 340 years for our constitutional and God-given rights. The nations of Asia and Africa are moving with jetlike speed toward gaining political independence, but we still creep at horse-and-buggy pace toward gaining of a cup of coffee at a lunch counter. Perhaps it is easy for those who have never felt the stinging darts of segregation to say, "Wait." But when you have seen vicious mobs lynch your mothers and fathers at will and drown your sisters and brothers at whim; when you have seen hate-filled policemen curse, kick, and even kill your black brothers and sisters; when you see the vast majority of your twenty million Negro brothers smothering in an airtight cage of poverty in the midst of an affluent society; when you suddenly find your tongue twisted and your speech stammering as you seek to explain to your six-year-old daughter why she can't go to the public amusement park that has just been advertised on television, and see tears welling up in her eyes when she is told that Funtown is closed to colored children, and see ominous clouds of inferiority beginning to form in her little mental sky, and see her beginning to distort her personality by developing an unconscious bitterness toward white people; when you have to concoct an answer for a five-year-old son who is asking: "Daddy, why do white people treat colored people so mean?"; when you take a cross-country drive and find it necessary to sleep night after night in the uncomfortable corners of your automobile because no motel will accept you; when you are humiliated day in and day out by nagging signs reading "white" and "colored"; when your first name becomes "nigger," your middle name becomes "boy" (however old you are) and your last name becomes "John," and your wife and mother are never given the respected title "Mrs."; when you are harried by day and haunted by night by the fact that you are a Negro, living constantly at tiptoe stance, never quite knowing what to expect next, and are plagued with inner fears and outer resentments; when you are forever fighting a degenerating sense of "nobodiness"—then you will understand why we find it difficult to wait. There comes a time when the cup of endurance runs over, and men are no longer willing to be plunged into the abyss of despair. I hope, sirs, you can understand our legitimate and unavoidable impatience.

You express a great deal of anxiety over our willingness to break laws. This is certainly a legitimate concern. Since we so diligently urge people to obey the Supreme Court's decision of 1954 outlawing segregation in the public schools, at first glance it may seem rather paradoxical for us consciously to break laws. One may well ask: "How can you advocate breaking some laws and obeying others?" The answer lies in the fact that there are two types of laws: just and unjust. Conversely, one has a moral responsibility to disobey unjust laws. I would agree with St. Augustine that "an unjust law is no law at all."

Now, what is the difference between the two? How does one determine whether a law is just or unjust? A just law is a man-made code that squares with the moral law or the law of God. An unjust law is a code that is out of harmony with the moral law. To put it in the terms of St. Thomas Aquinas: An unjust law is a human law that is not rooted in eternal law and natural law. Any law that uplifts human personality is just. Any law that degrades human personality is unjust. All segregation statutes are unjust because segregation distorts the soul and damages the personality. It gives the segregator a false sense of superiority and the segregated a false sense of inferiority. Segregation, to use the terminology of the Jewish philosopher Martin Buber, substitutes an "I-it" relationship for an "I-thou" relationship and ends up relegating persons to the status of things. Hence segregation is not only politically, economically and sociologically unsound, it is morally wrong and sinful. Paul Tillich has said that sin is separation. Is not segregation an existential expression of man's tragic separation, his awful estrangement, his terrible sinfulness? Thus it is that I can urge men to obey the 1954 decision of the Supreme Court, for it is morally right; and I can urge them to disobey segregation ordinances, for they are morally wrong.

Let us consider a more concrete example of just and unjust laws. An unjust law is a code that a numerical or power majority group compels a minority group to obey but does not make binding on itself. This is *difference* made legal. By the same token, a just law is a code that a majority compels a minority to follow and that it is willing to follow itself. This is *sameness* made legal.

Let me give another explanation. A law is unjust if it is inflicted on a minority that, as a result of being denied the right to vote, had no part in enacting or devising the law. Who can say that the legislature of Alabama which set up that state's segregation laws was democratically elected? Throughout Alabama all sorts of devious methods are used to prevent Negroes from becoming registered voters, and there are some counties in which, even though Negroes constitute a majority of the population, not a single Negro is registered. Can any law enacted under such circumstances be considered democratically structured?

Sometimes a law is just on its face and unjust in its application. For instance, I have been arrested on a charge of parading without a permit. Now, there is nothing wrong in having an ordinance which requires a permit for a parade. But such an ordinance becomes unjust when it is used to maintain segregation and to deny citizens the First-Amendment privilege of peaceful assembly and protest.

I hope you are able to see the distinction I am trying to point out. In no sense do I advocate evading or defying the law, as would the rabid segregationist. That would lead to anarchy. One who breaks an unjust law must do so openly, lovingly, and with a willingness to accept the penalty. I submit that an individual who breaks a law that conscience tells him is unjust, and who willingly accepts the penalty of imprisonment in order to arouse the conscience of the community over its injustice, is in reality expressing the highest respect for law.

Of course, there is nothing new about this kind of civil disobedience. It was evidenced sublimely in the refusal of Shadrach, Meshach and Abednego to obey the laws of Nebuchadnezzar, on the ground that a higher moral law was at stake. It was practiced superbly by the early Christians, who were willing to face hungry lions and the excruciating pain of chopping blocks rather than submit to certain unjust laws of the Roman Empire. To a degree, academic freedom is a reality today because Socrates practiced civil disobedience. In our own nation, the Boston Tea Party represented a massive act of civil disobedience.

We should never forget that everything Adolf Hitler did in Germany was "legal" and everything the Hungarian freedom fighters did in Hungary was "illegal." It was "illegal" to aid and comfort a Jew in Hitler's Germany. Even so, I am sure that, had I lived in Germany at the time, I would have aided and comforted my Jewish brothers. If today I lived in a Communist country where certain principles dear to the Christian faith are suppressed, I would openly advocate disobeying that country's antireligious laws.

I must make two honest confessions to you, my Christian and Jewish brothers. First, I must confess that over the past few years I have been gravely disappointed with the white moderate. I have almost reached the regrettable conclusion that the Negro's great stumbling block in his stride toward freedom is not the White Citizen's Councilor or the Ku Klux Klanner, but the white moderate, who is more devoted to "order" than to justice; who prefers a negative peace which is the absence of tension to a positive peace which is the presence of justice; who constantly says: "I agree with you in the goal you seek, but I cannot agree with your methods of direct action"; who paternalistically believes he can set the timetable for another man's freedom; who lives by a mythical concept of time and who constantly advises the Negro to wait for a "more convenient season." Shallow understanding from people of good will is more frustrating than absolute misunderstanding from people of ill will. Lukewarm acceptance is much more bewildering than outright rejection.

I had hoped that the white moderate would understand that law and order exist for the purpose of establishing justice and that when they fail in this purpose they become the dangerously structured dams that block the flow of social progress. I had hoped that the white moderate would understand that the present tension in the South is a necessary phase of the transition from an obnoxious negative peace, in which the Negro passively accepted his unjust plight, to a substantive and positive peace, in which all men will respect the dignity and worth of human personality. Actually, we who engage in nonviolent direct action are not the creators of tension. We merely bring to the surface the hidden tension that is already alive. We bring it out in the open, where it can be seen and dealt with. Like a boil that can never be cured so long as it is covered up but must be opened with all its ugliness to the natural medicines of air and light, injustice must be exposed, with all the tension its exposure creates, to the light of human conscience and the air of national opinion before it can be cured.

In your statement you assert that our actions, even though peaceful, must be condemned because they precipitate violence. But is this a logical assertion? Isn't this like condemning the robbed man because his possession of money precipitated the evil act of robbery? Isn't this like condemning Socrates because his unswerving commitment to truth and his philosophical inquiries precipitated the act by the misguided populace in which they made him drink hemlock? Isn't this like condemning Jesus because his unique God-consciousness and never-ceasing devotion to God's will precipitated the evil act of crucifixion? We must come to see that, as the federal courts have consistently affirmed, it is wrong to urge an individual to cease his efforts to gain his basic constitutional rights because the quest may precipitate violence. Society must protect the robbed and punish the robber.

I had also hoped that the white moderate would reject the myth concerning time in relation to the struggle for freedom. I have just received a letter from a white brother in Texas. He writes: "All Christians know that the colored people will receive equal rights eventually, but it is possible that you are in too great a religious hurry. It has taken Christianity almost two thousand years to accomplish what it has. The teachings of Christ take time to come to earth." Such an attitude stems from a tragic misconception of time, from the strangely irrational notion that there is something in the very flow of time that will inevitably cure all ills. Actually, time itself is neutral; it can be used either destructively or constructively. More and more I feel that the people of ill will have used time much more effectively than the people of good will. We will have to repent in this generation not merely for the hateful words and actions of the bad people but for the appalling silence of the good people. Human progress never rolls in on wheels of inevitability; it comes through the tireless efforts of men willing to be co-workers with God, and without this hard work, time itself becomes an ally of the forces of social stagnation. We must use time creatively, in the knowledge that the time is always ripe to do right. Now is the time to make real the promise of democracy and transform our pending national elegy into a creative psalm of brotherhood. Now is the time to lift our national policy from the quicksand of racial injustice to the solid rock of human dignity.

You speak of our activity in Birmingham as extreme. At first I was rather disappointed that fellow clergymen would see my non-violent efforts as those of an extremist. I began thinking about the fact that I stand in the middle of two opposing forces in the Negro community. One is a force of complacency, made up in part of Negroes who, as a result of long years of oppression, are so drained of self-respect and a sense of "somebodiness" that they have adjusted to segregation; and in part of a few middle-class Negroes who, because of a degree of academic and economic security and because in some ways they profit by segregation, have become insensitive to the problems of the masses. The other force is one of bitterness and hatred, and it comes perilously close to advocating violence. It is expressed in the various black nationalist groups that are springing up across the nation, the largest and best-known being Elijah Muhammad's Muslim movement. Nourished by the Negro's frustration over the continued existence of racial discrimi-nation, this movement is made up of people who have lost faith in America, who have absolutely repudiated Christianity, and who have concluded that the white man is an incorrigible "devil."

I have tried to stand between these two forces, saying that we need emulate neither the "do-nothingism" of the complacent nor the hatred and despair of the black nationalist. For there is the more excellent way of love and nonviolent protest. I am grateful to God that, through the influence of the Negro church, the way of nonviolence became an integral part of our struggle.

If this philosophy had not emerged, by now many streets of the South would, I am convinced, be flowing with blood. And I am further convinced that if our white brothers dismiss as "rabble-rousers" and "outside agitators" those of us who employ nonviolent direct action, and if they refuse to support our nonviolent efforts, millions of Negroes will, out of frustration and despair, seek solace and security in black-nationalist ideologies—a development that would inevitably lead to a frightening racial nightmare.

Oppressed people cannot remain oppressed forever. The yearning for freedom eventually manifests itself, and that is what has happened to the American Negro. Something within has reminded him of his birthright of freedom, and something without has reminded him that it can be gained. Consciously or unconsciously, he has been caught up by the *Zeitgeist,* and with his black brothers of Africa and his brown and yellow brothers of Asia, South America and the Caribbean, the United States Negro is moving with a sense of great urgency toward the promised land of racial justice. If one recognizes this vital urge that has engulfed the Negro community, one should readily understand why public demonstrations are taking place. The Negro has many pent-up resentments and latent frustrations, and he must release them. So let him march; let him make prayer pilgrimages to the city hall; let him go on freedom rides—and try to understand why he must do so. If his repressed emotions are not released in nonviolent ways, they will seek expression through violence; this is not a threat but a fact of history. So I have not said to my people: "Get rid of your discontent." Rather, I have tried to say that this normal and healthy discontent can be channeled into the creative outlet of nonviolent direct action. And now this approach is being termed extremist.

But though I was initially disappointed at being categorized as an extremist, as I continued to think about the matter I gradually gained a measure of satisfaction from the label. Was not Jesus an extremist for love: "Love your enemies, bless them that curse you, do good to them that hate you, and pray for them which despitefully use you, and persecute you." Was not Amos an extremist for justice: "Let justice roll down like waters and righteousness like an ever-flowing stream." Was not Paul an extremist for the Christian gospel: "I bear in my body the marks of the Lord Jesus." Was not Martin Luther an extremist: "Here I stand; I cannot do otherwise, so help me God." And John Bunyan: "I will stay in jail to the end of my days before I make a butchery of my conscience." And Abraham Lincoln: "This nation cannot survive half slave and half free." And Thomas Jefferson: "We hold these truths to be self-evident, that all men are created equal . . ." So the question is not whether we will be extremists, but what kind of extremist we will be. Will we be extremists for hate or for love? Will we be extremists for the preservation of injustice or for the extension of justice? In that dramatic scene on Calvary's hill three men were crucified. We must never forget that all three were crucified for the same crime—the crime of extremism. Two were extremists for immorality, and thus fell below their environment. The other, Jesus Christ, was an extremist for love, truth and goodness, and thereby rose above his environment. Perhaps the South, the nation and the world are in dire need of creative extremists. . . .

I have been so greatly disappointed with the white church and its leadership. Of course, there are some notable exceptions. I am not unmindful of the fact that each of you has taken some significant stands on this issue. I commend you, Reverend Stallings, for your Christian stand on this past Sunday, in welcoming Negroes to your worship service on a nonsegregated basis. I commend the Catholic leaders of this state for integrating Spring Hill College several years ago.

But despite these notable exceptions, I must honestly reiterate that I have been disappointed with the church. I do not say this as one of those negative critics who can always find something wrong with the church. I say this as a minister of the gospel, who loves the church; who was nurtured in its bosom; who has been sustained by its spiritual blessings and who will remain true to it as long as the cord of life shall lengthen.

When I was suddenly catapulted into the leadership of the bus protest in Montgomery, Alabama, a few years ago, I felt we would be supported by the white church. I felt that the white ministers, priests and rabbis of the South would be among our strongest allies. Instead, some have been outright opponents, refusing to understand the freedom movement and misrepresenting its leaders; all too many others have been more cautious than courageous and have remained silent behind the anesthetizing security of stained-glass windows.

In spite of my shattered dreams, I came to Birmingham with the hope that the white religious leadership of this community would see the justice of our cause and, with deep moral concern, would serve as the channel through which our just grievances could reach the power structure. I had hoped that each of you would understand. But again I have been disappointed.

I have heard numerous southern religious leaders admonish their worshipers to comply with a desegregation decision because it is the law, but I have longed to hear white ministers declare: "Follow this decree because integration is morally right and because the Negro is your brother." In the midst of blatant injustices inflicted upon the Negro, I have watched white churchmen stand on the sideline and mouth pious irrelevancies and sanctimonious trivialities. In the midst of a mighty struggle to rid our nation of racial and economic injustice, I have heard many ministers say: "Those are social issues, with which the gospel has no real concern." And I have watched many churches commit themselves to a completely other-worldly religion which made a strange, un-Biblical distinction between body and soul, between the sacred and the secular.

I have traveled the length and breadth of Alabama, Mississippi and all the other southern states. On sweltering summer days and crisp autumn mornings I have looked at the South's beautiful churches with their lofty spires pointing heavenward. I have beheld the impressive outlines of her massive religious-education buildings. Over and over I have found myself asking: "What kind of people worship here? Who is their God? Where were their voices when the lips of Governor Barnett dripped with words of interposition and nullification? Where were they when Governor Wallace gave a clarion call for defiance and hatred? Where were their voices of support when bruised and weary Negro men and women decided to rise from the dark dungeons of complacency to the bright hills of creative protest?"

Yes, these questions are still in my mind. In deep disappointment I have wept over the laxity of the church. But be assured that my tears have been tears of love. There can be no deep disappointment where there is not deep love. Yes, I love the church. How could I do otherwise? I am in the rather unique position of being the son, the grandson and the great-grandson of preachers. Yes, I see the church as the body of Christ. But, oh! How we have blemished and scarred that body through social neglect and through fear of being nonconformists.

There was a time when the church was very powerful—in the time when the early Christians rejoiced at being deemed worthy to suffer for what they believed. In those days the church was not merely a thermometer that recorded the ideas and principles of popular opinion; it was a thermostat that transformed the mores of society. Whenever the early Christians entered a town, the people in power became disturbed and immediately sought to convict the Christians for being "disturbers of the peace" and "outside agitators." But the Christians pressed on, in the conviction that they were "a colony of heaven," called to obey God rather than man. Small in number, they were big in commitment. They were too God-intoxicated to be "astronomically intimidated." By their effort and example they brought an end to such ancient evils as infanticide and gladiatorial contests.

Things are different now. So often the contemporary church is a weak, ineffectual voice with an uncertain sound. So often it is an archdefender of the status quo. Far from being disturbed by the presence of the church, the power structure of the average community is consoled by the church's silent—and often even vocal—sanction of things as they are.

But the judgment of God is upon the church as never before. If today's church does not recapture the sacrificial spirit of the early church, it will lose its authenticity, forfeit the loyalty of millions, and be dismissed as an irrelevant social club with no meaning for the twentieth century. Every day I meet young people whose disappointment with the church has turned into outright disgust.

Perhaps I have once again been too optimistic. Is organized religion too inextricably bound to the status quo to save our nation and the world? Perhaps I must turn my faith to the inner spiritual church, the church within the church, as the true *ekklesia* and the hope of the world. But again I am thankful to God that some noble souls from the ranks of organized religion have broken loose from the paralyzing chains of conformity and joined us as active partners in the struggle for freedom. They have left their secure congregations and walked the streets of Albany, Georgia, with us. They have gone down the highways of the South on tortuous rides for freedom. Yes, they have gone to jail with us. Some have been dismissed from their churches, have lost the support of their bishops and fellow ministers. But they have acted in the faith that right defeated is stronger than evil triumphant. Their witness has been the spiritual salt that has preserved the true meaning of the gospel in these troubled times. They have carved a tunnel of hope through the dark mountain of disappointment.

I hope the church as a whole will meet the challenge of this decisive hour. But even if the church does not come to the aid of justice, I have no despair about the future. I have no fear about the outcome of our struggle in Birmingham, even if our motives are at present misunderstood. We will reach the goal of freedom in Birmingham and all over the nation, because the goal of America is freedom. Abused and scorned though we may be, our destiny is tied up with the America's destiny. Before the Pilgrims landed at Plymouth, we were here. Before the pen of Jefferson etched the majestic words of the Declaration of Independence across the pages of history, we were here. For more than two centuries our forebears labored in this country without wages; they made cotton king; they built the homes of their masters while suffering gross injustice and shameful humiliation—and yet out of a bottomless vitality they continued to thrive and develop. If the inexpressible cruelties of slavery could not stop us, the opposition we now face will surely fail. We will win our freedom because the sacred heritage of our nation and the eternal will of God are embodied in our echoing demands.

Before closing I feel impelled to mention one other point in your statement that has troubled me profoundly. You warmly commended the Birmingham police force for keeping "order" and "preventing violence." I doubt that you would have so warmly commended the police force if you had seen its dogs sinking their teeth into unarmed, nonviolent Negroes. I doubt that you would so quickly commend the policemen if you were to observe their ugly and inhumane treatment of Negroes here in the city jail; if you were to watch them push and curse old Negro women and young Negro girls; if you were to see them slap and kick old Negro men and young boys; if you were to observe them, as they did on two occasions, refuse to give us food because we wanted to sing our grace together. I cannot join you in your praise of the Birmingham police department. . . .

I wish you had commended the Negro sit-inners and demonstrators of Birmingham for their sublime courage, their willingness to suffer and their amazing discipline in the midst of great provocation. One day the South will recognize its real heroes. They will be the James Merediths, with the noble sense of purpose that enables them to face jeering and hostile mobs, and with the agonizing loneliness that characterizes the life of the pioneer. They will be old, oppressed, battered Negro women, symbolized in a seventy-two-year-old woman in Montgomery, Alabama, who rose up with a sense of dignity and with her people decided not to ride segregated buses, and who responded with ungrammatical profundity to one who inquired about her weariness: "My feets is tired, but my soul is at rest." They will be the young high school and college students, the young ministers of the gospel and a host of their elders, courageously and nonviolently sitting in at lunch counters and willingly going to jail for consciences' sake. One day the South will know that when these disinherited children of God sat down at lunch counters, they were in reality standing up for what is best in the American dream and for the most sacred values in our Judaeo-Christian heritage, thereby bringing our nation back to those great wells of democracy which were dug deep by the founding fathers in their formulation of the Constitution and the Declaration of Independence.

Never before have I written so long a letter. I'm afraid it is much too long to take your precious time. I can assure you that it would have been much shorter if I had been writing from a comfortable desk, but what else can one do when he is alone in a narrow jail cell, other than write long letters, think long thoughts and pray long prayers?

If I have said anything in this letter that overstates the truth and indicates an unreasonable impatience, I beg you to forgive me. If I have said anything that understates the truth and indicates my having a patience that allows me to settle for anything less than brotherhood, I beg God to forgive me.

I hope this letter finds you strong in the faith. I also hope that circumstances will soon make it possible for me to meet each of you, not as an integrationist or a civil-rights leader but as a fellow clergyman and a Christian brother. Let us all hope that the dark clouds of racial prejudice will soon pass away and the deep fog of misunderstanding will be lifted from our fear-drenched communities, and in some not too distant tomorrow the radiant stars of love and brotherhood will shine over our great nation with all their scintillating beauty.

Yours for the cause of Peace and Brotherhood,
Martin Luther King, Jr.

Martin Luther King, Jr., *Why We Can't Wait* (New York: Penguin, 2000), pp. 64-84. The American Friends Committee first published this essay as a pamphlet.

It was the Roaring Twenties. And it was Los Angeles, boomtown of America's new century of postwar promise. Here is where one of the most interesting ministerial personalities of the twentieth century made her mark at Angelus Temple. Hollywood and showbiz glitz provided the context for the sprawling Angelus Temple. Here was a church like no other, built around the inimitable personality of Sister Aimee Semple McPherson. Sister Aimee attracted thousands with her dramatic sermons, caused a national scandal with her strange disappearances, and, in the end, became the mother of a whole new Christian church—the Church of the Foursquare Gospel. At her best, she was a creative, bold evangelist. At her worst, she capitulated to showbiz theatrics. In her attempt to reach the multitudes for Christ, Sister Aimee embodied a struggle that continued in the American church up through the present: When, in reaching out to the world, do we merely become indistinguishable from the world?

Sister Aimee
Daniel Mark Epstein

New Year's, 1923

At 2:30 in the afternoon Aimee Semple McPherson mounted an elevated platform just outside the central doors of Angelus Temple. Facing a crowd of more than 5,000, she opened her bible and read from the book of Kings, of the building of Solomon's temple, and the Lord's glory that filled it. After a song and a prayer, the evangelist was lowered to the pavement by two elders. Someone handed her a trowel to lay the corner plaques. She wept into the mortar. Two marble tablets were unveiled and set in place upon the center columns. One bore the name of the Church and its founder. The other tablet read: DEDICATED TO THE CAUSE OF INTER-DENOMINATIONAL AND WORLDWIDE EVANGELISM.

The tablet was to remind us that Angelus Temple was *not* a church in the parochial sense, any more than an evangelist is a parish priest. The Church of the Foursquare Gospel was conceived as a learning center for evangelism, whose chief object is the conversion experience. Insofar as it *became* a parish church, marrying and burying folks, the Temple veered from its founder's original intent. Sister Aimee wanted people who found salvation at her meetings either to become evangelists themselves or return to their parishes renewed with the power of the Holy Spirit.

The problem was that people became so attached to the pastor's vision, they never wanted to leave. They thought the Temple was magnificent. Fifty miles away the pilgrims could see a lighted cross rotating on top of the dome. In daylight the great dome sparkled from the crushed seashells mixed into the cement. Inside, the interior curve had been painted pale blue with wisps of clouds to resemble a bright sky. Five thousand three hundred seats in the auditorium and two balconies faced the stage, where the baptismal pool's backdrop represented the banks of the Jordan river.

Carved upon the proscenium were the words JESUS CHRIST, THE SAME YESTERDAY, TODAY AND FOREVER. At the top of the walls art-nouveau angels had been painted standing wing-to-wing, representing a vision she had had in 1917. The balcony facades bore a frieze of tilting bells.

It is curious that Aimee was more famous in Denver, St. Louis and Melbourne than she was in Los Angeles until that New Year's Day, 1923, when Angelus Temple was dedicated. In Los Angeles Aimee had kept a low profile while funds for the Temple poured in from the East and Midwest. Her invisibility at home may not have been calculated, but it was politically wise. No denomination in the city could have built such a church from the gifts of local constituents. Ministers looked at the construction in wonder and envy, driving by in their cars.

All this changed at the turn of the year. Ministers came from all over the country, spirit-filled Methodists, United Brethren, Baptists, and others who had worked with Sister Aimee, to share the pulpit with her at the dedication. The event received full coverage in *The New York Times*. Thousands of Aimee's fans, including five hundred Gypsies, made the pilgrimage to Echo Park. At sunrise they began gathering outside the Temple doors. By midmorning the traffic was so heavy that the anxious police began turning cars away from Echo Park, and they struggled to keep people off the streetcar tracks so the trolleys might pass.

While thousands were admiring Angelus Temple in Echo Park, hundreds of thousands saw a miniature of it glide past them in Pasadena. It was the day of the Tournament of Roses. Aimee had directed the creation of a float for the parade, a Temple replica made with roses and carnations. The float had a tiny organ playing hymns inside, and was surrounded by singing choir girls. Set on the flat bed of the largest truck they could find, the Angelus Temple float announced the dedication of the Church of the Foursquare Gospel. It received the parade's Grand Marshal Award.

Aimee's anonymity in Los Angeles was over.

What a long way she had come since the days when she battled to pitch her tent against the wind.

"The Gospel tent?" she recalled. "Its sloping poles are now pillars, its sagging roof a mighty dome. The openings that showed the evening stars have now become arched windows, and through them streams the Light of His blessing, even as it did then."

Like most blessings, it was mixed.

Building the Temple was an incomparable achievement. But the task that now faced her was even more difficult.

A stationary revival is almost a contradiction in terms. They had loved Aimee in San Jose, but after three weeks there her healings caused bitter controversy. Now a comparable "campaign" in Los Angeles had its opening on New Year's Day, 1923 and no date to close. How was she to keep it going?

Knowing she was happy only when she was working, Aimee put everyone to work. There was a sisterhood, with sewing circles that stitched layettes for poor mothers. A brotherhood found jobs for men released from prison. Her commissary, which would evolve into the greatest welfare agency in L.A. during the Depression, provided food, clothing, and rent money for the needy, regardless of race or religion. Nurseries cared for children too young for the Sunday school.

Most important of the volunteer activities was the prayer tower. This was the spiritual nerve center of Angelus Temple. From the day the Temple opened, a corps of volunteers prayed around the clock in two-hour shifts, surrounded by telephones. They prayed for God's Church, for the welfare of the nation; they prayed for themselves and their pastor and anyone who called in need. The Temple switchboard had a team of ministers who gave advice to parents, husbands and wives, alcoholics and drug addicts. They talked despairing wives out of suicide and drunken husbands out of homicide. Aimee referred to the prayer tower as the "dynamo of power" that kept Angelus Temple functioning.

Seventy years later, it is still radiating spiritual energy. You may call and ask them the time (theirs was the first telephone time service), or you may ask them to pray for you. They will cheerfully oblige. . . .

During the roaring twenties, journalists descended upon Hollywood like the proverbial locusts. By the decade's end four hundred correspondents from all over the world (including the Vatican) were covering the movie colony's escapades. When they ran out of juicy material on the Mary Pickfords and Rudolph Valentinos, they lit upon obscure but photogenic young players and gossiped about their love lives, making them famous.

On a dull day one of these journalists might wander into the crowd at Angelus Temple, to take note of the pretty evangelist who made men swoon.

The scandalmongers' effect on journalism in the 1920's is well known. They created a kind of "inflation" of news interest in personalities, lowering standards of privacy. It began with Hollywood. But reporters who covered Hollywood also covered City Hall, the racetrack, and Angelus Temple. . . .

Sister Aimee brought to Los Angeles her own brand of fantasy, just as powerful in its way as the moviemaker's fiction. She would prove herself no less inventive than Zukor and Lasky, and as energetic as Goldwyn and Fox—and these giants of the cinema admired her. Angelus Temple had perfect acoustics. In moments of envy certain producers in her audience hoped she might fail so they could take over the Temple and turn it into a theater.

But Aimee had already done that. Her years on the tent-show circuit had taught her that a religious service is sacred drama, a species of nonfictional theater, pure and simple. The problem with denominational churches, said Aimee, was that they had given in to their profane competitors—vaudeville, movies, and "legitimate theater"—and thereby had lost the attention of their congregations, who took their excitement wherever they could find it.

At first the climax of her services had been the altar call or, in smaller spaces, the baptism of the Holy Spirit. Then, from 1919 to 1922, her meetings culminated in prayers for the sick. But as of 1923 Aimee had so reduced her healing ministry, it could not attract the crowds she needed to sustain her.

The Temple was indeed a mixed blessing, a costly haven. She no longer had to leave her children and spend months on the road; but now she had to make sure that the crowds would come to *her*. She no longer had to strain her voice in drafty coliseums; but the 5,000-seat auditorium with its perfect acoustics cost a fortune to maintain. She was under pressure to create a religious theater that would guarantee an audience—and she could not repeat herself in her own pulpit.

As we have seen, she was a natural actress whose improvisatory power had quelled a Philadelphia riot in 1919. Now she would use the American revival meeting's dramatic structure to create a fluid form of religious theater that resembled, in all but content, a musical comedy.

On Easter in March of 1923 the temple organ, with its lofty pipes under the painted Savior's outstretched arms, was unveiled and dedicated. A fourteen-piece orchestra with a golden harp accompanied the organ's debut. Soon a choir of a hundred and a brass band of thirty-six—and numerous additional choral groups, trios, and quartets—would fill the sanctuary with their music. Aimee hired the talented Gladwyn Nichols away from the Salvation Army to be her musical director. The music was a mix of old hymns done in the traditional a cappella style and popular tunes with jazz arrangements. Sometimes Aimee would write religious lyrics for a current tune.

From Hollywood she could get costumes, props, and scenery to flesh out her message. After music, prayers, more music, and the offering, the audience would settle down for Aimee's sermon.

As she came to the story of Moses crossing the Desert of Zin, the organ played a dirge. The purple stage curtain opened on old Moses in his long Max Factor beard, in a blazing noonday spotlight. Toiling across the stage, he paused every few steps to lean upon his staff and wipe his brow. He raised his hands to Heaven, beseeching God's mercy upon his people. They were dying of thirst. Slowly the overhead lights focused on a gray rock upstage, and Sister Aimee read from Numbers 20:8 and 9.

"Take the rod, and speak ye unto the rock, and it shall give forth his water . . ." Watching the old man strike the rock with his staff, she cried out in horror, knowing the story's end—that this would cost Moses his entry into the Promised Land.

"Moses Crossing the Desert" was the first illustrated sermon played in the Temple. Aimee gave twenty-two other sermons a week, but it was the illustrated sermons that magnified her fame. They were so entertaining, it was nearly impossible to get within a block of Angelus Temple on Sunday nights, the crowds were so vast. For a decade the city had to schedule extra trolleys and detail special police to move traffic through Echo Park before and after services.

The tone of these little plays varied. By and large they were broadly humorous, poking fun at themselves, Satan, and human folly. The staging was professional, often superb; but in the 1920's the skits were shamelessly rough-hewn, full of missed cues and pratfalls. Aimee took every opportunity to use the actors' mistakes, and her own, as a good joke on herself to be shared with the audience.

Animals always got a laugh—they are natural comedians—and the former farm girl worked well with them. She made friends with Joe Flores, whose nearby stable supplied livestock for the horse operas. When time came for a sermon on the good shepherd and the hundredth lamb that went astray, Aimee telephoned Flores.

"Joe," she chirped in the little girl's voice she used on the telephone, "can you get me a lamb by the weekend?"

"Sure, Sister. As good as done."

The idea was that Aimee, in her shepherdess costume, would be surrounded by her painted flock, wailing in mock melodrama over the lost lamb. Suddenly the lamb would appear, wandering onstage from the wings, bleating forlornly. The shepherdess would shoulder the lost lamb and bear it around the stage in triumph.

Friday came. As Aimee had not heard from Joe Flores, she called him again to ask about the lamb. He told her he had not forgotten, and hung up. But Flores must have got very busy with something else, because Saturday came and went, and on Sunday morning Aimee called him in a panic.

"Joe, where's the lamb, Joe?"

Flores apologized all over himself: he was busy supplying a herd of cattle for a western. "What's the cue, Sister?" he asked. "I swear to God I'll deliver the lamb on cue."

So Aimee gave him the cue line. It was something like "Oh where, where can he be?" An indication of her faith—in the stable-keeper or her own improvisational genius—is that she went on with it. Dressed in her shepherdess costume, in front of more than 5,000 people, she preached toward the climax, which was to be the entrance of an animal she had never met. Aimee was probably prepared to pluck a child out of the audience, or a young man, and turn *him* into the lost lamb, down on his hands and knees making sheep sounds. That would do. Or maybe she would make comedy of the blown entrance, having an elaborate drumroll, fanfare, and spotlight upon—nothing, the absence of the delinquent hundredth lamb.

But Joe Flores was as good as his word. Aimee, dressed like Little Bo Peep, raised her big eyes to Heaven in mock despair over the hundredth lamb, crying out, "Oh where, where can he be?" The stage curtain ballooned ominously on the right as the animal blundered the wrong way before being turned toward the pulpit, bleating in the mature deep-throated tones not of a little lost lamb but of a disgruntled full-grown sheep.

She had forgotten to tell Flores she wanted a *portable* lamb.

Now it was too late. The animal eyed the shepherdess suspiciously as she approached, in a half-crouch, whooping and cheering and clapping her hands at the sight of her lost lamb. And the audience cheered, and then gasped at the thought she might try to pick it up. She did pick it up. Staggering hilariously back and forth, Sister Aimee regained her balance on those powerful legs, intoning from Scripture: "Even so it is not the will of your Father which is in heaven, that one of these—*little* ones . . ." She grunted, and the crowd laughed at the irony. ". . . should perish."

This made a wonderful show. So did the camel's entrance when Aimee preached upon the text: "It is easier for a camel to go through the eye of a needle, than for a rich man to enter into the kingdom of God."

The Eye of the Needle was a narrow gate to the walled city of Jerusalem. A camel could not squeeze through that gate until its burdens had been unloaded. Somehow Aimee staged the illusion of an enormous needle, tipped at such an angle that its eye might make a convincing passageway through which to lead the blinking camel, the smallest that the Barnes Zoo could supply. The camel was laden with bundles labeled Worldly Pleasure, Love of Riches, Selfishness, and Indifference to the Poor. Aimee made a comic business of trying to lead the camel through the passage with the burdens on, then removing them one by one to see if the beast could slip through, until all had been removed and the camel passed. We would find this hard to believe if Roberta Salter had not salvaged, from a crate of petty-cash receipts, one that amused her: From Barnes Zoo—$20.00, One Camel for the Eye of the Needle, May 12, 1925. And another invoice: Trucking—$12.70.

Roberta recalls the stage set for her mother's sermon on the Garden of Eden: papier-maché flowers and trees from end to end of the stage, in bold colors like a child's drawing. Aimee surveyed the designer's work, arms folded, foot tapping. "It needs . . . something," she thought out loud. "It needs something *alive* in it." And as Aimee overpronounced *alive*, her face lit up.

"The circus is in town," she exclaimed, snapping her fingers. "I'll get a macaw."

Why she thought the circus would be a reliable source of macaws we shall leave to the historians of the big top. In any case, this was the kind of impetuous decision that opened the door to the unexpected, the wellspring of comic improvisation. She got a macaw from the circus.

The gorgeous green bird with the long tail sat chained to his perch near the pulpit in silent dignity until the orchestra struck up its first tune. Then the macaw expressed his opinion, in words that revealed his unchristian education among circus roustabouts, barkers, and fire eaters.

"Oh, go to Hell," cried the macaw.

There was dead silence in the auditorium as the congregation wondered if they could believe their ears. The bird did not long keep them in suspense.

"Oh go to Hell," he repeated, a little louder than before. It was his only speech, evidently, but he knew it well.

Sister Aimee, hardly able to conceal her amusement, feigned horror. No one had ever dared to speak thus in her sanctuary, and now, here, in the Garden of Eden. . . .

Whatever the evangelist had planned for the evening, the hymns, the testimonies, the sermon, it would all now have to revolve around this running gag—Little Aimee versus the pagan macaw. If ever the show lagged and she needed a laugh, she would turn to the macaw and ask his opinion, and then gape, wide-eyed, as the bird delivered his inevitable judgment. She preached to him. She tried to convert him. She interpreted his sullen silences as acquiescence or as the deafness of the unrepentant. At last, in the play itself, she condemned the profane macaw, saying his voice was the voice of Satan that caused Adam and Eve to be banished from Paradise. But for his part in the little drama he would be granted absolution, a little perch in bird heaven.

The rich details of the early sermons are mostly lost, the pre-1930 skits and tableaus that built the Temple's membership. What has come down to us are their more spectacular effects, which legend has exaggerated. Aimee did *not* come thundering down the center aisle or the rampart of Angelus Temple on a motorcycle, as millions of people imagined she did. She was dressed in the uniform of a motorcycle cop, and she burst into the Temple from the lobby, cranking a hand siren. When she had got everyone's attention, she raised a white-gloved hand and shouted:

"Stop! You've been arrested for speeding."

That had been a rough week. The evangelist was so preoccupied with the administration of the commissary, the sisterhood, the Sunday School, the prayer tower, etc., that she could not find time to think about her Sunday sermon. She was suffering from a rare case of writer's block, when she took Roberta for a drive in the Oldsmobile. With her mind on the unwritten sermon, she heard the sound of a siren and over her shoulder saw a traffic policeman. The evangelist had been caught speeding.

The speeding ticket seemed a small price to pay for this lesson and the sermon it inspired. The sermon, in verse, was a long list of situations in which busy men and women might find themselves. You are preparing the house for a garden party, rushing here and there to shops for the perfect place settings . . . You are five days from the meeting of the board of the electric company to propose the adoption of your new invention . . . Suddenly your daughter becomes weak in the knees, faints with fever, and in the morning her legs are stiff, she cannot walk . . .

It was terrifying the way Aimee built, brick by brick, in her trumpeting voice, a glorious structure of worldly achievement, then wrecked it suddenly in a whisper of reference to human frailty—

sickness, shame, despair. When the auditorium was silent she cranked the horrible hand siren.

"Stop!" came the refrain. "You've been arrested for speeding."

God was the celestial traffic cop.

The sermon became so famous that a picture postcard of Aimee was printed, showing the evangelist leaning on a motorcycle with her hand up in the gesture of arrest. The postcard's effect is comic, and the motorcycle in the picture must have contributed to the legend that Aimee drove the vehicle through the church doors.

One night while Aimee was preaching on the theme that Salvation was available to anyone who would "step out in faith" and trust in the Lord, her sermon was interrupted by the screaming of a fire engine. The audience heard another scream, and another outside the building, the sirens overlapping their shrill rounds of alarm. The fear of fire in a crowded theater can turn so rapidly to panic, it is fortunate the firemen did not delay their entrance. With axes and ladders they burst through the temple doors.

They rushed toward the pulpit with a gigantic rescue net.

Spotlights hit a platform high above the stage, where a frail gentleman stood. He was in an obvious state of panic and indecision. Aimee explained to the congregation that the poor man trembling thirty feet above them like a treed kitten was a *sinner*. The audience exhaled an audible sigh of relief that this was all part of the show; and a wonderful show it was, too, as Aimee coaxed the sinner to step out.

That first step is a long one.

The firemen made a circle of strong arms around the net. Aimee stood by, calling to the sinner that God would save him, would save him from the flames of Hell if he would but step out, step out in faith and fly, "Fly into His safety net of refuge." This the man finally did, abandoning his timid posture, to execute the perfect swan dive of a trained acrobat.

This kind of shenanigans, and the jazz tunes, and the sprinkling of rose petals in the baptismal water, got Sister Aimee in trouble eventually with the Los Angeles Ministerial Association. She had joined shortly after the Temple opened, about the same time she joined the Chamber of Commerce. As an evangelist Aimee was welcomed; as a parish minister she was an unbearable intrusion.

Rose petals had no business in the holy water of the baptism, said the ministers. But their real, unspoken, quarrel with the rector of Angelus Temple was that she was raiding their church memberships. Since they couldn't come right out and say this, the preachers, in print and from the pulpit, denounced her "religious spectacles" as scandalous, exploiting the Gospel to attract attention to herself.

"Show me a better way to persuade willing people to come to church and I'll be happy to try your method. But please, please don't ask me to preach to empty seats," she said.

"Let's not waste our time quarreling over methods. God has use for all of us," she said. And:

"Remember the recipe in the old adage, for rabbit stew? It began, *First catch your rabbit.*"

At Home in Los Angeles, 1924

"No tourist who came to California in the twenties," says Roberta Salter, "felt his trip a success unless he could boast of hearing one of Aimee's sermons."

In the late 1920's her notoriety itself was a magnet—the mixture of achievement and scandal that had made her the most famous woman in America, more famous even than the actresses who came to sit at her feet and study her movements: Mary Pickford, Jean Harlow, Clara Bow. Roberta recalls: "Ambitious, social-climbing Hollywood hostesses, eager to provide their dinner guests with a new thrill, paid any price asked"—to scalpers who could guarantee good tickets for the Sunday night services.

But in the early years of the decade Sister Aimee was not yet a celebrity. She was well known, certainly, in religious circles, an emerging public figure. But people flocked to Angelus Temple for the sheer emotional intensity of the services, a blend of staged drama, music, and improvisational acting. Visitors never knew what to expect. Aimee was known for making theater of any human or animal eccentricity—a slip of the tongue, a foul-mouthed macaw, an obstinate sheep.

One night, before the offering, a poor woman stumbled up the aisle, her eyes shining. Hands outstretched, she announced in a musical voice that she was the blessed Mother of Christ, the Virgin

Mary. Hearing this, the white-garbed evangelist stepped down from the pulpit and met the woman's gaze. Aimee needed to make sure the woman was truly insane and not merely a heckler. Satisfied, she held out her arms to the pathetic woman. She embraced her warmly, saying, "Oh Mary, how blessed are we all, to have you here among us! Now come, come with me. As the mother of God you shall have the chair of honor above us all."

The madwoman beamed. She was overjoyed as Aimee led her up the steps to the stage and seated her in the carved minister's chair with such sincere respect, you would have thought the madwoman was indeed the Mother of God. From the seat of honor she watched in peaceful silence until the service was over.

Roberta and Rolf, now thirteen and eleven, often sat on the stage while Aimee preached. One Sunday night before the sermon began, they heard the sound of footsteps marching through the lobby. The doors burst open, several at once, and white-hooded figures entered, the white robes of Klansmen. A thousand of them filled four aisles of the Temple; a thousand people in the front rows silently gave up their seats to make way for the surprise visitors. The Klansmen sat in ominous silence, their arms folded across their chests, their breath whistling under the pointed hoods, as they waited for Aimee's sermon to begin.

Aimee turned to Roberta.

"Now you children go on home and study," she whispered. "You don't need to stay for the sermon tonight. Go home and do your schoolwork."

Roberta dutifully led her brother out the back door to the parsonage, where she left him with his books. But then she hurried back to the Temple and found a seat high in the last row of the top balcony.

The verses of a hymn were dying away as the sermon was about to begin. Aimee rose from her carved chair and slowly approached the pulpit, her open bible with the typed sermon balanced easily on her large hand.

Looking out at the congregation, she snapped the bible shut and laid it upon the lectern.

She spoke softly.

I have decided not to preach the sermon that has been announced all week. Unexpectedly, the Lord has placed a new message in my heart tonight.

But before I begin that sermon, I want to tell you a little story.

One day, in a city that shall be nameless, an aged Negro farmer came to see the sights. It was a warm, sunny Sunday, and he roamed the streets until he stood in the shadow of a beautiful church, far grander than any he had ever seen in his little country town.

The old Negro farmer stood gazing at the church spires pointing heavenward. And his heart filled with rapture as he listened to the sweet-voiced choir pouring out the praises of God.

"Oh I must go into *this* wonderful church," he told himself, "and worship my Master."

The actress rendered the cadence of the black man's voice so perfectly, the audience craned their necks to see if he stood behind her.

So very quietly he opened the door, and very quietly he sat down—in the *back* row.

Sister Aimee's eyes blazed as her audience took in the contrast between the humble farmer in the story and the bold intruders who now occupied all the front rows of this sanctuary.

She continued.

He sat, looking up in reverent wonder at the high ceiling and the stained glass windows, and the gold and silver ornaments on the altar. And he was about to find his place in the hymn book on the seat beside him.

All of a sudden an usher, in a frock coat, grabbed the old farmer by his elbow and jerked him to his feet. When the usher had led him outside, he said: "You can't come in here. There is a nice little Negro church on down the road about a mile."

"But I only wanted to worship the Lord," the old man said.

"Well," said the usher, "don't try to do it here. You'll have to go to your own church . . . Now get along."

And with that the usher turned on his heel and went back inside.

Now the old Negro was weary. He sat down on the stone steps of that magnificent church, and for a moment he was so hurt by what had happened to him, he began to weep. "All I wanted was to worship my Master."

Just then he felt the gentle warmth of someone's hand on his shoulder. He heard the sound of a kind but careworn voice.

"Don't feel sad, my brother," said the voice. It came from a fellow traveler who looked neither young nor old, but his clothes and boots showed the wear of many days and nights on the road.

"No, don't feel sad. I too have been trying to get into that church, for many, many years . . ."

As the stranger stroked his silky beard, his sad eyes twinkled merrily. And the old Negro farmer was suddenly thrilled and then comforted. For he knew down deep in his heart that he was looking into the compassionate face of Jesus Christ, the Master Himself.

She paused for a long beat to let the parable sink in.

The Klansmen had come to Angelus Temple to show Aimee the support they had promised her years earlier in Denver. They had come to worship in the Temple which their dollars (in clandestine donations) had helped to build. The hooded terrorists had not come to this public place in order to be terrorized and humiliated.

Aimee's voice rang out over the auditorium:

> You men who pride yourselves on patriotism, you men who have pledged yourselves to make America free for white Christianity, listen to me! Ask yourselves how is it possible to pretend to worship one of the greatest Jews who ever lived, Jesus Christ, and then to despise all living Jews?
>
> I say unto you as our Master said, *Judge not, that ye be not judged!*

This was the text of her sermon. But first she paused for a long time and looked into the eye slits of the hoods with a furious intensity that made the men rise, first one by one and then dozens at a time, until there was a virtual rout of the white-robed spooks up the aisles and out the doors, into the night from where they had come.

That is quite a story in itself, but it is not quite the end. Roberta recalls that as Aimee preached her impromptu sermon on the brotherhood of man, one by one and two by two "pale-faced men drifted back into the church and seated themselves quietly to listen . . ."

And next morning the park attendants found hundreds of white robes and hooded masks wadded up and abandoned in shrubs and bushes across the street and all around the lake in Echo Park.

Daniel Mark Epstein, *Sister Aimee: The Life of Aimee Semple McPherson* (New York: Harcourt Brace Jovanovich Publishers, 1993), pp. 247-63.

CHAPTER 12

The Pastor as Character

It is somewhat ironic that one of the noblest encomiums to Christian leadership was written by a man who was pleading that he had no business being a pastor, St. John Chrysostom. He loved the quiet monastic life and both feared and respected the peculiarly public demands of the priesthood. Was Chrysostom merely following the conventional "Nolo episcopare," "I do not want to be a bishop," humbly, but perhaps disingenuously, enumerating all the ways in which he was unworthy for such a demanding vocation as an expected first step toward assuming the very vocation he claimed not to seek? I prefer to think that Chrysostom was simply being honest. The pastoral ministry has its rewards, but it also is full of real difficulties. We have good reason to suspect the judgment of anyone who would too eagerly seek such a task. Even today, nearly twenty centuries after Chrysostom's eloquent defense of his reluctance to be a bishop, contemporary pastors hear from him an honest, cautionary word on the trials and tribulations of being a pastor.

Behind his eloquent apology for the priesthood lies what was to become a troublesome trend in thought about the ministry. Chrysostom falls into a trap that many commentators on the ordained ministry have been unable to avoid. In exalting this particular vocation, in praising the virtues required of priests, Chrysostom portrays the pastor as a spiritual giant, a different being than the lowly layperson. In so honoring the office of priest, Chrysostom undercuts the peculiar nature of ministerial leadership and becomes part of a tendency that has bedeviled the church through the ages—to regard the shepherd as ontologically, spiritually superior to the sheep in a way that is unfaithful to the Good Shepherd, who modeled leadership with a basin and towel. In asserting the power of the ministerial office, Chrysostom at times fails to carefully delineate the peculiarity of the pastor's power.

Yet the main moral of this great moralist is a solemn warning against what he regards as the two greatest dangers of ordained leadership—a desire for vainglory and pleasure in the praise of people. Written sometime around 386, On the Priesthood *still strikes a chord with today's pastors, still sounds a warning, even yet serves as a reminder of the nobility of "this sacred office."*

The Glory of the Priesthood
St. Chrysostom (trans. by Graham Neville)

The work of the priesthood is done on earth, but it is ranked among heavenly ordinances. And this is only right, for no man, no angel, no archangel, no other created power, but the Paraclete himself ordained this succession, and persuaded men, while still remaining in the flesh to represent the ministry of angels. The priest, therefore, must be as pure as if he were standing in heaven itself, in the midst of those powers.

The symbols which existed before the ministry of grace were fearful and awe-inspiring: for example, the bells, the pomegranates, the stones on the breastplate, the stones on the ephod, the mitre, the diadem, the long robe, the golden crown, the Holy of Holies, the deep silence within. But if you consider the ministry of grace, you will find that those fearful and awe-inspiring symbols are only trivial. The statement about the Law is true here also: "The splendour that once was is now no splendour at all; it is outshone by a splendour greater still."[1] When you see the Lord sacrificed and lying before you, and the High Priest standing over the sacrifice and praying and all who partake being tinctured with that precious blood, can you think that you are still among men and still standing on earth? Are you not at once transported to heaven, and, having driven out of your soul every carnal thought, do you not with soul naked and mind pure look round upon heavenly things? Oh, the wonder of it! Oh, the loving-kindness of God to men! He who sits above with the Father is at that moment held in our hands, and gives himself to those who wish to clasp and embrace him—which they do, all of them, with their eyes. Do you think this could be despised? or that it is the kind of thing anyone can be superior about?

Would you like to be shown the excellence of this sacred office by another miracle? Imagine in your mind's eye, if you will, Elijah and

---

1. 2 Cor. 3:10 (N.E.B.).

the vast crowd standing around him and the sacrifice lying upon the stone altar. All the rest are still, hushed in deep silence. The prophet alone is praying. Suddenly fire falls from the skies on to the offering. It is marvellous; it is charged with bewilderment. Turn, then, from that scene to our present rites, and you will see not only marvellous things, but things that transcend all terror. The priest stands bringing down, not fire, but the Holy Spirit. And he offers prayer at length, not that some flame lit from above may consume the offerings, but that grace may fall on the sacrifice through that prayer, set alight the souls of all, and make them appear brighter than silver refined in the fire. Can anyone, not quite mad and deranged, despise this most awe-inspiring rite? Do you not know that no human soul could ever have stood that sacrificial fire, but all would have been utterly annihilated, except for the powerful help of God's grace?

Anyone who considers how much it means to be able, in his humanity, still entangled in flesh and blood, to approach that blessed and immaculate Being, will see clearly how great is the honour which the grace of the Spirit has bestowed on priests. It is through them that this work is performed, and other work no less than this in its bearing upon our dignity and our salvation.

For earth's inhabitants, having their life in this world, have been entrusted with the stewardship of heavenly things, and have received an authority which God has not given to angels or archangels. Not to them was it said, "What things soever ye shall bind on earth shall be bound also in heaven; and what things soever ye shall loose, shall be loosed."[2] Those who are lords on earth have indeed the power to bind, but only men's bodies. But this binding touches the very soul and reaches through heaven. What priests do on earth, God ratifies above. The Master confirms the decisions of his slaves. Indeed he has given them nothing less than the whole authority of heaven. For he says, "Whose soever sins ye forgive, they are forgiven, and whose soever sins ye retain, they are retained."[3] What authority could be greater than that? "The Father hath given all judgement unto the Son."[4] But I see that the Son has placed it all in their hands. For they have been raised to this prerogative, as though they were already translated to heaven and had transcended human nature and were freed from our passions.

2. Cf. Matt. 18:18.
3. John 20:23.
4. John 5:22.

Again, if a king confers on one of his subjects the right to imprison and release again at will, that man is the envy and admiration of all. But although the priest has received from God an authority as much greater than that, as heaven is more precious than earth and souls than bodies, some people think he has received so slight an honour that they can imagine someone entrusted with it actually despising the gift. God save us from such madness! For it is patently mad to despise this great office without which we cannot attain to salvation or God's good promises.

For if a man "cannot enter into the kingdom of heaven except he be born again of water and the spirit,"[5] and if he that eateth not the Lord's flesh and drinketh not his blood is cast out of everlasting life,[6] and all these things can happen through no other agency except their sacred hands (the priests', I mean), how can anyone, without their help, escape the fire of Gehenna or win his appointed crown? They are the ones—they and no others—who are in charge of spiritual travail and responsible for the birth that comes through baptism. Through them we put on Christ and are united with the Son of God and become limbs obedient to that blessed Head. So they should properly be not only more feared than rulers and kings, but more honoured even than fathers. For our fathers begot us "of blood and the will of the flesh"; but they are responsible for our birth from God, that blessed second birth, our true emancipation, the adoption according to grace.

The priests of the Jews had authority to cure leprosy of the body, or rather, not to cure it, but only to certify the cure. And you know what rivalry there used to be for the priesthood then. But our priests have received authority not over leprosy of the body but over uncleanness of the soul, and not just to certify its cure, but actually to cure it. So people who look down on them are far more execrable than Dathan and his company and deserve more punishment. For although they claimed an office which did not belong to them, at least they had a marvellous opinion of it, as they showed by wanting it so much. But the people we are considering have done just the opposite at a time when the priesthood has been so embellished and enhanced. Their presumption, therefore, is far greater. In the assessment of contempt there is no comparison

5. John 3:5.
6. Cf. John 6:53.

between coveting an honour which does not belong to you and making light of it. Between one and the other there is all the difference between admiration and disdain. Who could be so beggarly-minded as to make light of these great blessings? No one, I should say, except the victim of some demonic impulse.

But, to return to the topic from which I digressed, God has given greater power to priests than to natural parents, not only for punishment, but also for help. The difference between the two is as great as between the present and the future life. Parents bring us into this life; priests into the life to come. Parents cannot avert bodily death nor drive away the onset of disease; priests have often saved the soul that is sick and at the point of death, by making the punishment milder for some, and preventing others from ever incurring it, not only through instruction and warning, but also through helping them by prayer. They have authority to remit sins, not only when they make us regenerate, but afterwards too. "Is any among you sick? Let him call for the elders of the Church, and let them pray over him, anointing him with oil in the name of the Lord. And the prayer of faith shall save him that is sick, and the Lord shall raise him up, and if he have committed sins, they shall be forgiven him."[7] Again, natural parents cannot help their sons if they fall foul of the prominent and powerful, but priests have often appeased the anger of God himself, to say nothing of rulers and kings.

Will anyone still dare to accuse me of arrogance after this? I think that after what I have said, such reverence must fill the minds of my hearers that they can no longer accuse of conceit and presumption those who avoid this honour, but only those who seek it of their own accord and are determined to get it for themselves.

The Difficulty of the Priesthood

If it is true that those who are entrusted with civic government subvert their cities and ruin themselves as well, unless they are wise and very watchful, what about the man whose task is to adorn the bride of Christ? How much strength in himself and from above do you think he needs to avoid complete failure?

---

7. Jas. 5:14-15.

No one loved Christ more than Paul; no one showed more earnestness than he; no one was endowed with more grace. Yet for all that he went in fear and trembling for his authority and those who were under it. He says, "I fear lest, as the serpent beguiled Eve, so your thoughts should be corrupted from the simplicity which is towards Christ."[1] And again, "I was with you in fear and in much trembling."[2] Yet he was a man who had been "caught up to the third heaven,"[3] and shared in the unspeakable things of God,[4] and endured "deaths"[5] every day he lived after his conversion. He was a man who did not want to use the authority given him by Christ in case one of the believers should be offended.[6]

If, then, one who did more than he was commanded by God and never aimed at any advantage for himself, but only for those under his direction, was always in fear, because he kept in view the magnitude of his responsibility, what will become of us, who often aim at our own advantage, and, so far from doing more than we are commanded by Christ, for the most part actually break his commandments? "Who is weak," he says, "and I am not weak? Who is made to stumble, and I burn not?"[7] That is what a priest should be like; or rather, not just like that, for even that is little or nothing in comparison with what I am going to say.

And what is that? "I could wish," he says, "that I were anathema from Christ for my brethren's sake, my kinsmen according to the flesh."[8] If anyone can say that; if anyone has a soul capable of that prayer, he would be to blame if he evaded the priesthood. But anyone who falls as far short of that standard as I do, deserves hatred, not for evading but for accepting it.

If it were a question of choosing someone for a generalship, and those responsible for conferring the honour dragged forward a coppersmith or a cobbler or some other workman of that sort, and tried to put him in charge of the army, I should not congratulate the

---

1. 2 Cor. 11:3.
2. 1 Cor. 2:3.
3. 2 Cor. 12:2.
4. Cf. 2 Cor. 12:4.
5. 2 Cor. 11:23.
6. 1 Cor. 9:12.
7. 2 Cor. 11:29.
8. Rom. 9:23.

poor man for not running off and doing all he could to avoid pitching himself into inevitable disaster.

If it is enough simply to be called a "shepherd of souls" and to undertake the work anyhow, without risk, blame me for vainglory if you like. But if, on the contrary, the man who accepts this responsibility needs great wisdom and, even before wisdom, the grace of God in good measure, and an upright character and a pure life, and more than human goodness, then do not withhold your forgiveness from me because I do not want to damn myself without rhyme or reason.

Suppose someone brought a merchant ship of great tonnage, fully equipped with rowers and loaded with valuable freight, and sat me at the rudder and told me to cross the Aegean or the Tyrrhenian Sea, I should jump off at his first words. And if anybody asked me why, I should say, "To save sinking the ship!" When it is only money that is at stake, and the risk is at most of bodily death, no one will blame a man for looking well ahead. But where the fate of the shipwrecked is to fall, not into the sea, but into the abyss of fire, and what awaits them is not the death which separates soul from body, but the death which consigns both together to eternal punishment, will you be angry with me and hate me for not throwing myself headlong into such a calamity? I beg and beseech you not to. I know how weak and puny my own soul is. I know the importance of that ministry and the great difficulty of it. More billows toss the priest's soul than the gales which trouble the sea.

First of all there is the dreadful rock of vainglory, more dangerous than the Sirens' rock of which the poets have marvellous tales to tell. Many have had the strength to sail past this rock and escape unscathed. But to me it is so dangerous that even now, when no necessity is driving me towards its cleft, I cannot keep myself untainted by the terrible thing. If anyone entrusted this charge to me, he would be as good as binding my hands behind my back and delivering me to the wild beasts that inhabit that rock, to savage me every day. And what are those beasts? Anger, dejection, envy, strife, slanders, accusations, lying, hypocrisy, intrigue, imprecations against those who have done no harm, delight at disgraceful behaviour in fellow priests, sorrow at their successes, love of praise, greed for preferment (which more than anything else hurls the human soul to destruction), teaching meant to please, slavish wheedling, ignoble flattery, contempt for the poor, fawning on the rich, absurd honours and harmful favours which endanger giver and receiver alike, servile fear fit only for the meanest of slaves, restraint of plain speaking, much pretended and no real humility, failure to scrutinize and rebuke, or, more likely, doing so beyond reason with the humble while no one dares so much as to open his lips against those who wield power. All these wild beasts and more are bred upon that rock. And people who are once seized by them cannot help being dragged into the kind of servitude which makes them do over and over again, even to please women, things that are too bad to mention.

The divine law excluded women from this ministry, but they forcibly push themselves in, and, since they can do nothing personally, they do everything by proxy. They have got such power that they appoint and dismiss priests at will. Topsy-turvy (you can see the truth of the proverb borne out) "the followers lead their leaders"—bad enough, if they were men; but they are women, the very ones who are not even allowed to teach. Do I say "teach"? St Paul did not allow them even to speak in church.[9] But I have heard it said that they have assumed such freedom of speech that they even rebuke the prelates of the churches and upbraid them more bitterly than masters would their slaves.

But do not let anyone think that I am bringing these charges against all the clergy. Many there certainly are who have escaped these entanglements—more indeed than those who have been caught in them. And I do not venture to blame the priestly office for these evils. God forbid that I should be such a fool! Wise men do not blame the knife for murder, nor wine for drunkenness, nor strength for insolence, nor courage for recklessness. No; they blame the men who make wrong use of the gifts of God, and punish them for it. The priestly office might well accuse us of not handling it rightly. It is not itself the cause of the evils I have mentioned. It is we on our part who have smirched it with stain upon stain, by entrusting it to commonplace men. And they eagerly accept what is offered to them, without first examining their own souls or considering the gravity of the matter. And when they come to exercise

---

9. 1 Cor. 14:34.

this ministry, their eyes are blinded with inexperience and they fill the congregations entrusted to them with a thousand and one troubles.

That was the very thing that all but happened to me—only that God quickly rescued me from these dangers, in mercy on his Church and on my soul. Tell me, where do you think all the disorders in the churches originate? I think their only origin is in the careless and random way in which the prelates are chosen and appointed. For the head ought to be the strongest member, in order to be able to control the evil exhalations which proceed from the rest of the body, and regulate them properly. But when it happens to be weak in itself, it cannot ward off those infectious attacks, becomes weaker than it naturally is, and destroys the rest of the body along with itself. To prevent this happening in the present instance, God has kept me safely in the category of "feet"—where I originally belonged!

St. John Chrysostom: Six Books on the Priesthood, trans. Graham Neville (London: SPCK, 1964), pp. 70-79.

CHAPTER THIRTEEN

The Pastor as Disciplined Christian

I first encountered Richard John Neuhaus when I was in seminary. He was one among a group of courageous young pastors who were leaders, with pastor Martin Luther King Jr., of the Civil Rights Movement. In his clerical collar, at press conferences, walking at the head of a protest march, Neuhaus was a model for many of us seminarians of the sort of pastors we hoped to be, speaking truth to power, mixing religion and politics, tackling the tough social issues, putting his faith on the line.

He served an inner-city Lutheran parish in Brooklyn while writing books that, with eloquence and remarkable theological discernment, spoke to the transitions of the American church in the late twentieth century. He embodied some dramatic transitions in his own ministry. Before the century ended, Neuhaus was a Catholic priest, saying that the best of his Missouri Synod Lutheran upbringing had formed him to be truly evangelical, truly Catholic, that the church that had nurtured him was not as catholic as it ought to be, that this was, to cite his 1987 book, The Catholic Moment. *In his writing, Neuhaus appeared to have made a lurch to the right, politically and theologically. He became a leader of the Christian anti-abortion movement. Those who had hailed him as a radical political activist now condemned him as America's most prominent neoconservative intellectual.*

In 1989 Neuhaus founded First Things: A Monthly Journal on Religion and Public Life, *a lively intellectual journal that demonstrated the dialogue between Christianity and politics that Neuhaus had practiced in important books like* The Naked Public Square *(1984).*

One of his most enduring and endearing books was written as a pastor to fellow pastors, Freedom for Ministry *(1979; revised, 1992). There, with his typical acerbic wit, eloquence, and deference to the evangelical and the catholic Christian faith, Neuhaus gave critique and encouragement to pastors. As might be expected of a great contemporary moralist* and social ethicist, the book concludes with a stirring call to clerical holiness of life that would have made Chrysostom proud.

The Pursuit of Holiness
Richard John Neuhaus

> "Are you now ready to take upon you this Holy Ministry. . . . Will you adorn the doctrine of Our Savior by a holy life and conversation?"
> "Yes, with my whole heart, the Lord helping me through the power and grace of His Holy Spirit."

In these or similar words, a minister promises at ordination to live a life in the pursuit of holiness. To "adorn the doctrine of Our Savior by a holy life and conversation" is a general phrase subject to many interpretations. It means at least the following:

1. The minister is called and pledged to be an exemplary person.
2. The pursuit of holiness is a lifelong process of actualizing what we already are in Christ.
3. There is not conflict but complementarity between the special vocation of the minister and the vocation of all Christians.
4. Holiness is not an abstract perfection but obedience in mission and, finally, nothing less than our union with the life of God.
5. The pursuit of holiness is not so much the observance of limits as the exercise of freedom.

[My purpose] is to clarify these five propositions with special reference to the particular temptations of Christian ministry posed by activism, ambition, sexuality, and money.

The Exemplary Person

. . . At an ordination in the Roman Rite, the bishop invites the congregation to testify to the candidates' "fitness for the priesthood." He announces: "If any one has any objection to urge against them, let him come forward boldly and speak." Then, remembering our common fragility and the charity without which life together is not possible, the bishop cautions the potential challenger: "But let him not forget the state of his own soul." Every Christian rite for ordaining to ministry includes some exchange between people and ordaining authority with respect to the worthiness of those being ordained. In the early Church and in some parts of the Church today, the people cry out *Axios!* ("He is worthy!"). . . . It is a solemn thing to promise the pursuit of an exemplary life. It is nothing less than a vocation to holiness. . . .

To adorn the gospel with a holy life is a pledge that engages the very core of the person. One is not only to behave in an exemplary manner but to be an exemplary person. "Therefore be imitators of God, as beloved children. And walk in love, as Christ loved us and gave himself up for us, a fragrant offering and sacrifice to God" (Eph. 5:1-2). The injunction is of course addressed to all Christians, but the ministry of the Church is to exemplify its meaning for all Christians. We are to walk in the light and do all things as in the day; there is to be a coherence between public and private person. These are hard sayings and it is little wonder that rites of ordination and consecration include prayers for a special measure of the Spirit's aid to those who are "set aside."

Today talk about "imitating" another person has unhappy connotations of mimicry and false consciousness. The intention is better caught in the word *emulate*. Most of us have encountered at crucial points in our lives people whom we try to emulate. Such encounters more often than not have a strong bearing upon our decision for the ministry to begin with. . . .

In writing to the churches, Paul is effusive in his use of maternal and paternal imagery to describe his relationship to the Christians for whom he is responsible. He does not hesitate to hold himself up as an example of one who follows *the* exemplar, Jesus Christ. The office that is entrusted to us inescapably carries with it that obligation and privilege of exemplification. The ongoing task is to strengthen the coherence between "office" and "person"; in other words, the person is to "adorn" the office. The language of adornment may seem superficial and even effete. Another way of putting it is that the coherence between office and person increases the *credibility* of that which the office represents. It has been said that saints are people whose lives prove that Christ is risen. That may be saying too much, but their lives are hard to explain apart from the risen Christ; maybe they are, maybe they aren't. One day we will see, and the whole creation will see along with us. But they do seem to be ambassadors, signaling a promise and a possibility from a future that is both far off and closer than each breath we draw.

In the third century, Origen excoriated bishops who failed to act as religious examples and sympathetic physicians of the soul but were rather worldly minded, pursued earthly occupations and affairs, longed for wealth, were haughty, quarrelsome, and self-assertive. They loved to be flattered, said Origen, and were less conscientious in the conduct of business than secular officials. As men in charge of penance, they were alternately harsh and impermissibly complaisant; and if anyone tried to bring them to account for their sins, they formed cliques and, if need be, anti-churches, so that they could hold on to their office. Clergy brag about their seniority, says Origen, and try to secure the best offices for friends and relatives. They refuse to take advice from their equals, much less from a layman or a pagan, and are, in sum, just like the Pharisees of old. This, von Campenhausen notes, is the first time in Church history that the comparison is made between the Christian clergy and the New Testament's unflattering portrait of the Pharisees.[1] It would be far from the last time.

Corruption takes many forms. The nuanced and eminently respectable slide into unbelief is the most common way in which we give up on the pursuit of holiness, probably without even knowing that we have given up. Corruption can also be more blatant. In my early years in Brooklyn, I was approached by the pastor of a large black church who invited me to join him in a scheme in which he worked with real estate interests to blockbust white neighborhoods and move more successful blacks into segregated suburbs. He preached racial integration while privately working to expand the all-black ghetto; he preached the responsibility of upwardly mobile blacks to help stabilize and strengthen the neighborhood while privately encouraging them to buy homes in suburbia. He received up to three thousand dollars as a "kickback" on each home purchased. He was amused by my shocked disapproval, writing it off to my youth, and reminding me that while man did not live by bread alone, it sure did help. In another instance, a white minister active in reform politics privately

---

1. Hans von Campenhausen, *Ecclesiastical Authority and Spiritual Power* (Stanford, Calif.: Stanford University Press, 1969), pp. 252–53.

pointed out the lucrative connections between political influence and the manipulation of real estate prices. He admitted to having done quite well and even quoted Reinhold Niebuhr in justification of his "ethical realism."

Of course these are gross examples, at least bordering on the criminal. Most ministers do not have such temptations, or opportunities. It is said that everyone has a price. Nobody knows whether it is true of him until he has been offered that price, and most of us are never offered it. But these are the conscious and overt corruptions. More common and subtle are other ways in which we confirm the wisdom of the warning that a bishop should not be a "lover of money" (1 Tim. 3:3). Especially among Protestant clergy, there is the question of wedding and funeral practices, for example. The yellow pages of any metropolis contain a listing of "Marrying Sams" available any time day or night at an appropriate fee. Similarly, clergy have their names listed with large funeral establishments, on call for a price. One hears such clergy rationalize their avarice with talk about "opportunities to preach the gospel" and "to help people in need." . . . In truth, marrying and burying for money is a form of prostitution. Where there is no significant pastoral relationship with the persons involved, such "ministry" is no more than a purchased service. One is merely selling the panache of piety, reducing Christian truth to sentimentality and the veneer of respectability.

The troubling words of Jesus about the love of Mammon (Mammon is almost personalized as a false god) remain terrifyingly pertinent today. The warnings in James and elsewhere against kowtowing to the rich should be pondered by every minister when he thinks about who are the "important" members of the congregation. One of my father's sterling memories is that as a very young pastor in northern Canada he refused to admit to communion a wealthy member who had been convicted for political corruption and, contrary to my father's certain knowledge of his guilt, had publicly denied any wrongdoing. This man and his relatives accounted for more than half of the church's offerings, and they all threatened to leave unless the pastor backed down. My father stood firm, insisting that the man admit his fault publicly and be received back into the fellowship as a forgiven sinner. The man refused, many members left, and, after a time of great financial difficulty, the congregation revived and was much the stronger for the ordeal.

In many churches today such a course of events is simply inconceivable. There are no adequate procedures for "church discipline" to be exercised by the pastor, deacons, or others in the congregation. Or if such procedures do exist, they have long since fallen into desuetude. . . . The demolition of the difference between good and evil is the secularized bastardization of Luther's *simul iustus et peccator*. The pursuit of holiness and the vitality of the churches in our day require a recovery of the practice of Christian discipline. . . .

For many people, Sinclair Lewis's *Elmer Gantry* still casts a shadow of suspicion over Christian ministry. Journalists relentlessly press the Gantry syndrome in connection with very prominent ministers, eagerly sniffing about for that financial motive that "explains what he is really up to." Much of this is outrageously unfair, and yet it reflects a popular intuition about the connection between money and integrity that is not too far removed from the teaching of the gospels. Most of us do not "sell out" by making crooked deals, or even by consciously compromising principle in order not to compromise financial security; we pay our tribute to Mammon in the minutes and hours spent in worrying about money and the things that money can get.

There are few decisions that a young pastor or pastoral couple make that are more important than the attitude toward money. One should as early as possible determine the top income one would ever want or strive to have. Of course there has to be a degree of flexibility in such a decision, but the question of money and the dangers it poses should be kept under the closest scrutiny. Otherwise the desire ineluctably grows, avarice feeds upon itself, and one ends up as the victim of an appetite that is in fact insatiable and consumes by worry, guilt, and discontent the hours and days that were once consecrated to ministry. It is not simply a matter of desire and avarice. The habits of a way of life become entrenched without our knowing it, and soon we discover that we have acquired all kinds of "needs" that can only be fed by more money. This is not the place for bromides about the wickedness of a consumer society; what we call the consumer society has likely been the greatest engine of economic distributive justice in the history of humankind, but the consumer*ism* that accompanies it is undoubtedly an enormous spiritual danger. For each of us, the answer to the peril is not—at least not chiefly—in calls for changing the economic system but in a pursuit of holiness that signals triumph over the ambiguities of prosperity.

It is not likely any time soon that most ministers will be required to take an oath of poverty. Yet there is today a happy reawakening to the liberation of living in simplicity of life, of breaking free from consumerism's grip. Very early we must determine whether we are going to live "the good life" of our own design, worked out in fear and trembling toward our destiny and our calling from God, or whether we are going to live the massified "good life" proffered on television and in the countless catalogues that constitute the daily reading of millions. And money is, of course, often related to career advancement. The late Saul Alinsky, famed guru of community organizers, once met with a group of seminarians interested in ministries among the poor. "The first thing you got to decide," said Alinsky, "is whether you want to be a priest or be a bishop. If you want to be a bishop, you might as well leave now because you'll never do anything else." Too many of the bishops of our churches, because they wanted to be bishops, never did or ever will do anything else.

Compare two pastoral couples. In the first case, there are six children and the family lives in gracious simplicity on an income that puts them at the lower edge of what is defined as middle class. The home is marked by a peacefulness that has everything to do with people having decided the life that is truly theirs. In the second case, there are two children and, although the parents think they are economically stretched, their two incomes put them in the top four or five percent of American families. Their family life is debilitated by anxiety, mainly about money. The reader can no doubt think of similar comparisons. The difference is not in economic needs. The difference is that one family is living its own good life and the other is living somebody else's good life. It is often said that it is much easier for celibates and single clergy, but that is not necessarily the case. Cars, traveling, expensive recreation and gimmicks can create a similarly debilitating economic pressure, and they often do. Whatever one's circumstance, unless one is born with or has discovered some special immunity, he is under pressure by the seductions of Mammon. This rule of thumb deserves at least respectful attention: If there is any dimension of ministry that you did or did not choose to pursue primarily for financial reasons, you probably chose wrongly. The pursuit of holiness is an exercise of freedom from bondage to Mammon, who, together with sexual fulfillment, is among the most imperious gods of the present age.

In biblical thought, holiness is the essential attribute of God, and God is unqualified freedom. His freedom takes the form of love, by which he first created all things and now engages his creation in faithful pilgrimage toward perfect union with himself. The Church is the community that knows and signals what the whole creation is about. The ministry is to exemplify that mission of the Church. The minister is to lead Christians in being different. The pursuit of holiness is nothing less than the pursuit of God. . . . Whatever our personal qualities or lack of qualities, we ministers are formally designated to bear a tradition that reflects and aspires to holiness. To lead in the pursuit of holiness—this is what the Church, at least ritually, says it wants us to do; and we are always surprised when people actually do it. The common ambivalence about the holy, its terror and its attractiveness, pervades also our own thinking.

There are signs of a welcome recovery of concern for "spiritual formation" in ministerial training today. Such training should help people to work through and to live with the ambivalence of holiness, the inescapable oddity of the ministerial vocation, the unavoidable "difference" that we are to exemplify. In some seminaries the talk is still about training "enablers," "facilitators," and the like. But what is needed is not the training of religious technicians but the formation of spiritual leaders. It is important for seminaries to impart skills and competencies; it is more important to ignite conviction and the courage to lead. The language of facilitation is cool and low-risk. The language of priesthood and prophecy and the pursuit of holiness is impassioned and perilous. We cover our fearful choice of the low-risk option with egalitarian talk about the priesthood of all believers. But those who have been touched by the burning coal from the altar, and whose touch has been ratified by the call of the Church, must not pretend that nothing special has happened to them. Such pretense is not humility but blasphemy; it is not modesty but ingratitude; it is not devotion to equality but evasion of responsibility. It is fear, the fear of being different. And when we are afraid to act upon the difference to which we are called, we inhibit others from acting upon the difference to which they are called.

To be exemplary is, by definition, to be different. What we make of the "difference" that ordered ministry makes is another matter. It can be a difference behind which we shield ourselves from genuine encounter with others. It can be a difference in the negative sense of more total conformity to the conventions and prevailing habits-of-soul in the group whose judgment we fear. Or it can be a difference in the intensity of venture, a challenge to the spiritual lethargy that now holds the churches in thrall. But whatever difference it makes, the difference should not be denied.

Actualizing the Holiness That Is Ours

The pursuit of holiness is not the quest for the Holy Grail. It is not a matter of looking for something that we do not have or of achieving something that we are not. It is rather a question of actualizing the gift that is already ours. . . .

. . . The pursuit of holiness is active engagement in the "now" and "not yetness" of Christian existence short of the Kingdom come. The indicative and imperative of salvation are not contradictory but speak to the continuity of the life lived in hope. The biblical assertion is that each human life is a response to vocation and destiny, which is God's gift to us even before we are born. With Isaiah we declare: "Listen to me, O coastlands, and hearken, you peoples from afar. The Lord called me from the womb, from the body of my mother he named my name" (Isa. 49:1). Sanctification is becoming what, by the grace of God, we are.

In ministry, as in life, we never arrive, for our ministries and our lives point beyond themselves. It is true, as they say in the abortion debate, that the fetus is merely a potential human being; but it is wrong to say "merely," for we are all potential human beings, growing into the fullness of humanity that is Christ. This note of preparation, of anticipation, of potentiality, should mark the whole of our ministry. This too is what Jesus meant by the necessity of being born again and becoming like a little child. The illusions of completeness and of having arrived must die, so that each day we begin anew the life of Christian hope. The pursuit of holiness means that our ministries are ever in process of formation.

The New Testament word for moral consecration or holiness is *agiasmos*. It is derived from the active verbal form and thus signifies "sanctifying" rather than "sanctification." The phrase *agiasmo pneumatos* might be better translated "Sanctifying Spirit" rather than "Holy Spirit," for it does not connote the moral status of the Spirit but rather what the Spirit is *doing*. The grace of God, then, is not compromised by good works; good works are the grace of God. The grace of God is an active gift, not just the static status of "being saved." To put it differently, we are saved and we are being saved. As important as understanding what the grace of God *is* is understanding what the grace of God *does*. "For the grace of God has appeared for the salvation of all men, *training us* to renounce irreligion and worldly passions, and to live sober, upright, and godly lives in this world, awaiting our blessed hope, the appearing of the glory of our great God and Savior Jesus Christ" (Titus 2:11). The pursuit of holiness is the Christian ever in training. . . .

As with the children of Israel in the wilderness, there are dry and difficult times in ministry. There are stale periods when mystical vision is smothered, prophecy seems pretentious, and even the apocalyptic sounds prosaic. One learns not to panic at the appearance of monotony. But neither should one be casual about the rot that can set in and finally rob ministry of its joy and venture. For very few people is life lived consistently on the felt edge of new discovery. Most of us know and expect the feeling that we are meeting events and ourselves coming around again in all too predictable a fashion. As preachers, for instance, we are properly depressed to hear ourselves repeating ourselves. The answer is not to feign excitement about exhausted ideas and emotions. There are few things so distasteful or so unpersuasive as forced enthusiasm. The better answer is to be prepared for such periods of weariness and to respond to them with a disciplined program of prayer, study, and hard thought.

On this score the wisdom of the saints has been confirmed in lives beyond number: When we least feel like praying, we most need to pray; when study seems unfruitful, we need the more intensely to study; and when thinking is dead-ended, think again. In times of spiritual and intellectual drought, the great temptation is to believe that renewal can be found in noise and action. This is the activism to which so many ministries fall prey. It is a frenetic effort to justify our ministries by doing things. Whether it is in parish programming, or evangelism, or community organization, activism is an attempt to forget the drought by expending energies; the result is to intensify the thirst and thus to intensify the need to forget. Or it takes the form of the stereotypical salesman, celebrity, politician, and media evangelist—hollow men and women who need their daily fix of admired hyperactivity in order to assure themselves that they are alive and that it matters that they are alive.

Activism is a form of decadence. Decadence is the decay that hollows out the forms of life, leaving them devoid of meaning and, even more fatally, flaunting such hollowness as virtue. As Paul put it, we boast of our shame. Mindless activism reduces the Church to a comfortable Rotarianism where grace is hustled at bargain prices, or it replaces the pursuit of holiness with the pursuit of narrow political, social, or psychological goals. Of course there are other forms of decadence. There are timorous, abstractly overintellectualized and overaestheticized ministries that give the appearance of churchy games played by curators of the monuments to past pieties. And, as discussed earlier, there is the decadence that confuses institutional failure with the Way of the Cross. But surely the most common and respectable form of decadence is the activism that becomes more frenetic as the direction of ministry becomes more uncertain.

In times of staleness, then, we need not to break out but to break in, to enter more deeply into the center of self and God and to renegotiate once again the terms of ambassadorship. We should neither deny our weariness nor defy it with the quick fix of self-willed enthusiasm and action. Rather, like the Psalmist, we entrust it to God, making no secret of what is no secret to him, unleashing the deep to call unto the deep, knowing that he is the cause both of our complaint and of our hope. There is no substitute for this renegotiation. If we accept substitutes, we end up in fraudulent ministries, and the fraud sooner or later becomes apparent to us, if not to others. "As a hart longs for flowing streams, so longs my soul for thee, O God" (Ps. 42:1). We must hold out for that, and learn to hold on while holding out. Spiritual integrity consists not in being satisfied but in being insistent.

We have said that activism is a form of forgetfulness, an alternative pursuit to the pursuit of holiness. A less respectable but perhaps equally common form of ministerial forgetfulness is the sin of sloth or acedia. It is a spiritual torpor and apathy that is not to be confused with ordinary and sometimes healthy laziness. Laziness can be enjoyed, like the extra hour of sleep stolen from an occasional morning; we tell ourselves that that call can be made at ten just as well as at nine. Laziness can be leisure created, delight's defiance of the schedule's harassment. Laziness is a reward bestowed on oneself, sinking into the hammock of a summer's afternoon, with a cool drink and half-believed self-assurances that that meeting was not very important anyway. In fact, you comfort yourself, it will probably do them good to get along without you for once.

Such "laziness" can be liberating. It is quite different from sloth. If it could speak, laziness might say, "I know I should be doing this or that, but I'm just too lazy today." Acedia, to the extent that it could articulate itself at all, might say, "Should I really be doing that? Why? What difference does it really make?" Laziness is time resistant to the pressure of duty; acedia is the temper that undermines the duty. Laziness can be defiance; acedia is pure forgetfulness. Laziness is, at least in part, a decision; acedia is an addiction. Laziness is on friendly terms with time, using it to a different purpose; acedia is the enemy of time, consuming it in nothingness.

Acedia is all of Friday consumed in getting out the Sunday bulletin. Acedia is two hours dawdled away on *Time* magazine, which is then guiltily chalked up to "study." Acedia is evenings without number obliterated by television, evenings neither of entertainment nor of education but of narcoticized defense against time and duty. Above all, acedia is apathy, the refusal to engage the pathos of other lives and of God's life with them.

The sin of acedia is hardly unique to the clergy, but the temptations can be peculiar and severe. Unlike most other occupations, the meaning of what we do has to be largely reconstructed by ourselves day by day. In this sense our situation is like that of the writer or creative artist. Nobody tells the novelist what the next chapter must be or can even convince him that the novel is worth doing. The reliance on what is called inner-directedness is frightening. So, if we are honest about it, the external demands and definitions of what is required of us as ministers are often quite minimal. In many—perhaps most—situations, one can "get away with" doing very little. Ministers resent the old jibe about their only working one day a week, but we may protest too much. In truth, many full-time pastoral positions are not full-time in what is externally or structurally required of them. This is not to say that we cannot fill the time. Here, too, Parkinson's Law applies: Work expands in proportion to the time available for doing it. But filling time is not a very fulfilling ministry. Nor would I suggest that many ministers are not fearfully overworked. But here we must understand that hyperactivity and sloth are twin sins. They are both escapes from the daily renegotiation of our ambassadorship, from the daily resumption of the pursuit of holiness. Acedia is activism grown weary. Activism is the effort to justify ministry by busyness, which is no justification at all, while acedia has given up on the search for justification.

Acedia, like activism, feeds on the fear of uncertainty. The remedy is the courage of uncertainty, knowing clearly that everything we do and everything we are is premised upon a hope not yet actualized. We should not try to shore up the believability of what we do by borrowing legitimations from other professions and other enterprises. Again, nothing can finally vindicate the Church and our ministries in the Church but the coming of the Kingdom of God, and that vindication is assured in the Word which is the Risen Christ. The pathos of the present moment and of all history is God's working out of the vindication of his own holiness. By entering into that pathos we join him in his work. That God is the Holy One of Israel and that Israel, including the Church, is the signal of the future of all humankind—that is the most important single truth in the whole of creation. All of our prayer, meditation, study, teaching, and loving service are to articulate that truth. In light of that truth we dare to call the Church a holy people (1 Peter 2, following Exod. 19). Thus the pursuit of holiness is the actualization of who we are; but even more ultimately and to the minds of many absurdly, it is the actualization of who God reveals himself to be. Any understanding of the pursuit of holiness that falls short of this extravagant claim is only moralism and leads either to self-righteousness or to despair—which is to say, it leads to death.

Ordination and the Vocation of the Church

The vocation of the Church is to sustain many vocations. The ordained minister, the one set aside and consecrated, is to illuminate the vocation of the Church and the vocations of the many people who are the Church. That means that ordination is not exclusionary but exemplary. Such a statement is easily made, but it is and always has been hard to live out in the life of the Church. The popular suspicion persists that the minister is more fully a Christian than "ordinary" members of the Church. Ordination, it is thought (even if it is unsupportable theologically), represents "first-class" spiritual status. Of a religiously serious adolescent it is said that perhaps he should be a priest. As though religious seriousness can only be usefully employed (or protected?) in holy orders. In some traditions it is said of someone who is ordained that "he went into the church." As though we did not all enter the Church in baptism. . . .

Paul persistently emphasized the diversity of gifts. The New Testament nowhere supports a leveling egalitarianism in the life of the Church. Rather the whole Body is strengthened as each part becomes more fully what it is called to be. The pursuit of holiness is not a zero-sum game, as though there were only so much holiness to go around. One member's gain is not another's loss, but rather a gain for the whole Body, making it more whole. The destiny or vocation of each member is not limited but infinite, the possibilities of actualization inexhaustible. In other words, the pursuit of holiness is premised upon the belief, indeed the Divine promise, that there is a complementarity of excellences. The vocation of each member is unique, and each member should sustain all other members in discerning and pursuing their peculiar callings. Conflicts arise only when people try to pursue vocations that belong to somebody else. . . .

The ministerial vocation, then, is not exclusionary but exemplary, not in competition with but complementary to the vocations of others. The minister should persistently lift up, enhance, and exalt instances of lay vocations pursued with courage and faithfulness. In the local church the excessive attention given those who compete for the pastor's vocation and its responsibilities detracts from the public celebration of those who pursue their own vocations. We should gladly and publicly make clear that, while we are called to be spiritual leaders, we are not necessarily in the lead in the actualizing of God's call. The Sanctifying Spirit in the lives of others may be making much more headway than in our own lives, and we should urge sisters and brothers on to even greater progress, knowing that we are all enriched by their advance. Concern for the vocations of laypersons also requires great sensitivity to the myriad ways in which their dignity and integrity are under assault in the everyday world. . . .

. . . In the leadership of the church, the pastor who encounters hostility and conflict may on rare occasions be forced to conclude that he is confronted by sheer evil, by the demonic. In such instances his hope lies in whatever rites of exorcism are available to him, or in rugged perseverance, or in talking to the bishop about a transfer. But, as a general rule, the operative assumption is that such conflict results from people seeking an importance and a vocation other than their own. The appropriate action is for the pastor to recall them to their own vocation and strengthen them in it by the exemplary pursuit of his vocation.

Finally, the complementarity of vocations requires that we really want, that we really pray for, the Sanctifying Spirit in the lives of others. We should pray and pray urgently for the success of other ministries. If we are afraid of competition from the church up the street, our own ministries will become defensive holding actions. Above all, we should be praying for our own people. Many times a week, people ask the pastor to pray for them or for their loved ones. "Yes, I will pray for you," he responds. But what if he doesn't? Perhaps he should say to such people, "No, I'm sorry but I don't pray." Such a healthy jolt might get intercession written into the minister's contract, as it is already and most certainly in the calling. A grand old pastor who died several years ago first impressed upon me the importance of praying for one's people. He would go into the church or some quiet place alone, taking with him the list of all his parishioners, and devote no less than an hour a day to praying for them one by one.

It does not matter whether one is in a "prayerful mood," whatever that may be. And all inhibitions about whether or not prayer "works," whatever that may mean, must be rejected as temptations from the Evil One. We are not likely to announce on a Sunday morning that we are not in the mood to preach, or that we have our doubts about the efficacy of preaching, and therefore there will be no sermon this morning. It is to be suspected that we preach because the people know and care if we do not preach, while only God knows and cares if we do not pray. The ministry of intercession is an integral part of our own pursuit of holiness, and it is the clearest evidence of our faith in the complementarity of all vocations within the Body of Christ.

Abstract Perfection Versus Obedience in Mission

We are commanded to be perfect as the Father is perfect. The meaning of that is exemplified in the life of Christ, which is the life of obedience. To speak positively of obedience today is to be profoundly countercultural. The valid suspicion of talk about obedience is grounded in the experience of authoritarianisms, both past and present. Obedience is confused with "blind obedience," which is morally odious. Obedience is confused with conformity, with going along, with asking no questions. But obedience really means responsiveness; it is related to the Latin *audire*, to hear, to listen, to respond appropriately. Obedience is not the surrender of responsibility but the acceptance of responsibility for what we respond to and how. Obedience is not conformity. Indeed, we must refuse to conform in order that we may obey. Conformity means accepting a direction or destiny that belongs to someone else; obedience is the actualization of our own destiny.

Obedience, then, is not the enemy of freedom but the exercise of freedom. Contrary to much popular thinking, we are not most free when we are least responsive to the commands, invitations, and directions which beckon us. Liberation is not the absence of duty but deciding which duty is ours. We are liberated by that which we accept as obligation. Again, we are freed when we discover the pleasure of duty rather than the duty of pleasure. There is no more onerous bondage than to be liberated from any obligation that is truly ours. The discovery of our true selves is the emergence of ourselves in free decision and fidelity to the obligations that are ours. The pursuit of holiness is not the pursuit of an abstract perfection—whether that be the perfection of our "authentic selves" or the perfection of moral behavior. The pursuit of holiness is rather a life-time of responsive listening, of obedience, to our vocation.

This insight is powerfully expressed by Dietrich Bonhoeffer in his poem-prayer, "Who Am I?" written during his imprisonment. He reviews the ways in which he is perceived by others—by his family, by jailers, by church and government authorities, by fellow prisoners—and the ways in which he perceives himself. Of all these different and sometimes contradictory perspectives, he asks, which is the real me? It is impossible to tell; there is a measure of truth in each. Then Bonhoeffer concludes triumphantly, "Thou knowest, O Lord. I am thine!" Who am I, really? I am the one who, in the particularities and confusions of this one life, lives in respon-sive listening, in obedience, to you, O Lord.

We want to be known for who we really are, not for the "roles" we play. But that way of thinking is dead-ended. Who we are is defined by that to which we are obedient. Imagine a first-century person in Galilee wanting to know Jesus for who he really is, apart from what he came to do. Always he *is* the one who came to do the will of the Father. To know him is to know his work, to know him is to follow him. There is no other way. He does not wish to be known, indeed he cannot be known, apart from his mission, apart from his obedience, apart from his cross.

"Am I not free? . . . Though I am free from all men, I have made myself a slave to all, that I might win the more. . . . I have become all things to all men, that I might by all means save some" (1 Cor. 9:1, 19, 22). This offends contemporary sensibilities. It is compro-mise, it is false consciousness, it is inauthentic existence. But Paul knew that the self that we are, when separated from the loyalties, commitments, and obligations that we have freely accepted, is an abstracted and false self. Today's human potential therapies that thrive on such separation are dead wrong—that is, they are lethally wrong. "You are what you think you are." "You are what you want to be." "You are what you feel you are." No, we *are* what we are called to be in obedience to the vocation we have accepted as ours. "I do it all for the sake of the gospel, that I may share in its bless-ings." We *are* what the gospel promises we will be.

The pursuit of holiness means singleness of heart. We all live far short of that purity of heart that wills one thing; it is important to remember that and thus to know that we live by grace. Just as important to remember is that the one thing we should will is not some abstract moral perfection for ourselves but the perfect rule of God, the Kingdom of God. What the particulars of the perfect rule of God might be eludes us at this preliminary point in history. But, for each one of us, that perfection is discovered in part by single-minded, single-hearted obedience to doing what he has called us to do. Anything that divides our hearts and minds, such as ambition, is to be seen as the enemy.

From ambition we should draw back as from lethal poison. But, it is countered, we should be ambitious for doing good. If the attainment of some position of greater power and influence can increase the good we can do, what could possibly be wrong with that? It is a seductive line of reasoning. It is the reasoning that underlies the corruption of careerism in the ministry, that makes it almost automatic that successful ministries move on to successively larger churches until they are crowned by executive posts, honorary doctorates, and the bishop's mitre. Whoever ministers in one place with an eye on the next is ministering with a divided heart.

Of course, few people stay in one place their whole lives; we have to make decisions when changes are proposed to us. We say that we move on to "greater challenges for the Lord"; but such challenges are usually shadowed by the suspicion created by the greater satisfactions offered. A good general rule by which to test our singleness of heart is that, when faced with choices, we give greater weight to the one that will require the greater sacrifice. And another general rule: Choose the one that others would be less likely to choose. Were these rules more honored, the Church would have more exemplary ministries in the inner cities, among the rural poor, with a great host of society's marginal people. Does this mean that pastors of large and prosperous churches, denominational executives, seminary deans, and bishops cannot be saved? Of course not. With God all things are possible. There might even be legitimacy in the sentiment attributed to one pope, "Since God has seen fit to give us the papacy, let us enjoy it." But only when, after great resistance, one is forced to conclude that God has given it. They carried a protesting Ambrose to the church in order to make him a bishop. The corruption of the present-day Church would be greatly reduced were more of its leaders compelled to office by obedience rather than attracted to office by ambition.

The Observance of Limits or the Exercise of Freedom

Activism, ambition, money, and sexuality—these are among the chief forces dividing the ministerial heart, crippling the pursuit of holiness, and compromising the vocation to exemplary life. The temptations are quite different in the ways they affect the relationship between ministry and people. Activism, for example, is often approved and rewarded. There are seldom severe strictures against ambition and the love of money, unless they become overweeningly overt. But with respect to sexuality, sensitivities are heightened and censures are strong. In Christian thinking in this area, the line between prejudice and piety, between fear of God and fear of the unfamiliar, is hard to draw.

But here too the pursuit of holiness cannot be dominated by fear or by negative limitations. The question is not, "What can I get away with?" but "What am I called to do in order to actualize what, by the grace of God, I am?" In short, here too we are called to the exercise of freedom in the courage of uncertainty. The freedom of obedience always comes hard. Much easier is conformity to clear-cut rules and unchallengeable prohibitions. Especially in the interstices of the erotic, where are engaged our deepest longings for companionship, for loving and being loved, for ecstatic loss of self in another, here we would readily surrender our freedom. Freedom can be surrendered either in conformity to the expectations of others or in conformity to our own passions. Legalism and libertinism are but two sides of the coin we pay to be freed from freedom.

Obedience is responsive listening for the will of God. On the basis of the Spirit's promise to the Church, we listen for God's speaking also through his people. The pursuit of holiness means living in sensitivity to the sensitivities of God's people. In sensitivity to their sensitivities, but not in subservience to their prejudices. Again, holiness is not some bland and respectable "goodness"; it is the radically disturbing pressing on to the Good. It challenges more than it confirms; it fascinates and it terrifies.

In the service of satisfying passion, we can call upon an almost infinite reservoir of rationalization. After all, we tell ourselves, our peccadilloes are precisely that: small infractions that hurt no one. In discussion of social policy today, we hear much about "victimless crimes." In public policy the concept is dubious, in ministerial ethics it is disastrous. We are to live as in the day, so that we need not fear exposure to the light of all that we do. It is a hard saying. And woe to us if we offend one of these little ones whom he calls his own. It would be better for us that a millstone be hung about our necks and we be cast into the depths of the sea. It is a very hard saying.

Moral theologians in some traditions have made much of the distinction between "giving offense" and "taking offense." We should not submit to those who use their weakness as a weapon. We dare not let our lives be inhibited by those who would take offense at every infringement of their prejudices. We dare not because we have no right to surrender our freedom, and because we should not confirm them in their petty legalism. To offer people our subservience is to deny them the strength of our obedience. This is nasty in its complexity, this relationship between freedom and obligation. It is also majestic. Refusing to surrender our freedom on the side of legalism or of libertinism, we conclude with the seventeenth-century poet, " 'Tis glorious misery to be born a man."

"Ich kann nicht anders," Luther declared at Worms, lighting up the modern world with an exemplary instance of the freedom of obedience, whatever our view of the substance of his protest. "I cannot do otherwise": The emphasis is upon the *ich*, which is not mere feeling or what is usually meant by conscience but is a judgment born from self-understanding. This is not individualistic whimsy or self-assertion; contemporary twaddle about "doing your own thing" could hardly be more foreign to Luther's intent. He declares that he holds himself accountable to those who differ, calling on them to correct him by scripture, by witness of the tradition, or by clear reason. Barring such correction, he has no choice but to obey, to exercise freedom in the courage of uncertainty. In a similar vein, many in our times have raised the question of civil disobedience, and it was argued that this was not really disobedience but obedience of a different order.

It is often remarked that the gospels have relatively little to say about sexual sins, and that is true. In the reported words of Jesus there is at least ten times as much on the dangers of money and the oppression of the poor by the rich. One must point this out when the discussion of Christian ethics is too confined to sexuality and one would direct attention to issues of justice. At the same time, however, we cannot belittle the emphasis upon sexuality in the New Testament. It is much easier to call for social transformation than to be personally transformed. Critics who rail against the dishonesties of government or corporations may be tempted to cheat on the love and justice owed to their families and the People of God. Almost all the scholars agree that the biblical passages on holiness and sanctification are closely and inseparably connected with sexuality. Typical are the warnings of Ephesians 5 against "immorality and all impurity . . . For it is a shame even to speak of the things that they do in secret." So pervasive is the emphasis that it is said that Paul and the pastorals are "obsessed" by sexuality. The same critics who make that claim sometimes also assert that the New Testament writers, living in a pre-Freudian era, could not appreciate the pervasiveness and nuance of sexuality in human behavior. It is hard to have it both ways.

Or it is said that the New Testament writers were "culturally conditioned" and that therefore their ideas about sexuality need not be taken too seriously. This is a curious argument indeed. Does it mean that *we* are not culturally conditioned, or that we are conditioned by a superior culture? Both propositions are implausible. Or perhaps we are looking for principles that transcend culture. But that is what the earlier gnostics thought they had found, enabling them to be disdainful of the beliefs and rules and orders of a given time in history. True, ours is a living tradition, and the Spirit is leading the Church into fuller truth, illuminating the meaning of obedience in this moment. To cite the most common example, our attitude toward human slavery may not be Paul's, yet we are confident that it is obedient to New Testament teaching in relation to our historical moment. The Sanctifying Spirit is not to be confused with the spirit of the times; yet those led by the Spirit are to be creatively responsive to the questions and opportunities posed by the times.

If it is proposed that the Spirit is leading the Church to change its understanding of the exemplary life, it must be clear that what is being proposed is not greater permissiveness but truer obedience. This intent is not always manifest among those who propose changes in attitudes towards celibacy, homosexuality, marriage as a lifelong union, and other dimensions of sexual behavior. At the same time, it is far from clear that those who resist such changes are interested in true obedience, as distinct from conformity.

The purpose here is not to treat these questions in detail. Books have been written on them, and the debates will no doubt continue for some time. The point here is the connection between the pursuit of holiness and the minister's pledge and call to live an exemplary life. If that pledge and call are agreed upon, then what is being debated today is the definition of the exemplary life. The question is not what is permissible but what is exemplary. . . .

. . . Ministers are not "just like everybody else." Ministers who plead to the contrary simply fly in the face of everything that the Church—and that they in their more sensible moments—intend by Christian ministry. Is the burden of being different unfair? Not really; not if we have freely affirmed the vocation and pledge to adorn the gospel with a holy life.

The purpose here is not to affirm conventional morality; it is to affirm concern for the Church and the role of the ministry in the Church. Conventional morality may be the received wisdom that has stood the test of time and, in the view of most Christians, is backed by Divine ordinance. What is conventional, what is the accepted thing, in many communities today is the unconventional. Millions of people, including many Christians, take for granted recreational sex, regular genital exercise as an essential part of mental and physical fitness, and the acceptability of serial polygamy and polyandry. They could not be unconventional if they tried, for they have quite forgotten the conventions. In the churches that keep alive a tradition of sexual morality, however, the situation is different. Minority views have a venerable record of sometimes turning out to be acclaimed as right. What is exemplary in the realm of sexuality, one might argue, is subject to change. If one's effort is to redefine the exemplary concept of marital fidelity, that could be a worthy intention. That would seem to require that one's behavior be public, if it is to have any effect on changing attitudes. One should then, to borrow a phrase from another debate, come out of the closet. But in fact the defense of marital infidelity, when it is made, is usually framed in terms of satisfying irresistible needs or of winking at the marginally permissible; in short, it is defended in the language of limit observance rather than of the exercise of freedom in the pursuit of holiness. If we are unfaithful in this way, we have, at least in that one area, abandoned the pursuit; and of course the nature of compromises makes it difficult to contain the corrosive damage to that one area. . . .

In its countercultural role as radical critic, the Church has an enormous contribution to make in relativizing, and thus shattering, the tyranny of sex over so many lives in our society. Like consumerism, indeed as a species of consumerism, sexual satisfaction is presented as a categorical imperative. American society is in a constant state of what moral theology used to call "sexual commotion." This imperious commotion should be challenged by a community that is heir to a much more comprehensive and subtle understanding of what it means to be human. We must insist that virginity is not a perversion, restraint is not inhibition, desires are not necessarily needs to be met, biological capacity contains no imperative to action. Against the myriad manuals for sexual fulfillment, the Church's witness should be clear that persons are never to be subordinated to sexual performance, nor love to lust.

Perhaps all times are times of sexual commotion, ours being different only in that the commotion is culturally celebrated and established as social and psychological orthodoxy. Of course the Church is caught up in the commotion, but that need not mean it is captive to it. Fidelity, homosexuality, changing sex roles, marriage and celibacy—all are questions that will continue to claim the attention of the churches. The Christian contribution is to understand these questions not in terms of liberation from limits but in terms of that true liberation which is the exercise of freedom in the pursuit of holiness. If the Church and its ministry have the nerve for it, the commotion can be tempered and transformed by a renewed vision of the exemplary life, and that could be the real sexual revolution of our time.

Conclusion and Beginning

At whatever point we are in ministry, whether we are just starting out or are veterans of visions lost and visions only partially fulfilled, we are at a point of change, of formation, of potentiality, of promise. The harder we work at this ministry, the less easily satisfied we are with ourselves. The more we know the value of the treasure, the more keenly we know the earthenness of the vessel. "We are afflicted in every way, but not crushed; perplexed, but not driven to despair; persecuted, but not forsaken; struck down, but not destroyed; always carrying in the body the death of Jesus, so that the life of Jesus may also be manifested in our bodies" (2 Cor. 4:8-10).

At the beginning and at the end of every day, we offer up our ministries. We are responsible for the offering, and God is responsible for the consequences, and his is the infinitely greater responsibility. We tinker and tune and experiment and resolve and fail and try again, in the happy assurance that, when all is said and done, it is the awesome recklessness of his love and not our ambition that called us to the seeming absurdity of this work. Because of our infidelities, we have a lot to answer for. Because of his promise, God has a lot more to answer for. "[Even when] we are faithless, he remains faithful—for he cannot deny himself" (2 Tim. 2:13). We affirm our place in the tradition of fidelity, and of infidelity, that is the Church. In that tradition we proclaim the presence of the One who seems to be absent. We are the stewards of the mysteries of his presence, and of his absence.

The pursuit of holiness is holding out for the fullness of God's rule in our lives and in our world. And it is learning to hold on while holding out. Christian ministry is freedom's exercise and aspiration. It is Paul in 1 Corinthians 4. Once again he has tried to explain what his ministry is about. Once again he suspects that he has failed to be entirely persuasive. He has done his best and he hopes the Corinthians will think better of him than they did before. And then he adds: "But with me it is a very small thing that I should be judged by you or by any human court." Then this statement of most perfect liberation: "I do not even judge myself . . . Let no one judge before the time" (1 Cor. 4:3-5).

Let no one judge before the time. At that time it will be revealed to us and to all that we were indeed the ambassadors of a sovereignty then no longer disputed. That is the promise, and that promise is the source of freedom for ministry.

Richard John Neuhaus, *Freedom for Ministry* **(Grand Rapids, Mich.: Wm. B. Eerdmans, 1979), chap. 11.**

Full of insight, practical wisdom, humor, and common sense, Charles Haddon Spurgeon's Lectures to My Students *is perhaps this master preacher's most beloved legacy. He had a reputation for having the largest congregation in Victorian London. His writings, mostly sermons as well as lectures to his students, comprise the largest body of evangelical writings in the English language. In his time, he was called "Prince of Preachers," and in our time, his advice to pastors still rings true. This great Baptist pulpiteer here lectures upon the power to be had through the pastor's private prayer. His grand voice fell silent in 1892.*

The Preacher's Private Prayer
Charles Haddon Spurgeon

Of course the preacher is above all others distinguished as a man of prayer. He prays as an ordinary Christian, else he were a hypocrite. He prays more than ordinary Christians, else he were disqualified for the office which he has undertaken. "It would be wholly monstrous," says Bernard, "for a man to be highest in office and lowest in soul; first in station and last in life." Over all his other relationships the pre-eminence of the pastor's responsibility casts a halo, and if true to his Master, he becomes distinguished for his prayerfulness in them all. As a citizen, his country has the advantage of his intercession; as a neighbour those under his shadow are remembered in supplication. He prays as a husband and as a father; he strives to make his family devotions a model for his flock; and if the fire on the altar of God should burn low anywhere else, it is well tended in the house of the Lord's chosen servant— for he takes care that the morning and evening sacrifice shall sanctify his dwelling. But there are some of his prayers which concern his office, and of those our plan in these lectures leads us to speak most. He offers peculiar supplications *as a minister*, and he draws near to God in this respect, over and above all his approaches in his other relationships.

I take it that as a minister *he is always praying*. Whenever his mind turns to his work, whether he is in it or out of it, he ejaculates a petition, sending up his holy desires as well-directed arrows to the skies. He is not always in the act of prayer, but he lives in the spirit of it. If his heart be in his work, he cannot eat or drink, or take recreation, or go to his bed, or rise in the morning, without evermore feeling a fervency of desire, a weight of anxiety, and a simplicity of dependence upon God; thus, in one form or another he continues in prayer. If there be any man under heaven, who is compelled to carry out the precept—"Pray without ceasing," surely it is the Christian minister. He has peculiar temptations, special trials, singular difficulties, and remarkable duties; he has to deal with God in awful relationships, and with men in mysterious interests; he therefore needs much more grace than common men, and as he knows this, he is led constantly to cry to the strong for strength, and say, "I will lift up mine eyes unto the hills, from whence cometh my help," Alleine once wrote to a dear friend, "Though I am apt to be unsettled and quickly set off the hinges, yet, methinks, I am like a bird out of the nest, I am never quiet till I am in my old way of communion with God; like the needle in the compass, that is restless till it be turned towards the pole. I can say, through grace, with the church, 'With my soul have I desired thee in the night, and with my spirit within me have I sought thee early.' My heart is early and late with God; "tis the business and delight of my life to seek him." Such must be the even tenor of your way, O men of God. If you as ministers are not very prayerful, you are much to be pitied. If, in the future, you shall be called to sustain pastorates, large or small, if you become lax in secret devotion, not only will *you* need to be pitied, but your people also; and, in addition to that, you shall be blamed, and the day cometh in which you shall be ashamed and confounded.

It may scarcely be needful to commend to you the sweet uses of private devotion, and yet I cannot forbear. To you, as the ambassadors of God, the mercy-seat has a virtue beyond all estimate; the more familiar you are with the court of heaven the better shall you discharge your heavenly trust. Among all the formative influences which go to make up a man honoured of God in the ministry, I know of none more mighty than his own familiarity with the mercy-seat. All that a college course can do for a student is coarse and external compared with the spiritual and delicate refinement obtained by communion with God. While the unformed minister is revolving upon the wheel of preparation, prayer is the tool of the great potter by which he moulds the vessel. All our libraries and studies are mere emptiness compared with our closets. We grow, we wax mighty, we prevail in private prayer.

Your prayers will be your ablest assistants *while your discourses are yet upon the anvil*. While other men, like Esau, are hunting for their portion, you, by the aid of prayer, will find the savoury meat near at home, and may say in truth what Jacob said so falsely, "The Lord brought it to me." If you can dip your pens into your hearts, appealing in earnestness to the Lord, you will write well; and if you can gather your matter on your knees at the gate of heaven, you will not fail to speak well. Prayer, as a mental exercise, will bring many subjects before the mind, and so help in the selection of a topic, while as a high spiritual engagement it will cleanse your inner eye that you may see truth in the light of God. Texts will often refuse to reveal their treasures till you open them with the key of prayer. How wonderfully were the books opened to Daniel when he was in supplication! How much Peter learned upon the house-top! The closet is the best study. The commentators are good instructors, but the Author Himself is far better, and prayer makes a direct appeal to Him and enlists Him in our cause. It is a great thing to pray one's self into the spirit and marrow of a text; working into it by sacred feeding thereon, even as the worm bores its way into the kernel of the nut. Prayer supplies a leverage for the uplifting of ponderous truths. One marvels how the stones of Stonehenge could have been set in their places; it is even more to be enquired after whence some men obtained such admirable knowledge of mysterious doctrines: was not prayer the potent machinery which wrought the wonder? Waiting upon God often turns darkness into light. Preserving enquiry at the sacred oracle uplifts the veil and gives grace to look into the deep things of God. A certain Puritan divine at a debate was observed frequently to write upon the paper before him; upon others curiosuly seeking to read his notes, they found nothing upon the page but the words, "More Light, Lord," "More light, Lord," repeated scores of times: a most suitable prayer for the student of the Word when preparing his discourse.

You will frequently find fresh streams of thought leaping up from the passage before you, as if the rock had been struck by Moses' rod; new veins of precious ore will be revealed to your astonished gaze as you quarry God's Word and use diligently the hammer of prayer. You will sometimes feel as if you were entirely shut up, and then suddenly a new road will open before you. He who hath the key of David openeth, and no man shutteth. If you have ever sailed down the Rhine, the water scenery of that majestic river will have struck you as being very like in effect to a series of lakes. Before and behind the vessel appears to be enclosed in massive walls of rock, or circles of vine-clad terraces, till on a sudden you turn a corner, and before you the rejoicing and abounding river flows onward in its strength. So the laborious student often finds it with a text; it appears to be fast closed against you, but prayer propels your vessel, and turns its prow into fresh waters, and you behold the broad and deep stream of sacred truth flowing in its fulness, and bearing you with it. Is not this a convincing reason for abiding in supplication? Use prayer as a boring rod, and wells of living water will leap up from the bowels of the Word. Who will be content to thirst when living waters are so readily to be obtained! . . .

Prayer will singularly assist you in the delivery of your sermon; in fact, nothing can so gloriously fit you to preach as descending fresh from the mount of communion with God to speak with men. None are so able to plead with men as those who have been wrestling with God on their behalf. It is said of Alleine, "He poured out his very heart in prayer and preaching. His supplications and his exhortations were so affectionate, so full of holy zeal, life and vigour, that they quite overcame his hearers; he melted over them, so that he thawed and mollified, and sometimes dissolved the hardest hearts." There could have been none of this sacred dissolving of heart if his mind had not been previously exposed to the tropical rays of the Sun of Righteousness by private fellowship with the risen Lord. A truly pathetic delivery, in which there is no affectation, but much affection, can only be the offspring of prayer. There is no rhetoric like that of the heart, and no school for learning it but the foot of the cross. It were better that you never learned a rule of human oratory, but were full of the power of heavenborn love, than that you should master Quintilian, Cicero, and Aristotle, and remain without the apostolic anointing.

Prayer may not make you eloquent after the human mode, but it will make you truly so, for you will speak out of the heart; and is not that the meaning of the word eloquence? It will bring fire from heaven upon your sacrifice, and thus prove it to be accepted of the Lord.

As fresh springs of thought will frequently break up during preparation in answer to prayer, so will it be in the delivery of the sermon. Most preachers who depend upon God's Spirit will tell you that their freshest and best thoughts are not those which were premeditated, but ideas which come to them, flying as on the wings of angels; unexpected treasures brought on a sudden by celestial hands, seeds of the flowers of paradise, wafted from the mountains of myrrh. Often and often when I have felt hampered, both in thought and expression, my secret groaning of heart has brought me relief, and I have enjoyed more than usual liberty. But how dare we pray in the battle if we have never cried to the Lord while buckling on the harness! The remembrance of his wrestlings at home comforts the fettered preacher when in the pulpit: God will not desert us unless we have deserted him. You, brethren, will find that prayer will ensure you strength equal to your day.

As the tongues of fire came upon the apostles, when they sat watching and praying, even so will they come upon you. You will find yourselves, when you might perhaps have flagged, suddenly upborne, as by a seraph's power. Wheels of fire will be fastened to your chariot, which had begun to drag right heavily, and steeds angelic will be in a moment harnessed to your fiery car, till you climb the heavens like Elijah, in a rapture of flaming inspiration.

After the sermon, how would a conscientious preacher give vent to his feelings and find solace for his soul if access to the mercy seat were denied him? Elevated to the highest pitch of excitement, how can we relieve our souls but in importunate pleadings. Or depressed by a fear of failure, how shall we be comforted but in moaning out our complaint before our God. How often have some of us tossed to and fro upon our couch half the night because of conscious shortcomings in our testimony! How frequently have we longed to rush back to the pulpit again to say over again more vehemently, what we have uttered in so cold a manner! Where could we find rest for our spirits but in confession of sin, and passionate entreaty that our infirmity or folly might in no way hinder the Spirit of God! It is not possible in a public assembly to pour out all our heart's love to our flock. Like Joseph, the affectionate minister will seek where to weep; his emotions, however freely he may express himself, will be pent up in the pulpit, and only in private prayer can he draw up the sluices and bid them flow forth. If we cannot prevail with men for God, we will, at least, endeavour to prevail with God for men. We cannot save them, or even persuade them to be saved, but we can at least bewail their madness and entreat the interference of the Lord. Like Jeremiah, we can make it our resolve, "If ye will not hear it, my soul shall weep in secret places for your pride, and mine eye shall weep sore and run down with tears." To such pathetic appeals the Lord's heart can never be indifferent; in due time the weeping intercessor will become the rejoicing winner of souls. There is a distinct connection between importunate agonising and true success, even as between the travail and the birth, the sowing in tears and the reaping in joy. "How is it that your seed comes up so soon?" said one gardener to another. "Because I steep it," was the reply. We must steep all our teachings in tears, "when none but God is nigh," and their growth will surprise and delight us. Could any one wonder at Brainerd's success, when his diary contains such notes as this: "Lord's Day, April 25th—This morning spent about two hours in sacred duties, and was enabled, more than ordinarily, to agonize for immortal souls; though it was early in the morning, and the sun scarcely shone at all, yet my body was quite wet with sweat." The secret of Luther's power lay in the same direction. Theodorus said of him: "I overheard him in prayer, but, good God, with what life and spirit did he pray! It was with so much reverence, as if he were speaking to God, yet with so much confidence as if he were speaking to his friend." My brethren, let me beseech you to be men of prayer. Great talents you may never have, but you will do well enough without them if you abound in intercession. If you do not pray over what you have sown, God's sovereignty may possibly determine to give a blessing, but you have no right to expect it, and if it comes it will bring no comfort to your own heart. I was reading yesterday a book by Father Faber, late of the Oratory, at Brompton, a marvellous compound of truth and error. In it he relates a legend to this effect. A certain preacher, whose sermons converted men by scores, received a revelation from heaven that not one of the conversions was owing to his talents or eloquence, but all to the prayers of an illiterate lay-brother, who sat on the pulpit steps, pleading all the time for the success of the sermon. It may in the all-revealing day be so with us. We may discover, after having laboured long and wearily in preaching, that all the honour belongs to another builder, whose prayers were gold, silver, and precious stones, while our sermonisings being apart from prayer, were but hay and stubble.

When we have done with preaching, we shall not, if we are true ministers of God, have done with praying, because the whole church, with many tongues, will be crying, in the language of the Macedonian, "Come over and help us" in prayer. If you are enabled to prevail in prayer you will have many requests to offer for others who will flock to you, and beg a share in your intercessions, and so you will find yourselves commissioned with errands to the mercy-seat for friends and hearers. Such is always my lot, and I feel it a pleasure to have such requests to present before my Lord. Never can you be short of themes for prayer, even if no one should suggest them to you. Look at your congregation. There are always sick folk among them, and many more who are soul-sick. Some are unsaved, others are seeking and cannot find. Many are desponding, and not a few believers are backsliding or mourning. There are widows' tears and orphans' sighs to be put into our bottle, and poured out before the Lord. If you are a genuine minister of God you will stand as a priest before the Lord, spiritually wearing the ephod and the breast-plate whereon you bear the names of the children of Israel, pleading for them within the veil. I have known brethren who have kept a list of persons for whom they felt bound especially to pray, and I doubt not such a record often reminded them of what might otherwise have slipped their memory. Nor will your people wholly engross you; the nation and the world will claim their share. The man who is mighty in prayer may be a wall of fire around his country, her guardian angel and her shield. We have all heard how the enemies of the Protestant cause dreaded the prayers of Knox more than they feared armies of ten thousand men. The famous Welch was also a great intercessor for his country; he used to say, "he wondered how a Christian could lie in his bed all night and not rise to pray." When his wife, fearing that he would take cold, followed him into the room to which he had withdrawn, she heard him pleading in broken sentences, "Lord, wilt thou not grant me Scotland?" O that we were thus wrestling at midnight, crying, "Lord, wilt thou not grant us our hearers' souls?"

The minister who does not earnestly pray over his work must surely be a vain and conceited man. He acts as if he thought himself sufficient of himself, and therefore needed not to appeal to God. Yet what a baseless pride to conceive that our preaching can ever be in itself so powerful that it can turn men from their sins, and bring them to God without the working of the Holy Ghost. If we are truly humble-minded we shall not venture down to the fight until the Lord of Hosts has clothed us with all power, and said to us, "Go in this thy might." The preacher who neglects to pray much must be very careless about his ministry. He cannot have comprehended his calling. He cannot have computed the value of a soul, or estimated the meaning of eternity. He must be a mere official, tempted into a pulpit because the piece of bread which belongs to the priest's office is very necessary to him, or a detestable hypocrite who loves the praise of men, and cares not for the praise of God. He will surely become a mere superficial talker, best approved where grace is least valued and a vain show most admired. He cannot be one of those who plough deep and reap abundant harvests. He is a mere loiterer, not a labourer. As a preacher he has a name to live and is dead. He limps in his life like the lame man in the Proverbs, whose legs were not equal, for his praying is shorter than his preaching. . . .

I would seriously recommend to you, when settled in the ministry, the celebration of extraordinary seasons of devotion. If your ordinary prayers do not keep up the freshness and vigour of your souls, and you feel that you are flagging, get alone for a week, or even a month if possible. We have occasional holidays, why not frequent holy days? We hear of our richer brethren finding time for a journey to Jerusalem; could we not spare time for the less difficult and far more profitable journey to the heavenly city? Isaac Ambrose, once pastor at Preston, who wrote that famous book, *Looking unto Jesus*, always set apart one month in the year for seclusion in a hut in a wood at Garstang. No wonder that he was so mighty a divine, when he could regularly spend so long a time in the mount with God. I notice that the Romanists are accustomed to secure what they call "Retreats," where a number of priests will retire for a time into perfect quietude, to spend the whole of the time in fasting and prayer, so as to inflame their souls with ardour. We may learn from our adversaries. It would be a great thing every now and then for a band of truly spiritual brethren to spend a day or two with each other in real burning agony of prayer. Pastors alone could use much more freedom than in a mixed company. Times of humiliation and supplication for the whole church will also benefit us if we enter into them heartily. Our seasons of fasting and prayer at the Tabernacle have been high days indeed; never has heaven-gate stood wider; never have our hearts been nearer the central glory. I look forward to our month of special devotion, as mariners reckon upon reaching land. Even if our public work were laid aside to give us space for special prayer, it might be a great gain to our churches. A voyage to the golden rivers of fellowship and meditation would be well repaid by a freight of sanctified feeling and elevated thought. Our silence might be better than our voices if our solitude were spent with God. That was a grand action of old Jerome, when he laid all his pressing engagements aside to achieve a purpose to which he felt a call from heaven. He had a large congregation, as large a one as any of us need want; but he said to his people, "Now it is of necessity that the New Testament should be translated, you must find another preacher: the translation must be made; I am bound for the wilderness, and shall not return till my task is finished." Away he went with his manuscripts, and prayed and laboured, and produced a work—the Latin Vulgate—which will last as long as the world stands; on the whole a most wonderful translation of Holy Scripture. As learning and prayerful retirement together could thus produce an immortal work, if we were sometimes to say to our people when we felt moved to do so, "Dear friends, we really must be gone for a little while to refresh our souls in solitude," our profiting would soon be apparent, and if we did not write Latin Vulgates, yet we should do immortal work, such as would abide the fire.

C. H. Spurgeon, *Lectures to My Students* (Grand Rapids, Mich.: Zondervan, 2001), pp. 42-52.

Index of Names

Subject Index

Made in the USA
Middletown, DE
25 February 2020